THE COMPLETE BOOK OF BATON TWIRLING

THE COMPLETE BOOK OF

Baton Twirling

by FRED MILLER and GLORIA SMITH

with Perri Ardman

PHOTOGRAPHS BY BREWSTER STROPE

DRAWINGS BY EVELYN RODBERG

DOUBLEDAY & COMPANY, INC., Garden City, New York

Library of Congress Cataloging in Publication Data

Miller, Fred W
The complete book of baton twirling.

Includes index.
1. Baton twirling. I. Smith, Gloria, joint author.
II. Ardman, Perri, joint author. II. Title.
MT733.6.M54   785'.06'7108
ISBN 0-385-12394-9
Library of Congress Catalog Card Number 77–82769

CONTENTS

I would like to take this opportunity to express my thanks and appreciation to Perri Ardman for all the work and effort she extended in making this book possible. Working with Perri on *The Complete Book of Baton Twirling* was a real joy, and I was amazed at how quickly she began to learn and understand what baton twirling and its related activities are all about. She has that innate knack of putting into words such simple how-to-do explanations that it is impossible for a person not to understand exactly what she is talking about.

Without Perri Ardman, this book would have been impossible to put together. On behalf of Gloria Smith and myself, we wish to say a very special thanks to Perri, a most talented and gifted author.

Fred J. Miller

INTRODUCTION

You may be a championship twirler, a high school majorette, or a gal who has never laid hands on a baton. But chances are you've experienced in one way or another the thrill of baton twirling. Even if you've never twirled, you've certainly seen twirlers in action—either in person or on TV. After all, who hasn't witnessed a parade or a half-time show at a sporting event?

Think back to how you felt when you saw a twirler throw her baton in the air. You probably gasped and crossed your fingers, then sighed with relief when the catch was completed—or felt a pang of disappointment if the baton fell to the ground.

If you've twirled yourself, no matter what your degree of proficiency, you know first hand the joy of perfecting a trick and achieving mastery over a baton.

It's an exhilarating feeling. This is why baton twirling is one of the fastest-growing activities for girls today. It is both an art and a sport. And to hundreds of thousands of girls and young women, from two to twenty-four, being a twirler is a dream come true.

However, twirling wasn't always a young girl's dream. In the early part of the century, twirlers were mostly boys and men—because the batons were very heavy.

In the late 1930s the majorette made her debut. The role became so popular that high school girls all over the country wanted to participate. Shorter, lighter batons were developed for the rash of feminine twirlers springing up. Through the '40s, '50s, and '60s, more and more girls became majorettes. The involvement of girls and young women made twirling a more graceful, artistic form of self-expression than it had ever been before.

In the middle 1950s incorporated baton-twirling associations began to develop. The associations organized baton competitions on both state and national levels.

Two of the largest associations today are the United States Twirling Association (USTA)* and the National Baton Twirling Association (NBTA). Both hold national competitions every year and officiate at competitions at local, state, and regional levels. You can think of the two associations as being similar to the National and American Baseball Leagues. There hasn't yet been a World Series of baton twirling, but it's something we'd very much like to see happen.

Today's twirlers, 99 per cent female, are far more talented and creative than twirlers of the past. Modern twirling barely resembles what went on forty years ago—or even fifteen years ago, for that matter. Each year, twirling progresses, capturing the fancy of more and more young people who are developing their skills to levels previously unimagined.

Why Twirl?

Twirling is one of the most wholesome, involving activities available to young people today. Many of you, if you're not connected with twirling, may think of it as a silly accomplishment, with little intrinsic value. But if you hold this view, you might as well take the same attitude toward any other activity—school sports, dancing lessons, whatever. Intrinsically, being able to put a ball into a hoop or do a pirouette is no more or less worthwhile than being able to twirl a baton.

The real value of activities such as these is that they are all useful tools leading to self-development and personal growth. In this area, baton twirling offers exceptional opportunities.

* References in this book to competition rules and procedures refer to USTA only. For information regarding competition specifics of other associations, write to them. Names and addresses of all twirling associations are in the Appendix.

Twirling builds self-confidence. Learning to do something gives a young-ster faith in his abilities and belief in himself. For a shy child who has little confidence, twirling is a marvelous booster—because it doesn't take very long to learn the simple basics. Since twirling is not nearly as difficult as it looks, students feel a sense of accomplishment early on.

Many young students are pathetically shy. They are socially immature and often have difficulty conversing, even with their peers. Once they begin to master some of the basics, though, we often see their personalities begin to change.

The activities open to beginners can bring even the most retiring girl out of her shell. Skirt-clingers start leading parades. Lonely teens start perform-ing in twirling lines. This recognition adds to the twirler's feeling of well-being.

Since twirling is a group activity, as well as an individual skill, it gives young people an immediate sense of belonging, which adds to their confidence. One of the most dramatic coming-out stories concerns one of Fred's former students, a slightly retarded girl we'll call Sarah.

Sarah was having great difficulty, even in her special school, intellectually as well as socially. She was not working up to her abilities, but even more disturbing, she was quite violent. A strong girl, she frequently beat up her classmates, sometimes injuring them despite the teacher's efforts to control her.

Desperate, Sarah's mother enrolled her in a twirling class—just after Sarah's school had threatened to expel her. Surprisingly, Sarah did more than just learn the basics of twirling. She also became much calmer and bet-ter behaved.

Sarah worked hard at twirling for many years, and she eventually became an excellent intermediate twirler. She also decided she wanted to be a member of the corps.

When she tried out, she couldn't even march in time to the music. She was always out of step. But she was very determined, and something told Fred that if she were willing to make the effort to succeed, then he should be willing to work with her. Over resistance from other parents, who felt the corps championship status would be threatened if Sarah joined, Fred let her in. It wasn't easy for either of them, but it paid off.

Although Sarah was a good twirler, twirling in the line was beyond her. But she did learn to march well and keep in step. She remained in the corps until she was twenty-one, eventually becoming captain of the color guard.

Through twirling, Sarah developed the self-confidence and sense of belonging she needed. She settled down in school and graduated.

Of course, few retarded people have the chance to twirl. Sarah was unusual. First, she did have the opportunity. And second, with strong guidance and much encouragement from her teacher, she used all of her energy and her limited intelligence to stretch herself, mentally and physically. Certainly not all retarded people could learn to twirl as well as Sarah did. But we wanted to tell you about her because her needs—to feel a part of something and to believe in herself—are basic human needs. Twirling helps to satisfy them for everyone, and provides an environment in which the individual can truly blossom. We've seen it happen time and time again.

Twirling teaches discipline, builds drive and motivation. Unlike other skills, which may be more difficult to master initially, twirling pays off almost immediately. Small children really dig twirling, from the very first lesson. We both like to get them marching around the room in time to the music. They learn how to hold the baton and how to salute and stand at attention. They're on top of the world before they even learn the simplest twirl. They run home, very excited and very proud. "Hey, look at me," they say to their parents. "Look what I can do!"

Few youngsters who begin twirling lessons quit because it's too hard, too boring, or because they've got to put in five years before they can have any fun with it. They get hooked pretty fast, becoming involved in any of several activities open to beginners.

Even children who usually discourage easily, who have given up quickly on other endeavors, will persist with twirling. Of all students who start lessons, 75 per cent continue and keep on twirling in one capacity or another throughout high school.

Many parents with hard-to-motivate children are surprised at how willing they are to practice with the baton, over and over again until they're doing it properly. No one has to force them. It's completely voluntary. They want to do it, and they give it all they've got.

And it does take plenty of practice. We said twirling is easier than it looks, but we never said it doesn't take hard work. In twirling, young people learn early that discipline and concentrated effort bring their own rewards. Practice brings visible improvement, and young people, like anyone else, take special delight in consistently beating themselves, in striving to do their best, in sweating and struggling over a trick until they finally triumph.

Each achievement is important to a twirler's later life, whether she stays in the field or not. People who strive for and meet with success at an early age usually have the necessary confidence, motivation and know-how to apply themselves successfully in other areas as they grow older.

Both of us keep in touch with many of our former students, if not directly, then through the parents. Not long ago, Fred was working late in his studio when a mailman brought him a special delivery package. He looked familiar, and when Fred said so, the mailman reminded him that his daughter had been a twirling student.

"My wife and I used to argue about you all the time," the man told Fred. "She always thought you worked the kids too hard, not letting them quit until they got it right. I told her the discipline was healthy.

"Well, let me tell you, my daughter learned to buckle down. She's a doctor now, practicing in North Carolina. And my wife's got a whole different outlook on what you were trying to do with those kids. She doesn't think you were too tough anymore."

Twirling is one of the few activities that gives the *majority* of people who try it a real taste of early success. Most young twirlers we've watched grow up have become spirited and determined young adults. They're not discouraged easily and they've learned to stick things out, even when the rewards aren't so immediate. Most of our students go on to college, and a large number do graduate work as well.

Twirling develops team spirit and promotes social responsibility. Most twirlers, even those who are good enough to win solo championships, find that twirling in a group is the most rewarding aspect of the art. Many groups are formed primarily to entertain, but others compete at every level from local to national. Every year more and more groups go abroad to perform in twirling exhibitions.

Team sports have traditionally been restricted mostly to boys, and despite recent progress in this area, girls are still not getting their fair share. Twirling helps even up the score. It not only offers opportunities to compete individually, but also gives a tremendous number of girls and young women all the benefits of team competition. It awakens the competitive spirit, develops sportsmanship, provides travel opportunities, offers scholarships.

Being in a twirling group, competitive or not, helps children develop close, lasting friendships and gives them a sense of team spirit. It builds their cooperative skills and helps them function efficiently within a group.

Not long ago Gloria was judging a contest in another state and a little non-twirler was in the audience. Gloria heard her say to her mother, "If I learn how to twirl, I'll be too scared to do it alone. But I'd like doing it with other people."

One of the greatest things about twirling is that you don't have to perform alone to enjoy it or to get recognition. And you don't have to be a superstar to feel important—even if you're in a competitive group. A very average twirler can be a member of a championship corps. Few other activities offer this type of opportunity to youngsters who are not outstandingly talented.

When you're in a twirling line, you quickly learn the importance of each individual. Every member of your group depends on you, just as you depend on each of them. No matter how many people are on the team, each one counts equally.

Twirling not only builds self-respect, but also a basic belief in the worth of every individual. Furthermore, twirling helps children develop a strong sense of responsibility—to themselves and their teammates—which can stand them in good stead throughout their adult lives.

Twirling strengthens the family unit. When one child in a family becomes involved in twirling, it's common for others to follow suit. Even boys still learn to twirl. (Fred recently judged a contest in which four brothers competed against each other in the boys' division.) More often, though, boys will learn to play an instrument, join the band, and become a member of the corps that way.

But it's not only the children who make twirling an important part of their lives. Parents become as fascinated and involved as younger people. For example, behind every corps is an active parents' organization. Among other things, this group raises funds to keep the corps in existence.

We find that people involved in twirling spend a lot of time with their families. They enjoy being together and have lots of fun. One of the things twirling families often do is travel together. Often, the annual National competitions serve as family vacations. The 1976 USTA Nationals were held in Miami Beach, and the travel package included a side trip to Disney World. Twirling students, their parents, siblings, uncles and aunts, and even grandparents took advantage of this offer. The trip was far less expensive than it would have been had they gone on their own. In fact, many wouldn't have been able to afford to go any other way.

We've had so many parents tell us that the years their kids were in twirling were the happiest times of their lives. At a party given for Gloria's corps after the New York State competition, the parents of a corps member going off to college in the fall came over to speak to her. They were almost sorry to see their child leaving for college because it would mean the end of all the twirling experiences the family had shared. Much of their social life had revolved around corps activities, and their friends also had children active in twirling. Both parents had worked hard in the booster club and had gotten great pleasure from their own activities, as well as from their child's accomplishments.

With twirling as a mutual interest, the lines of communication between the generations become more open. Parents gain new respect for their children when they see them working hard to improve themselves. And kids love it when their parents share their interests. It really helps them thrive and makes them more responsive and loving, not only as children, but as teen-agers and adults.

Twirling builds physical fitness. Become physically fit through baton twirling? Ridiculous, you might say, but just watch a twirler at work—or better yet, try it yourself—and you'll see what we mean.

Because twirling is—from the beginning—something you do with your hands, it's an excellent way of developing motor control. Many doctors recommend it for children who have not adequately refined their motor skills. Furthermore, because in twirling you're doing different things simultaneously with your hands and your feet, it builds your coordination. Hand-to-eye coordination is another skill that twirling develops because throwing the baton in the air and catching it is basic to even the most elementary twirling routine.

The farther you go in twirling, the more difficult and strenuous it becomes. Marching, strutting, dancing, even acrobatics can be included in a twirler's performance. Twirling develops grace and poise, and it gets your body into good overall condition.

Many twirlers, because they're gradually tuning their bodies without the drudgery of calesthenics, don't even realize what terrific shape they're in. When Gloria's corps went to Switzerland to perform last year, she wanted one of her daughters to perform with the group. She'd been away at college for two years and hadn't been twirling much during that time.

The first few days of corps practice really exhausted her, and she couldn't understand why since twirling had never made her so tired before. But as her stamina gradually returned, she realized she was simply out of condition. By the time she got to Switzerland, she'd gotten herself into shape again, just by daily practice. She'd even knocked off a few extra pounds.

While it's true that twirling can help you slim down, it's not only the chubbies who can benefit. If you're too skinny, twirling is a great body developer. You can always tell a twirler's legs, for example. They're very nicely built—not overly muscled.

It may sound strange, but we've noticed that twirling can change a person's entire appearance. It not only improves the body, making it healthier and more attractive, it even changes facial expressions and grooming habits.

People who never cared enough about themselves to pay attention to their appearance begin wearing more becoming clothes, fix their hair neatly, smile more. They begin to radiate, not only during performances, but all the time. There's an aura of confidence about them, and this is reflected in their appearance and carriage. Most baton twirlers aren't really any better looking than other girls, but sometimes they seem to be.

Time after time we've seen children and teen-agers who are gawky, clumsy, sloppy, too fat, or too thin undergo remarkable changes. There's one student in particular Gloria remembers. She was very overweight, and because she never combed her hair or took care of her clothes she looked even worse. In addition, she had family and social problems. To be frank, she was very unattractive and few people wanted to associate with her.

Gloria sometimes wondered whether she'd ever amount to anything. She'd work like the devil in corps rehearsal, huffing and puffing twice as much as anyone else, because she was heavier than all the other members. Then she'd drown her sorrows in huge amounts of food, negating the value of all that exercise.

But she finally pulled herself together. Today, she's a very successful teacher of baton twirling. Although she still hasn't really licked her overeating problem, she's got it under much better control. She's slimmed down to a normal size and now wears clothes and make-up to accent her best features. And she gets along famously with her students and their parents. Gloria sees her from time to time at state contests and can hardly believe she's the same person.

Twirling builds mental skills. Physical as twirling is, about 40 per cent of the work is mental. You don't have to be a genius to twirl, but you've got to be able to think fast, concentrate on several things at once and, above all, stay alert. You'll develop and refine these mental skills as you practice your twirling.

You've got to memorize routines, listen to music, keep time with the beat, and recover quickly if you make a mistake. Speed and timing are everything. When you throw your baton in the air, you've got to be able to judge time and distance. How long is it going to stay up there? Where is it going to come down? How can you be sure you'll be in the right spot to catch it?

If you're twirling in a group, you've got to learn complicated maneuvers, keep track of where you're supposed to be at all times in relation to everyone else's position on the floor. And you've got to be confident enough so that your neighbor's mistake won't foul you up.

Twirling sharpens your mind and can help you become better at whatever you do—not only twirling. For example, we find that most twirlers do well in school. Sometimes parents express fears that their children will fall behind in school if they take twirling lessons. They'll spend less time doing homework and more time practicing twirling. What usually happens is that the quality of school work doesn't suffer, although time spent on it may decrease. Homework usually gets done with less dawdling and more efficiency.

This often holds true even for children who have never been whizzes scholastically. Once they begin twirling, their marks often improve. In cases like this, it was never lack of intelligence that caused the problems, only lack of motivation.

Twirling offers college and career opportunities. Nearly every college that has a band has one or more featured twirlers, and most colleges and universities in the West, Midwest, and South offer scholarships to their featured twirlers. If you're an advanced twirler, all you have to do is write to the band director of the colleges you'd like to attend and find out when tryouts are being held. Many advanced twirlers do get accepted to a college of their choice, so don't pass up the opportunity to try out. (A list of colleges that offer such scholarships is included in the Appendix.)

We have many, many students who've been awarded full scholarships to major universities. One of Fred's students became the first female twirler at the University of Alabama. The band director was so impressed when she tried out that he broke the precedent of only having men march with the band. Exactly the opposite situation occurred at the State University of Indiana. There the twirlers had always been women until one of Fred's male students tried out, floored the band director, and got himself a scholarship.

Whether or not you go to college, you can remain in the twirling field by becoming a teacher. We'll tell you more about how to do this later, but suffice it to say now that the demand for twirling teachers is far greater than the supply. Many young women are finding it a profitable, fast-growing career. Twirling teachers can also become contest judges. As judges, they enjoy good pay and plenty of expense-paid travel opportunities.

So you don't have to think of twirling as something you'll have to stop doing once you're beyond legal competition age. Being able to twirl is like having money in the bank. It's a skill that's there for you to use whenever you want or need to.

If you're already a twirler, then you're probably aware of all the benefits twirling has given you, and you can vouch for everything we've written here. And if you're thinking about twirling, either for yourself or your children, then perhaps we've inspired you to go past the thinking stage—and actually begin.

Whatever your experience or twirling level, this book is for you: student, parent, twirling teacher. We've written it to serve many purposes:

- To teach novices the fundamentals.
- To help intermediate twirlers better their skills and become advanced.
- To show advanced twirlers how to get into top-notch form.
- To guide those who want to twirl competitively—in group or solo events.
- To give twirling teachers additional techniques and help them to be better able to reach their students.
- To help band directors, teachers, students, and parents interested in organizing a corps to get the group off the ground.
- To provide sample routines for all twirlers (majorettes, soloists, teams, and corps).
- To teach all twirlers the basics of creating original routines that will make their performances more exciting.

You'll find you can use this book in several ways:

As a self-contained curriculum and workbook—with or without a partner or a teacher—grading yourself along the way, measuring your own improvement.

As a refresher course in particular areas that may need work.

As a compendium of electives, choosing those sections that interest you and skipping the ones that don't.

As a source book, to further explore the whole field of twirling.

What you make of what you're about to read, then, depends on you and you alone.

The beginning section of the book is mostly for beginners. But even if you're an experienced twirler, you should skim it anyway. You might pick up some useful tips that will improve your style and help you get more out of the intermediate and advanced sections.

THE COMPLETE BOOK OF BATON TWIRLING

ONE

Before You Begin

Let's assume you've never twirled a baton. You've certainly thought about it, or you wouldn't have bought this book.

But still, you've got dozens of questions. Am I too young or too old to begin? How will I find a teacher? What if there isn't a teacher in my area? How long will it take me to become a good twirler? How much time should I spend practicing? Is it expensive? What equipment do I need? When I put the baton in my hand, what do I do with it?

Let's begin at the beginning. Is there any reason you shouldn't learn to twirl? Probably not. As we said before, nearly anyone can learn. The average age of a beginning twirler is seven or eight—some start as early as three or four. Most likely, if you're reading this book, you're older than the average starting age. But don't let that stop you. Neither of us started until we were in our teens, and we can assure you, that's not too late. Many girls don't get interested in twirling until they get to junior or senior high school, at which time they think about becoming majorettes.

Equipment. Although you've probably seen twirlers in fancy costumes, you don't need anything out of the ordinary if you want to learn. Shorts and T-shirt or a plain leotard are the best things to wear because they allow you to move freely and don't get in the way of your baton.

You can also forget about fancy boots or ballet slippers or anything special for your feet. The preferred footwear for twirlers is a pair of white gym shoes, but any flat-heeled, non-slip shoe will do until you can get them.

Of course, the one thing you can't twirl without is a baton. You'll need a real baton, not something you can pick up at the five and dime, and it will cost you from $6.00 to $10. If you can't buy one from your teacher (or if you don't have a teacher to buy a baton from), then try a music store, especially one that sells instruments as well as sheet music. Or you can order one from any of the manufacturers listed in the Appendix.

When you compare a real baton to a toy, you'll not only see the difference, you'll also feel it. The baton you'll use is very lightweight, but probably a bit heavier and far more sturdy than a toy. It must be balanced at its center point. You'll notice that the shaft (chrome stick part) is thinner in a balanced baton than it is in most toys. Actually, it's as thin as a golf club shaft and made the same way.

Many twirlers today use batons with a shaft that's textured, or sand-blasted, in the middle. This improves the grip and makes it less likely for the baton to slip out of a hand that's damp from perspiration.

At each end of the baton is a piece of rubber. The smaller piece is called the tip and the larger piece is called the ball. Baton balls used to be completely rounded, but today they also come squared-off in several different styles. This modification helps prevent the baton from rolling clear across to the other side of the room when you drop it.

You'll have to be sure your baton is the right length for you. If you're buying your baton from your teacher or in a store, you can measure with the baton itself. Extend your arm straight out and place the tip of the baton against your underarm. The ball should extend slightly beyond your fingertips.

If you're ordering by mail, measure from your underarm to your fingertips, preferably with a wooden yardstick. If your arm measures 25½", order the 26" baton.

Lessons. To take or not to take. We designed this book so you can use it to teach yourself to twirl. But no book, no matter how thorough it is, can completely substitute for good personal instruction, and if you can get it, you should. With someone to coach you, you'll learn more quickly and more accurately.

A teacher will give you necessary feedback. Scheduling lessons at a particular time each week helps to establish discipline. But if this book is your only resource, then by all means rely on it. And if you can study with a teacher, use this book in conjunction with your lessons.

Finding a teacher. Most twirling teachers usually like to know how their students find them. One little seven-year-old came to Gloria for her first lesson, and said, "I followed a twirler I saw in a parade. I chased her all the way down the street and when the parade ended I asked who her teacher was."

You may not have to follow a parade to get a recommendation, but if you don't know of a teacher, asking someone who twirls is always a good idea. If you live in a town where lots of kids twirl, then it will be pretty simple to get a list of teachers. Just ask around.

If you don't know anyone who twirls, then you can look in the Yellow Pages. Or write to the USTA, or any of the other twirling associations listed in the Appendix. Ask for a list of certified baton teachers in your area.

Another way to find a teacher is to attend a baton-twirling contest in your area. These events are open to the public and are usually announced in the newspapers and in poster displays around town. At the contest, ask the winners who gives them lessons. Of course, this method isn't foolproof since some good instructors may not have entered students in that particular competition. You can check with the contest officials, making sure there's a wide representation of teachers at the event. Also, talk to other people in the audience. They probably know something about twirling and might be able to give you the names of well-known instructors.

If you're fortunate enough to have more than one teacher available to you, then you'll have to weigh several factors in making your selection. One of the most important things for a beginner is to have a teacher who is close by. You'll be more likely to attend your lessons regularly if it's not a hassle for you to get there.

Cost will also be a consideration. Group lessons are less expensive than private, and they usually run about $2.00 a person. Private lessons may cost anywhere from $4.00 to $15, depending on the experience of the teacher.

At first you may not want to invest a lot of money in lessons. After all, you're just trying it out. Even if you can afford it, you don't have to spend a fortune to get good results. Once you see just how deep your interest is, and you learn something about what your capabilities might be, you can consider spending a little more. Maybe you'll want to switch from group classes to private lessons. Or take two lessons a week instead of one. It's possible that you'll want a more experienced teacher as you progress, or one who specializes in a certain aspect of twirling that appeals to you.

How long will it take me to learn? That depends on you. Some twirlers are born into it. They have an abundance of natural ability and pick it up very quickly. Others—the majority—will progress more slowly, even though they practice diligently. Let's assume you're an average beginner and you're going to practice from twenty to forty minutes a day. If you're taking lessons in a group, your teacher will probably get through all the rudiments, the most basic moves, within three months or so. You'll learn them a little sooner if you take private lessons.

But it will probably take you a year to achieve mastery over the more difficult beginner moves. You see, there's learning, and then there's learning *well*. Learning the basics well—making them smooth, speedy, effortless, and automatic—is crucial. This takes plenty of practice and lots of patience. But if you don't do it right, you're never going to be much of a twirler.

Nearly all the advanced twirling moves are no more than combinations or variations of things you learn as a beginner. Taking short cuts, cheating, letting sloppy work pass won't do. It will show up in your performance.

Beginners are always tempted to rush through the basics and get to the fancy stuff. Just keep in mind that you're going to look ridiculous doing hard tricks if you can't execute the basics smoothly. And remember too that even the simplest maneuvers, done well, look very impressive. You've got plenty of time to get fancy later.

But you said twirling is easy. We said it's not as difficult as it looks. If you've ever seen really sharp twirling, you know that it can look unbelievably hard. The main reason for this is that in twirling, everything is happening so fast that someone who doesn't know how to twirl can't really tell what's going on.

For one thing, the action is mainly in the wrist, not in the fingers. Once you're aware of this, things that seemed impossible become plausible. Second, much of baton twirling is illusion. The baton really isn't spinning as often or as fast as it seems to be. It just looks that way. Third, most of the fancy tricks are just one simple move connected to another simple move connected to another simple move, with a variation thrown in here and there. You'd see this in an instant if you watched twirling in slow motion.

That's entertainment. Like dancing, singing, playing an instrument, or acting, twirling is a performing art. It allows you to express yourself, develop your own style, be creative, and use your skill and talent to entertain others.

You don't have to become an intermediate or advanced twirler before you start performing. There are plenty of opportunities for beginners. It will probably surprise you to know that most majorettes are beginners. Besides trying out for majorette, you can twirl in parades, perform at school- or community-sponsored events (fairs, sporting events, etc.), or entertain at dances, fund-raising dinners, local talent shows, and the like. If you want, you can also try your hand at competitive twirling. Local contests are held often. Since beginners only compete against each other, you've got as good a chance as anyone else to win a trophy or medal.

As a beginner, you'll have to gear yourself to performing alone, because twirling with a group usually requires a lot more skill. But beginners can still become members of corps in non-twirling roles (color guard, pompon line), with an eye to joining the twirling line later on.

There's more to twirling than twirling. Baton twirling doesn't merely involve what your hands do with the baton. Learning how to maneuver the baton is only the beginning. Twirling involves your entire body. How you carry yourself, how gracefully you move, what you do with your feet, what you do with your free hand (the one that's not twirling), your smile, your eye contact with the audience, your energy and enthusiasm—all these are important to your presentation, and they're no less important than your actual twirling skill.

We realize you're not going to be able to think about eye contact or footwork as you're first learning a baton maneuver. But once that move is mastered, you've got to concentrate on performing with style and pizzazz.

Unfortunately, many beginning twirlers never realize there's anything more to twirling than the actual twirling itself. They see other twirlers looking sharper or winning more contests, but they don't understand why. No one has ever told them about projecting their personalities, developing a style, building qualities of showmanship, sharpening their performances down to the most minute detail, or creating an exciting, dramatic routine.

Let's face it. We'd all be bored to death watching a twirler who just stands stiffly and fiddles around with her baton—no matter how well she fiddles. So in this book, you'll not only learn baton maneuvers, but also the finer points of twirling.

The goals of twirling are smoothness and speed, in that order. As a twirler, you should strive for a graceful, flowing performance, and although you're a beginner, you can achieve it—if you don't try to race ahead of your ability and sacrifice smoothness for speed.

It will help you to think of yourself and your baton as a single, constantly moving unit, rather than as two separate entities that are at odds. You should learn to move your body and your baton at the same tempo, and you should twirl at a pace you'll be able to maintain throughout your routine. Remember, a beginner who is silky-smooth looks more professional and experienced than one who is clumsy and jerky. When you begin practicing the basics, start off slowly and keep your speed down until you've really got control of the baton. Then gradually pick up the pace.

What if I drop it? Every beginner is afraid she'll embarrass herself by dropping the baton. But there's no way you can become a twirler without dropping. Even the most advanced students drop their batons—and not only during practice. It happens right in front of the judges' eyes at every contest.

Don't let your fear of dropping inhibit you. Some beginners hold the baton too tightly, thinking that will prevent a drop. What it prevents is a twirl. You've got to have a loose, relaxed grip, or you won't be able to move your wrist freely. Ultimately, you want to have as little continuous contact with your baton as possible. This means being willing to let go of it.

Dropping the baton is a necessary part of learning. Every time you attempt a new trick, expect lots of drops. Every time you increase your speed on an old trick, expect some drops. But with practice they'll become less frequent, the exception rather than the rule.

And now it's time to begin. Grab your baton and turn the page.

TWO

Ready-Set-Go: Tricks for Beginners

This chapter is for beginners. But even if you've been twirling awhile, it's a good idea to skim over it and make sure you can do everything here. Mastery of the fundamentals as they're presented in this book is crucial.

Just what is a beginner? Well, if you've never twirled, you're certainly a beginner. You should also consider yourself a beginner if you've never twirled competitively, or if you've won fewer than three first-place awards in competitions. That means that even some of you who have twirled are still considered beginners—at least as far as this book is concerned.

The average student takes a year or so to move out of the beginner class. If you don't have a teacher in addition to this book, it could take you a little longer. But don't get discouraged. Remember, almost everyone who wants to learn to twirl can do it, but not everyone will learn at the same rate.

This chapter is divided into ten lessons, but that doesn't necessarily mean you'll be through with it in ten weeks. Some of you will be able to do a whole new lesson every week. Others may have enough twirling experience to cover two lessons in a week. And there will be some of you who may need two or three weeks for some lessons, but only one week for others.

However fast you progress, try to add a minimum of one new trick every week, even if you don't cover a whole lesson. This way, you'll have at least one new thing to practice each week (along with everything you learned during the previous weeks), and you won't get bored.

At the end of this chapter are some sample routines beginners can use. When you can do them smoothly, in the allotted time, you will probably be very close to winning enough awards to move into intermediate. If you're not competing or planning to compete, practice these routines anyway. You can use them in your performances, and you'll be able to tell from the way you do the beginner routines just how ready you are to move into the intermediate chapter and when to begin adding harder tricks to your repertoire.

So, ready. Get set. Go!

LESSON ONE

Positions

It's important for every twirler to hold and carry her baton properly. Practicing the positions will help you feel familiar and comfortable with the baton and will also make you look professional.

Marching

If you can walk, you can march. It's not difficult. Before you try marching, walk across the room a few times, as you normally do. Notice how your arms swing automatically as you walk. Your right arm moves forward with your left leg; your left arm swings forward with your right leg.

Marching is similar to walking, only all the movements are exaggerated. In marching, foot movements break down into a definite heel lift, toe lift, toe down, heel down action. In marching, you lift your knees higher than you do when you walk. Your arm swings will be more pronounced. In marching, *always* start with the *left* foot.

But don't try to march yet. Just walk. Now try to get a constant rhythm into your walk. You can put on a marching record, if you have one. Or set a metronome. You can even hum a simple tune (like "Yankee Doodle")— something with beats you can count off evenly in twos. Your walk should have a nice even rhythm as you move across the floor. Count ONE (left foot lifts and hits floor all on this count), two (right), ONE (left), two (right). Be sure your foot doesn't hit the floor between the beats, but right

	2	3	4	5

1. **AT EASE:** Stand with feet about 18″ apart, toes pointed slightly out. You should feel stable and comfortable. Keep your shoulders back, but don't be stiff. Hold baton lightly in both hands, behind your back, with your right hand near the ball.

2. **ATTENTION:** From the at-ease position, snap left foot so feet are as shown, toes pointed out at 45° angle. Snap baton to right hip as shown, holding it like a pencil. The shaft of the baton rests in crook of right elbow. Hands are on hips, fingers pointing toward opposite knees. Head up, shoulders back. Coming from at ease to attention takes just one count, with all the snap you can muster.

3. **SALUTE:** From attention position, on first count of salute, bring baton so tip comes down forward and points to floor.

4. On second count, raise tip up so it points forward at shoulder level.

5. On count of "three," continue moving baton so tip comes up and over toward nose, inverting hand so you can place baton, tip first, into an imaginary holster in front of left shoulder. Stop when back of your hand is against front of left shoulder. Keep your left hand and feet in attention position. (Hold salute position for two counts. You'll do this at the beginning and ending of a routine, during the playing of the National Anthem, taps, or the American flag ceremony.)

SALUTE: Pattern of baton during salute. Tip moves in direction of arrows.

on the beat. In the time between one beat and the next, say the word "and" to help keep even spaces between each beat.

(One)	(and)	(Two)	(and)	(One)	(and)	(Two)	(and)
Yan	- kee	Doo	- dle	Went	- to	Lon	- don

Make sure you move your foot fast enough to get a definite heel lift, leg lift, toe return, heel return all completed in one beat. No matter how fast you're marching, each part of the stride should be distinct.

6   7   8   9

6. **MARCHING:** Hold baton in right hand, in attention position. Your body should be erect, but not stiff. Shoulders are back, chest out, chin up. To do a complete march step with each foot will take up one whole beat of "Yankee Doodle." Instead of just lifting your whole foot and setting it down as you did when you were walking, you should divide each beat into four definite foot movements, or four parts.

7. Part one is to lift your left heel off the floor.

8. Part two is to lift your leg until upper leg and knee are parallel to the floor. Strong downward point of the toe is a must. Right arm swings out in a good stretch, with baton resting on it, ball forward. Treat the baton as if it is part of your arm. Left arm stretches out to the rear.

Part three is to return left toe to the floor. Your left foot will look just like it did during part one. The last (fourth) part of the beat is to put left heel on the floor. Repeat with right leg following same procedure.

9. With right leg lifted, left arm is in front, right arm to the rear. Baton continues resting on right arm, moving with the arm as though it's permanently attached.

Before you begin to march, keep knees and feet close together, and bring feet together between strides. The length of your stride will depend on what feels comfortable to you.

Planes

When you're twirling, you will be holding your baton in one of six different planes. Two of the planes are under the overall designation of *horizontal*, or *flat*. This means that the baton's shaft is parallel to the floor. It remains parallel to the floor throughout the twirl. If the trick is performed with your arm extended upward so the baton is above your waist or head, it's in the *flat up* plane. If you're twirling the baton below your waist or close to the floor, you're twirling in the *flat down* plane.

While there are only two horizontal planes (up and down), there are four *vertical* planes, in which the baton is twirling with the shaft perpendicular to the floor. If you're twirling in front of your body, you're twirling

11   12   13

14   15

PLANES

10. Flat down. Shaft remains horizontal throughout trick.

11. Flat up. Shaft remains horizontal throughout trick.

12. Right side. The twirler in this photo uses right hand in right plane. Baton in left hand stretched over to right side would also be in right plane.

13. Left side. Right hand can also twirl in left-side plane by holding baton over to twirler's left side.

14. Front plane.

15. Back plane. Baton can either be behind back, or directed to twirler's rear with either hand.

in the *front plane*. If you're holding the baton behind your back or toward your rear, then you're using the *back plane*. Twirling maneuvers done with the baton at your right side are done in the *right-side plane*, while those done with the baton to your left side are in the *left-side plane*.

If you're having trouble grasping this concept, imagine yourself in an enclosed box, with six walls. Four walls, those to the right and left, front and rear, are vertical walls and represent the four vertical planes. The top and bottom walls, or floor and ceiling of your box, represent the horizontal planes.

Some baton maneuvers can be done in more than one plane. Maneuvers that must remain in the horizontal plane are called horizontal or flat maneuvers. As you begin to learn the specific twirls, you'll become accustomed to the different planes.

Body Directions

When you twirl, you don't always face the same direction. Your routine is much more diversified and interesting if you occasionally change the direction your body faces. There are four body directions that twirlers use, and they're shown in the photographs below.

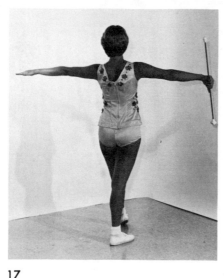

16   17   18   19

BODY DIRECTIONS

16. Front. You face the audience.
17. Rear. Your back is toward the audience.
18. Right, or one-quarter right. Turn from facing front one-quarter turn to the right. This puts you at a 90° angle to the audience, with your left side toward the audience.
19. Left, or one-quarter left. Turn from front, one-quarter turn to the left. Right side now faces the audience.

Vertical Wrist Twirls

Now it's time to learn your first real twirling maneuver. This move depends on keeping your fingers loose and relaxed enough for you to twist your wrist. Keep in mind that the main action is in your wrist, and that's why we call it a wrist twirl. (Some teachers call it an underarm twirl because the ball of the baton travels along a path under your arm.)

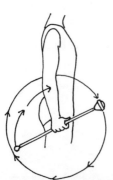

WRIST TWIRL: Pattern is the same for right-hand and left-hand wrist twirls. Ball moves along inside of arm, tip travels along outside. When ball and tip return to starting point, baton has made one revolution. Each wrist twirl constitutes one revolution of the baton.

 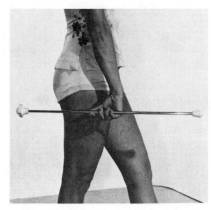 

20   21   22

RIGHT-WRIST TWIRL

20. Hold baton thumb to ball, in right hand. Ball is toward floor.
21. Turn wrist so ball revolves up and then down toward rear.
22. Keep turning wrist so ball continues up along inside of arm, while tip follows path on outside of arm, until baton returns to position in photo 20, making one revolution. Keep repeating wrist twirl, using pumping motion of arm for continuous spin.

In the beginning, your twirls will probably be a little jerky. Don't try to increase your speed until you can do sixty continuous wrist twirls smoothly. Don't stop between the end of one twirl and the beginning of the next. Eventually, you should be able to complete sixty wrist twirls in a minute, but it will take you at least several weeks of practice before you'll be able to twirl smoothly at this speed.

Most teachers teach right-hand twirls first, whether you are right- or left-handed. Right-handed twirlers should not wait too long before going on to the left-hand wrist twirls. Both right-handed and left-handed twirlers may have to devote more practice time to the weaker hand, and it's important to do this right away. If you do, you'll soon feel comfortable twirling with either hand. A twirler's goal is to become ambidextrous—to do all twirls equally well with both hands.

Horizontal Wrist Twirls

The wrist twirl you just learned was in the vertical plane. Now you're going to do a wrist twirl in the horizontal, or flat plane. Just remember that the main action is still in the wrist, but you'll have to keep your fingers loose enough to turn along with your wrist.

RIGHT-HAND HORIZONTAL WRIST TWIRL: In the right hand, ball of the baton travels over arm, while tip travels under. Baton moves counterclockwise, ball going to the left.

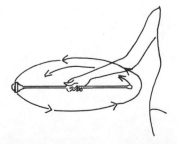

23   24   25

RIGHT HORIZONTAL WRIST TWIRL

23. Hold baton thumb to ball, with ball pointing directly in front of you. Keep arm at shoulder level throughout twirl.

24. Start ball moving to left, or counterclockwise. Keep fingers loose, so baton can keep turning and still remain horizontal.

25. Keep turning baton until ball travels over your arm. Repeat the twirl by continuing to move ball to left, with tip traveling along a path under your arm.

Now that you've tried the twirl, you'll notice that the looser your grip on the baton, the more smoothly you can twirl it. Keep wrist and fingers as loose as possible. Your wrist will become more flexible as you practice. But you can also exercise your wrists without the baton by doing circles from the wrist with your hands, moving both hands in each direction. If you're having trouble, loosen up your wrists by doing this a few times before you begin your baton practice each day.

For the left-hand horizontal wrist twirl, the baton also moves in a counterclockwise direction, with the *ball end of the baton moving* to the *left*. Beginners often forget this, and do the left-hand horizontal wrist twirl clockwise, instead of to the left. Watch out.

Moving the baton in the same direction with both hands makes it possible to pass it from hand to hand without stopping the smooth flow of motion.

Practice horizontal wrist twirls with both hands and work up to 60 smooth revolutions a minute.

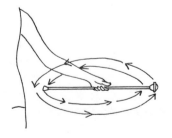

LEFT-HAND HORIZONTAL WRIST TWIRL: Counterclockwise motion of the baton continues. The ball still moves over the arm, while tip travels under.

Practice everything from Lesson One for at least 20 minutes a day for a week. If you practice for an hour a day, of course, you'll learn faster. If you divide your practice time into two or three sessions a day, you'll get less tired.

Begin Lesson Two a week from now. You won't be doing 60 wrist twirls a minute by then, but you should start on something new anyway. Continue practicing Lesson One, even after you've advanced to future lessons. Keep working for smoothness, and eventually you'll be able to increase your speed without sacrificing the smooth, even flow of motion.

LESSON TWO

Forward Figure Eight (Open Version)

There are several figure-eight patterns you can make with the baton. The simplest of them is called a forward figure eight.

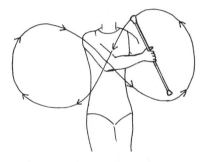

FORWARD FIGURE EIGHT: Pattern baton makes in open version (right hand). Follow arrows from the ball. Try drawing a big figure eight in the air, in front of you, using the ball as pencil point. Definite arm and baton movements are shown in photos that follow.

RIGHT-HAND FORWARD FIGURE EIGHT

26, 27, 28, 29. Hold baton thumb to ball, ball up, as in 26. Ball travels forward and down, toward left side of body and up to start position, as in 27. Baton has now made one revolution. Turn palm up, so ball travels forward and downward as arm moves back to right side of body, as in 28 and 29. Continue turning so ball comes back up to start position. This completes the second revolution, or last half of the figure eight.

26

27

28

29

When you do the figure eights, your arm should make a dipping motion as it moves from left to right, as though the ball of the baton is scooping out ice cream from a giant container on your left and dumping it out into a giant dish on your right. Keep scooping up the ice cream and dumping it out as you repeat the figure eight.

There's nothing complicated or difficult about doing the forward figure eight with your left hand. Simply hold the baton in your left hand, out in front of you, ball up, thumb to ball. Begin your figure eight by moving the ball forward and down to the right side. Just remember to think of the ball as the point of your pencil, and draw an imaginary figure eight in the air. Move your imaginary container of ice cream over to your right side when you practice the left-hand forward figure eight.

Forward Figure Eight (Closed)

Continue practicing figure eights, but as you do them, make your arm movements from side to side less and less sweeping, until eventually, you're not moving your arm from side to side at all, but keeping it straight out in front of you. At this point, you'll notice that the baton spins close to your arm. Instead of making the figure-eight pattern from the left side of your body to the right side of your body, the baton is making the figure eight from the left side (inside) of your *arm* to the right side (outside) of your arm. Be sure to practice this with both hands.

Side Figure Eights

The only difference between a side figure eight and a closed forward figure eight is the position of your arm. Instead of holding your arm in front of you, keep it stretched out to the side. In the right-side figure eight, right arm extends to right side. In the left-side figure eight, left hand does the twirling with left arm extended out to left side.

Two-hand Spin

In the two-hand spin, the baton will make two complete revolutions, starting in the right hand, transferring to the left, and back into the right

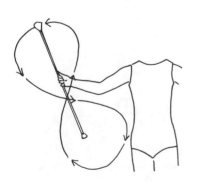

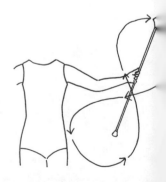

RIGHT-SIDE FIGURE EIGHT: Ball follows direction of arrows, moving down then around and completing one revolution along inside of arm. Second half of the figure eight has ball again starting down and coming around to finish second revolution along outside of arm.

LEFT-SIDE FIGURE EIGHT: Ball travels path shown by arrows. Procedure is same as for right-side figure eight, with ball traveling down first, then around and up, one revolution on inside of arm, the other revolution along outside of arm.

30   **31**   **32**

TWO-HAND SPIN

30. Hold baton in right hand, thumb to ball. Baton is horizontal, ball to left.

31. Turn wrist as far right as possible, until palm is up and baton has done three-quarter revolution. Ball is now down, tip up. You're supporting the baton between your thumb and hand. Next, the shaft is going to roll over your right thumb, tip leading to right.

32. Right hand can't turn any farther to right, but left hand helps keep baton moving. Place left hand, palm up, in palm of right hand. Keep left hand to left of baton. Left hand will touch baton, just below your little finger.

33. With side of left hand, push baton. It will begin to roll over your right thumb, moving into a horizontal position with tip at right.

34. As baton continues revolving, with ball coming up, it will begin to roll over your left hand, between thumb and first finger. Ball is leading, revolving to right.

35. As soon as baton is vertical (ball up), give it a little push with your left thumb, to keep it revolving until it's horizontal, ball at right. As baton comes around to the right, close left hand around. You'll now be holding it in your left hand, thumb to tip, palm up. Your hand will be slightly off center, toward ball. (When you begin doing this fast, baton won't need push from left thumb. Its momentum will carry it over into your left hand.)

36. Turn left hand over, so palm is down, returning baton to start position (tip right, ball left). Twirler in photo is getting ready to grab baton with right hand as soon as it comes back to horizontal start position. Grasp baton in right hand, palm down, thumb to ball. Keep turning right hand to right to repeat maneuver.

34   **35**   **36**

hand at the end. Although the baton is changing hands, it continues to revolve in the same direction—to the right—throughout the entire maneuver.

During this maneuver, the baton will be carried along by its own momentum as well as by the action of your hands. The photographs on page 17 break the maneuver down into steps and show you how to place your hands at various points.

Once you memorize the procedure, try to do the two-hand spin without stopping the baton, so that the flow of motion is *uninterrupted*. Do it very slowly so you don't jerk the baton or lose control if it starts to move too fast. When you can do 5 continuous two-hand spins smoothly, try for 10, then 15, then 20. Eventually, you should be able to do 30 in a minute, but this may take several weeks of daily practice.

Two-hand-spin Back Pass

This is a way to get fancy with your two-hand spin. The maneuver looks more impressive than the two-hand spin because it creates the illusion that the baton is spinning behind your back. Actually, it isn't.

Once you've learned the steps, practice this maneuver slowly, without stopping, until you can do it smoothly and continuously. Always remember to aim for smoothness first, then pick up speed. Keep in mind that your goal in twirling is to keep the baton constantly in motion.

Back-pass Variations

Here are a few ways to make your routine more interesting and to make you look as though your twirling skills are more advanced than they really are.

It's no more difficult to pass the baton between your legs or behind your legs than it is to pass it behind your back. Be sure to turn your left wrist just as you do for the back pass. Let the tip of the baton lead, and grasp the baton in your right hand—just as in the back pass.

Keep practicing the two-hand spin, without the back pass, with the back pass, and with all the variations. When you can do it smoothly, try doing 7 or 8 in a row, with a different back-pass variation each time. Keep the baton in motion throughout all the maneuvers, and don't stop between the end of one pass and the beginning of the next spin.

If you're having trouble with the split jump, forget it for now. But if you can do it well, then an effective combination is to alternate the two-leg pass with the split-jump pass.

After you've been twirling awhile, you'll begin to learn which tricks and

37   **38**   **39**   **40**

41

TWO-HAND-SPIN BACK PASS

37. Here's your position at the end of the regular two-hand spin, just before right hand grabs baton.

38. Instead of transferring baton to right hand, continue turning baton to the *right*, with the left hand, bringing *ball end up* and over. You'll end up in this position, with baton horizontal. This takes considerable twist of left wrist.

39. Move hand around left side of body to rear, tip leading, baton remaining horizontal as you pass baton behind your back to the right hand.

40. Rear view of 39. Notice both palms are out. Grab baton in right hand, thumb to ball. (You remain facing front.)

41. Bring baton out from behind back, tip leading. Baton remains horizontal, close to body, until it's completely out from behind your back. (This will bring it in front of you for an instant, as shown.) Whipping the baton in front of you like this helps create the illusion that i. did spin behind your back.

Ball then travels down and continues moving in same direction until it is up . . .

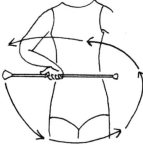

42

42. . . . in this position, baton vertical, thumb to ball.

43

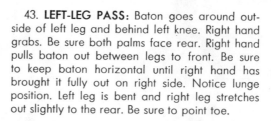

43. **LEFT-LEG PASS:** Baton goes around outside of left leg and behind left knee. Right hand grabs. Be sure both palms face rear. Right hand pulls baton out between legs to front. Be sure to keep baton horizontal until right hand has brought it fully out on right side. Notice lunge position. Left leg is bent and right leg stretches out slightly to the rear. Be sure to point toe.

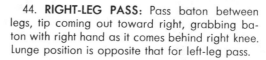

44. **RIGHT-LEG PASS:** Pass baton between legs, tip coming out toward right, grabbing baton with right hand as it comes behind right knee. Lunge position is opposite that for left-leg pass.

44

45. **TWO-LEG PASS:** Simply bend knees and lean body slightly forward, as tip leads to right side. Keep legs and feet together or this will look very awkward.

46. **SPLIT-JUMP PASS:** Begin jump feet together, knees bent, almost squatting. The deeper the knee bend, the higher the jump. Jump, legs in spread-eagle position, as you pass baton front to back between legs. Keep body erect, head up, legs straight, toes pointed. Land feet together, *knees bent*—a return to start. This is called the "cushion" position, because it cushions your body as you land. Cushioning is essential. Without it, you can hurt yourself.

45

46

variations best show off your particular skills and personality. When you make up routines, you'll use these to highlight your performance.

Keep practicing everything from the first two lessons every day. With regular daily practice, you'll improve very quickly. Within two or three weeks, you'll be twirling as well as many majorettes. Lots of them don't know any more maneuvers than we've just shown you in Lessons One and Two.

Don't expect to do everything perfectly before you start Lesson Three. But do give yourself at least a week of practice between lessons if you've never twirled before.

LESSON THREE

Right Whip

This maneuver follows a right-side figure eight. Do one figure eight, but instead of beginning another as you finish, you're going to quickly bring the baton behind your back, then whip it out in front of you. The baton stays in your right hand the whole time.

47

48

49

50

RIGHT WHIP

47, 48, 49, 50. Do right-side figure eight. After completing second revolution, let ball continue down to behind right side of body, to a horizontal position, as in 47 and 48. Whip baton at front, keeping it horizontal, tip leading until baton is in front of your waist, tip to left, as in 49. Then bring ball down, around, and up to position, as in 50. (This is the same motion that is used in the back pass following the two-hand spin.) Do continuous right whips by repeating only the last half of right-side figure eight before bringing baton behind back and whipping out in front of you.

51   52   53

RIGHT REVERSE FIGURE EIGHT

51. Starting position, thumb to ball, ball forward.
52. Ball travels up, then toward nose.
53. Ball continues down along inside (or left side) of arm and . . .

Reverse Figure Eight

Make sure you're fully familiar with the forward and side figure eights before you learn this one. The reverse figure eight is just like the others, except it begins with ball coming *up* first.

Now that you've tried it, you can see that the whole direction of the baton is backward, or the reverse of the regular figure eight. Don't get confused, though, by trying to imagine the pattern backward. Just remember to move the ball up first on *both* revolutions and you will automatically do it right.

Practice reverse figure eights in both hands. (The left-hand reverse is identical to the right—ball moving *up* first on both revolutions.)

Now practice the reverses out to the sides of your body, right arm extended straight out to right side for the right reverse, left arm extended out to left side for left reverse.

You should also become familiar with the right reverse at your left side (cross right arm in front of your body over to the left), and with the left reverse at right side. You'll find it more natural to do the outside revolution first in these positions.

Later on, as you begin doing routines, you'll notice that the left hand usually uses a reverse figure eight, while the right hand usually does a regular figure eight. This allows both hands to keep the baton flowing in the same direction.

55

56

54. . . . back to start position. First revolution, or first half of reverse figure eight is now completed.

55. Now bring ball up again, toward nose, but this time, turn palm out, so ball can continue along *outside* (right side) of arm.

56. Ball continues down and around, back to start position.

Figure-eight and Reverse Figure-eight Variations

The following tricks combine figure eights and reverses in new ways. If you've practiced all the figure eights we've given you so far, you won't have much trouble with these variations.

1. Right-hand Circles

In this maneuver, your right arm will make a complete circle moving from left to right. Begin with right arm extended across your body toward your left side. In this position, do a reverse figure eight (outside revolution first).

57

58

RIGHT-HAND CIRCLE, BODYWORK

57. Left lunge position (left knee bent, right leg extended to side with pointed toe). Keep left arm outstretched throughout maneuver.

58. As you move your right arm around in the circle, stretch it to the limit throughout entire maneuver. It makes your performance more graceful and eye-catching. This bodywork is effective and attractive, but you don't need to limit yourself to our suggestions. Devise your own bodywork if you want.

Complete the reverse (inside revolution), and as you do so bring your arm up over your head and extend it straight out to your right side.

Go directly into a regular right-side figure eight, again with the outside revolution first. Complete the figure eight with an inside-arm revolution. As you do this, swing your arm down and back over to your left, starting another right reverse figure eight at your left side.

2. Left-hand Circles

Begin with left arm extended across your body to right side. In this position, do a complete figure eight, starting with inside revolution.

After completing outside revolution, swing arm down and out to left side. The downswing begins the inside revolution of left reverse. Complete reverse (outside revolution) with arm outstretched to left side.

We suggest bodywork that is the reverse of right-hand circle bodywork shown. Lunge to right and keep right arm extended out to your right side.

LESSON FOUR

More Figure-eight and Reverse Variations

1. Full Circles

Full circles involve two passes of the baton from one hand to the other. The first pass is from right to left hand, behind back. The second pass is from left to right hand, overhead.

Begin with right-side figure eight, outside revolution only. Bring baton behind back, ball leading. Grab baton with left hand (both palms out), and bring it out on your left side, tip leading into left reverse figure eight (outside revolution only), with left arm outstretched to left side. Bring baton overhead to right, tip leading. Grab the baton overhead with right hand (both palms out) and begin another right-side figure eight (outside revolution only). Repeat for continuous full circles.

2. Rear Combination

Rear combinations also involve two passes of the baton, both behind the back. The first pass is from right hand to left, and the second is from left back to right. The second pass is identical to the back pass you learned in Lesson Two.

Begin with baton in right hand. Do an outside revolution of a figure eight. Pass baton behind back to left hand, exactly as you did for the full circle, and do outside revolution of a left reverse. So far, the entire maneuver is identical to the first half of a full circle.

Upon finishing left reverse, pass baton behind back as in back pass. Bring it out, tip leading across front of waist (tip will be at your left), then swing right arm so ball leads up and over, going into another outside revolution of a figure eight at your right side.

3. Figure-eight Turnaround

In this maneuver, you'll combine figure eights and reverses with a complete body turn to the right. Baton remains in right hand the whole time. The entire maneuver should be completed in four counts. You spin your body around on the middle two counts.

1. Begin with right reverse figure eight (both revolutions, outside first) at your left side, in left lunge position.

2. Begin spin by transferring weight from left foot to right, and turn body to right. As your body comes to one-quarter right position, do outside revolution of figure eight.

3. By the count of three, your body should be at one-quarter left. Do inside revolution of reverse and end up facing front again.

4. Left foot hits floor, either resuming lunge or next to right foot. Extend right arm out to right side and do outside revolution of a figure eight.

Once you get the hang of it, don't stop at each count. Your spin, which takes up counts two and three, should be smooth and continuous and fast. You'll find that the baton naturally goes into the correct revolutions as your body spins around.

LESSON FIVE

Now you're ready to let go of that baton and release it into the air. Be prepared to drop it. These moves take lots of practice, and there's no way you're going to learn them without many drops along the way. Keep at it.

Thumb Flip

This is a two-count maneuver. Hold the baton horizontally in your right hand, thumb to ball, ball to your left. On count one, ball travels up and around one revolution. On count two, shaft rolls over your thumb as you

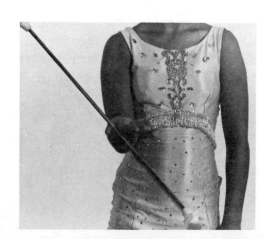

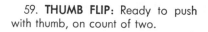
59. THUMB FLIP: Ready to push with thumb, on count of two.

lift your thumb to flip the baton into the air. Baton should do one revolution in the air.

Accent the count of two, to give your thumb the necessary thrust to force the baton up. But remember, you need only enough push to keep it up for one revolution.

Don't try to recover (get it back into your hand) yet. Keep practicing the thumb flip and let the baton fall to the floor, making sure it does one revolution in the air. Not a half a revolution and not one and a half, but *one*. After a little practice, you'll discover just how hard you have to push with your thumb to flip it.

Recoveries

There are two basic recoveries. The palm-down recovery is called a grab; the palm-up recovery is called a catch.

60. **RECOVERY:** Ready for grab (palm down).

61. **RECOVERY:** Ready for catch (palm up).

60   61

Thumb-flip Recoveries

You've already practiced the thumb flip to a count of two. Now you're going to recover it on the count of three, after the baton had done *one* revolution in the air. There are four ways to recover a thumb flip.

1. Grab right (for continuous thumb flips). Remember, palm down. *Thumb* must be *to ball* each time. If you grab with thumb to tip, your baton has not done one revolution.

2. Catch left (to go into a different move). Remember, palm down, *thumb to ball* each time.

3. Catch left with follow-through (keep arm moving), into left reverse figure eight and back pass.

4. Grab right with follow-through, into right reverse at left side, in lunge position.

62. **RECOVERY:** Grab right with follow-through.

Now practice thumb flips with your left hand. Follow the same procedure as for the right-hand thumb flip, beginning with left-hand thumb to ball. (Ball should be to your right, so baton travels in opposite direction of right-thumb flip.) Practice left-thumb flips with a right-grab recovery.

Reverse-cartwheel Thumb Flip

Turn body one-quarter left and stay in this body direction throughout entire maneuver. Do right-thumb flip at your right side and catch left, at your right side. Ball continues up and toward you into a left-reverse revolution as you carry arm over to your left side. Then do a left-thumb flip at your left side and *catch* right at your left side.

To repeat, do a right-reverse revolution as arm moves back to your right side. Repeat entire maneuver for continuous baton movement from side to side. Practice until you can do the whole reverse cartwheel without stopping between each part of it, so everything flows.

Reverse-cartwheel Thumb-flip Variations

In these variations, do the reverse-cartwheel thumb flip exactly as described above, but recover the baton as in any of the photos that follow.

All the reverse-cartwheel thumb flips are difficult to do smoothly. In the beginning you'll drop a lot, but you'll notice, as you keep practicing

27

63
64

OUTSIDE LEG CATCH

63. Left hand catches under and outside right leg.
64. Right hand catches under and outside of left leg.

65
66

INSIDE LEG CATCH

65. Right hand reaches from outside and under right leg to catch.
66. Left hand reaches outside and under left leg for catch.

regularly, that the maneuver becomes more and more smooth and you drop less and less often. Don't become discouraged. Keep working, and you'll get it.

LESSON SIX

Aerials

An aerial is two or more revolutions in the air. To get the baton up, use a thumb flip, but with more push than before. Always recover an aerial thumb to ball. With practice, you'll learn just how much power your flip needs to give you the exact number of revolutions you want.

While the baton is in the air, it should spin in front of you, and up, with height depending on the number of revolutions you want. If the baton is flying all over the place, you'll have to run like a bunny to catch it.

The way to keep the aerial where you want it is to look up when you flip the baton. In the beginning your tendency will be to look at the baton as you flip it. *Don't.* Imagine a dot in the air, exactly where you want the baton to go, and look at that spot. Aim for it as you flip the baton. You'll find you can recover much more easily, keeping your eye *on the baton as it comes down*. This is the secret to a good aerial.

Avoid reaching up over your head to recover aerials. There is no way we can tell you how high your baton should be during an aerial. This depends on how many revolutions you want, how tall you are, and how fast the baton is spinning. You'll figure it out yourself with practice.

Throws

A throw is a kind of aerial, but it's not done the same way as the other aerials we've taught you so far. To do a throw, you don't use a thumb flip. And you won't be holding the baton in the center when you release it.

Hold the baton thumb to ball, but place your hand near the tip end of the baton. Lift your hand over your head and release the baton when your arm is where the hands of a clock are at noon. This is called the 12-o'clock position. The release is actually a throwing motion of your hand, but the

67. **THROW:** Arm in 12-o'clock position.

29

thrust that gets the baton into the air comes from the motion of your arm as you're lifting it to the 12-o'clock position.

A throw has fewer revolutions for the baton's height than an aerial does. That is, an aerial 8′ in the air will have more revolutions than a throw 8′ in the air.

For throws, as for aerials, look up as you release the baton. Throws are normally executed from a back pass or a knee pass.

Throw Variation

Any throw over 15′ in the air is called a steeple throw. Obviously, you have to practice steeple throws outdoors. In *all* throws, the baton should come down directly in front of you. In the steeple throw, descent accuracy is more difficult than in other throws. It's also more important, because if the baton doesn't come down in front of you, it can come down on top of your head—or on top of someone else. Believe it or not, people watching twirling exhibitions have on occasion been hit by a baton descending from a steeple throw.

Remember, the secret of accuracy is looking up as you release. But you can look up till you're blue in the face—you won't get accuracy without plenty of practice.

Horizontal Toss

A horizontal toss is executed from a horizontal wrist twirl that you do at shoulder level. The baton must remain in the horizontal plane while it's in the air, and tossing it from shoulder level is the best way to insure this. (If it starts slanting in the air, you'll get points off in competition.)

68. **HORIZONTAL TOSS:** Baton must remain in horizontal plane while it's in the air, as in this photograph.

Execute the toss by lifting your arm and releasing the baton simultaneously. Always recover thumb to ball. Horizontal tosses are recovered from underneath the baton as it descends, so catch it palm up. A horizontal toss can have any number of revolutions, but it must have at least one.

Practice horizontal tosses in the following combinations, beginning with a horizontal wrist twirl in tossing hand and ending with a horizontal wrist twirl in recovery hand.

(1) Toss and catch right; (2) Toss and catch left; (3) Toss right, catch left; and (4) Toss left, catch right.

LESSON SEVEN

This lesson will teach you how to do basic rolls. A roll is a maneuver in which the baton does a revolution over a part of your body. It takes a lot of practice to learn to do a roll. Expect to drop the baton often until you get the hang of it. Just remember to practice every day, and soon you'll be doing the rolls without much trouble.

Wrist Roll

A wrist roll is a single-hand maneuver, during which the baton does one revolution. Start with palm down and keep it down throughout the whole maneuver.

Begin with a right-wrist roll. Start with baton horizontal, thumb to ball, ball to your left. Hold the baton slightly off-center, with your hand a little closer to the tip end.

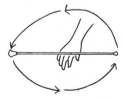

RIGHT-WRIST ROLL: Baton follows this path. Palm stays down the whole time.

31

69 70 71

RIGHT-WRIST ROLL

69. Starting position. From here, ball travels up and shaft rolls across back of hand. Palm stays down.

70. Baton in mid-roll. Second half of revolution has begun.

71. Revolution completed. Hand grasps shaft near ball end as baton finishes rolling over back of hand into full hand.

Ball comes up and around, shaft rolling over the back of your hand and into full hand as it completes the revolution. You grasp it very slightly off-center—not toward the tip, as when you started, but closer to the ball end. Remember to keep your palm down the whole time.

The procedure for the left-hand wrist twirl is the same, but the baton will move in the opposite direction. Begin with thumb to ball, ball to your right. Your hand is slightly toward tip end of center.

Hand Flips

The hand flip is very similar to the wrist roll. It's a single-hand maneuver, one revolution, with baton shaft rolling across the back of your hand. The major difference is that you begin and end with palm up.

For a right-hand flip, follow the same procedure, beginning thumb to ball, palm up, hand slightly to ball end of center. Tip begins traveling down. Baton will be moving in the opposite direction from a left-hand flip.

Left-elbow Roll

Place your left hand on your right shoulder, and lift left arm (now bent) so that it's parallel to the floor. If your elbow is tilted up or down, you won't be able to do the roll correctly. In this maneuver, the baton will leave your right hand as it rolls over your bent left arm and back into right hand.

32

LEFT-HAND FLIP

72. Begin with baton horizontal in left hand, palm up, thumb to ball, slightly off-center toward ball end. Ball is left. Tip starts traveling down . . .

73. . . . and around as shaft starts to roll over back of hand. As the shaft starts rolling over your hand, your hand will automatically turn slightly under to facilitate roll.

74. Release baton as it continues rolling over the back of your hand.

75. As baton completes revolution, rolling into full hand, grasp palm up, a little toward tip end of center.

72

3

74

75

76 **77** **78**

LEFT-ELBOW ROLL

76. Hold baton in right hand, thumb to ball, near tip end. Ball leads as you pass baton under left arm.

77. Ball continues leading as shaft rolls over bent left arm and your right hand releases baton.

78. As ball continues down and shaft rolls over forearm, grasp baton with right hand, thumb to tip, near ball end.

Left-elbow-right-elbow Combination

This maneuver will take you longer to learn than the left-elbow roll. Don't expect to do it without many a drop until a week or more of daily practice helps you get the knack. Don't be discouraged. It will suddenly click for you one day.

In the combination, the baton is going to roll over both elbows. The first half of the maneuver is identical to the left-elbow roll, except that you won't grasp the baton in your right hand as ball comes down over left forearm.

Instead, you'll bend your right arm with elbow parallel to floor, so baton can roll over bent right arm, tip leading.

HINT: When you first begin to practice the left-elbow-right-elbow combination, don't try to catch the baton. Let it drop to the floor until you can do the roll over both arms comfortably, relatively smoothly, and with some degree of confidence. Then begin to practice the maneuver with the catch. Remember, expect lots of drops the first several weeks of practice.

LEFT-ELBOW-RIGHT-ELBOW COMBINATION

79. When baton becomes vertical after completion of left-elbow roll, bend right arm to pick it up and let tip lead as shaft begins to roll across right forearm.

80. Shaft rolls over entire arm, tip leading.

81. Tip continues down. Left hand is preparing to catch behind the back.

82. As baton comes off right arm, bring left arm completely around to your back, so your left hand can break fall of baton. Baton has made one revolution in air, beginning with photo 81 and ending with the catch.

| 79 | 80 | 81 | 82 |

LESSON EIGHT

In this lesson we're going to describe some maneuvers we call wraps. Actually, wrap is just another word for roll, and some teachers don't even use it. So you can call the tricks in this lesson wraps or rolls or whatever you like. If you have a teacher, use the same term she uses.

In these wraps, it's very important that your baton is the correct size. You won't be able to do them if your baton is too short.

Horizontal Neck Wrap

In this maneuver the baton wraps around the back of your neck. You begin the neck wrap with baton in your right hand and finish with it in the left hand. Do this to a count of three while you're learning. Later, you'll complete the whole maneuver in one count. The important thing to remember is to keep the baton horizontal at all times.

83   84   85

HORIZONTAL NECK WRAP

83. Begin with both arms outstretched as shown. Keep arms at shoulder level to help avoid drops and keep baton horizontal. Hold baton off-center toward tip end, in right hand, thumb to ball, ball to right.

84. On count of "one," swing right arm over to the left, keeping baton horizontal. Ball will travel in an arc in front of you as you swing your arm over. Ball leads as baton, on count of "two," starts wrap across back of neck. You should be able to feel your neck with the side of your hand. Once you're "skin to skin," release right hand. Baton will continue around neck.

85. On count of "three," catch ball end with left hand, palm down, thumb to tip, as it completes wrap around back of neck. As you release right hand, stretch it out to the right side. Do not place your left hand on the baton until you've released the right hand. This is cheating, and will not help you to learn rolls. Expect lots of drops at first. If you don't drop it in the beginning, you're probably cheating.

HORIZONTAL WAIST WRAP

86. Hold baton in left hand, as close to the ball as possible, with thumb to tip. (When learning, it helps to hold the baton ball itself. Later you should move your hand to the correct position as shown here.)

87. On count of "one," left arm swings around to back, tip leading in an arc so baton remains horizontal. When hand and back are "skin to skin," release left hand on count of "two."

88. Tip will lead as baton rolls across your body at waist level. Reach right arm behind your back as far as possible, to prepare for behind-back catch.

89. On count of "three," catch—palm out at tip end, thumb to ball.

90. Rear view of catch. Left arm remains behind back. (Body stays facing front throughout entire maneuver.)

86

Horizontal Waist Wrap

During the horizontal waist wrap, you're going to start with the baton in your left hand, bring it behind your back, let it roll across the front of your waist, and catch it behind your back in your right hand.

Again, remember to keep baton in the horizontal plane throughout. Learn it first to a count of three and practice so that you can do it in a single count as you increase your speed.

This is a fairly difficult maneuver, and you should expect to practice daily for several weeks before you can do it without a drop.

HINTS: When learning, point left toe in front of you and lean body very slightly back. After you can do the waist wrap, straighten up.

Practice counts one and two alone first, letting the baton fall to the floor as it completes its roll across your waist. Then add the catch.

Be sure the baton is touching your body as it comes around your waist at the front. It's nearly impossible to catch otherwise. If you remember "skin to skin" before you release your left hand, the baton will touch body correctly as it wraps.

Leg-wrap Variations

All leg wraps begin with the baton in the left hand and end with it in the right. You can do wraps around either one leg or around both at once. Single leg wraps aren't very difficult, so try them first.

87   88   89   90

Then go on to the double-leg wrap. It's somewhat harder than the singles, but the procedure is identical to the waist wrap. If you can do a waist wrap, then the double-leg wrap isn't far behind.

HINT: The lower you can squat, the easier the double-leg wrap will be. Get your chest as close to your knees as possible.

RIGHT-LEG WRAP

91. Baton is in left hand, toward ball end, thumb to tip. Assume deep lunge as shown. On count of "one," bring baton between legs, tip leading from *front to back*. When left hand and outside of right leg are "skin to skin," release left hand and reach right hand under right leg from outside the leg, as shown, to prepare for catch.

92. On count of "two," catch—inside leg, palm up, thumb to ball, as baton rolls across shin tip first.

91   92

93

94

LEFT-LEG WRAP

93. Start with baton in left hand, as for right-leg wrap. On count of "one," bring baton between legs, tip leading from *back to front*. When left hand is "skin to skin" with inside of left leg, release baton and reach right hand under right leg from inside of leg, as shown. Right hand is now ready to catch—outside left leg.

94. On count of "two," catch palm up, thumb to ball, as baton completes roll across shin with tip leading.

95

96

DOUBLE-LEG WRAP

95. Procedure is same as for waist wrap. Stand feet together, knees bent as shown. On count of "one," bring baton behind knees with left hand, tip leading. As tip leads baton around shins . . .

96. . . . catch behind knees with right hand.

RIGHT HORIZONTAL TWO-FINGER TWIRL

97. Hold baton thumb to ball, ball at rear, with index finger around shaft, as shown. Ball will move up and forward to . . .

98. . . . second finger, making half a revolution.

99. Ball continues down as baton proceeds to next finger. Then ball comes up and . . .

100. . . . forward as baton reaches pinky, or fourth and final finger.

101. Let baton roll over back of hand and catch, thumb to ball, to finish maneuver.

97

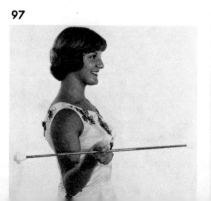

98

The wraps and variations from this chapter can be combined effectively in a routine. Try alternating neck wraps with a left-leg wrap and a right-leg wrap. Another exciting combination is a neck wrap, a waist wrap, and then a double-leg wrap.

LESSON NINE

Finger Twirls

Most non-twirlers think all baton maneuvers are done with the fingers, but as you know, this isn't true. Most beginning maneuvers rely on wrist action.

But some baton maneuvers do involve the fingers, more and more of them the more advanced you become. Tricks that rely on the fingers are called fingerwork, or finger twirls.

The basic idea of finger twirls is to keep the baton traveling between your fingers, half a revolution at a time, as it proceeds from one finger to the next.

If you study the photos, you'll quickly grasp the idea of what happens during the various finger twirls. It's simple enough to understand, but not so simple to execute. Regular practice is a must.

While you're learning, practice step by step, just as the twirl has been broken down in the photos. But remember, your ultimate goal is to make each step flow into the next with no stops in between.

The key to a quick, smooth finger twirl is keeping your fingers *relaxed*. You may find this difficult at first and will no doubt drop the baton a lot. But that's okay. You can't learn to twirl without first dropping. Pretty soon you'll develop dexterity and you'll be able to do finger twirls without stops and drops.

There are four different finger twirls in this lesson. We suggest learning the first two this week (both hands) and waiting another week before attempting the last two.

Vertical Four-finger Twirl

In this twirl, baton moves in the direction of a bicycle wheel going forward. It proceeds through four fingers as it travels, beginning with the index

100

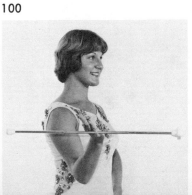
101

finger (first), moving on to middle (second), then to ring finger (third), and finally on to the pinky (fourth).

Left hand follows same procedure, at left side of your body. Be sure to practice with both hands.

Vertical Two-finger Twirl

In the vertical two-finger twirl, the baton moves through your first two fingers and back again. Tape your ring finger and your pinky together while you learn two-finger twirls. Take tape off only after you can do it smoothly.

RIGHT VERTICAL TWO-FINGER TWIRL

102. Tape last two fingers on your right hand together. Eventually, these two fingers will form a "hook."

102

103. Hold baton thumb to ball, ball up, as shown. Index finger is around shaft.
104. Ball goes forward and down, through middle finger, to "hook."
105. Grab baton with hook, which you will use . . .

103   104   105

To do the left vertical two-finger, follow the same procedure, beginning at the left side of the body.

Horizontal Two-finger Twirl

Again, tape your last two fingers together for learning. Remember it's important to keep baton in horizontal plane all the time.

For the left-hand horizontal two-finger, follow same procedure, only begin overhead, holding the baton in index finger, ball leading counterclockwise. See photographs on pages 42–44.

Horizontal Four-finger Twirls

As in the horizontal two-finger twirl, it's important to keep the baton in the flat plane. The baton moves counterclockwise.

Once you get the hang of it, try combining the left flat four-finger with some effective bodywork. We suggest a complete turn to the left on your toes, with right arm extended out to right side.

Practice the flat four-finger twirl in your right hand, also, keeping the direction of the baton counterclockwise.

106. . . . to carry baton across to left side of your body.
107. Baton stays on left side of body as ball moves up, then forward and down toward front as shaft goes back through middle finger . . .
108. . . . and continues to index finger. You're back to start position. Carry baton over to right side to begin again.

107   108

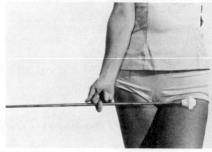

109 **110**

109. Thumb to ball, holding baton in right index finger, palm out.

110. Ball travels in horizontal plane, forward to front, over to left side as shaft moves between index finger and middle finger. Notice that palm remains facing out.

RIGHT HORIZONTAL TWO-FINGER TWIRL

113. Ball continues under arm, making half a revolution.

114. Lift to flat overhead position, completing the revolution.

113 **114**

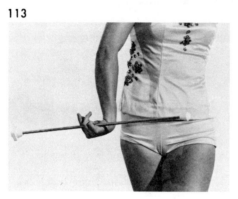

BODYWORK FOR RIGHT HORIZONTAL TWO-FINGER

117. On two-finger down, assume deep lunge, left arm out to side. Back straight, head up, point right toe.

118. On hook coming up to overhead position, snap up on toes, left arm out to side . . .

119. . . . and remain up on toes for overhead two-finger up.

117

112

111. Proceed to "hook" fingers, which now guide baton. Ball still moves counterclockwise and palms turn in toward body.

112. "Hook" still guiding, ball proceeds toward body.

115. Ball proceeds from "hook" back to middle finger and index finger.

116. Still moving counterclockwise, baton proceeds between index finger and thumb, back to starting point. By bringing baton straight down to start position, you can do this in continuous motion: two-finger down, two-finger up; two down, two up.

116

119

120. Start thumb to ball, palm down.

121. Move arm out and up as you roll shaft into index finger. Ball moves counterclockwise.

122. In directly overhead position, proceed through to middle finger.

123. Baton continues counterclockwise to ring finger . . .

124. . . . and on to pinky.

125. Extend three fingers so baton can do half a revolution over the backs of them to return to full-hand starting position, as in photo 120.

LESSON TEN

Connecting Moves

Connecting moves are used between tricks to enable you to go from one trick to another without interrupting the flow of motion. You can use connecting moves to get the baton from one plane to another, or to get the baton into the correct hand for beginning a new trick.

1. Flat Overhead One-hand Whip. Baton begins in right hand and stays there throughout, ready to begin new trick in right hand. Hold baton thumb to ball, close to tip end. Keeping baton in flat plane, circle it over your head, counterclockwise, a revolution and a half. You have your choice of keeping your body facing front or turning one complete spin to the left as baton circles over your head.

2. Flat Overhead Two-hand Whip. Baton goes from right hand to left hand. It does two complete circles over your head, while you turn your body one complete turn to the left.

127   128   129

130

FLAT OVERHEAD TWO-HAND WHIP

126. Circle baton over head with right hand . . .

127. . . . . as in one-hand whip.

128. As you complete first circle overhead, place left hand on baton with right hand, as shown.

129. Keep circling baton, counterclockwise (always horizontal), as you turn your body to the left.

130. End facing front again. Bring baton out to left side in your left hand as you finish the second circle.

131   132   133

LEFT-SHOULDER ROLL

131. Model is facing one-quarter right. Hold baton near tip end, in right hand, thumb to ball.

132. Bring your arm down and behind your back, ball leading toward left shoulder.

133. Ball will lead as shaft rolls over shoulder. Catch in left hand, palm up, toward ball end. In this photograph, twirler has placed left hand on baton before releasing right hand. You can practice this way in the beginning, but eventually you must release your right hand and let baton actually roll over shoulder before you catch left.

3. Shoulder Rolls. Shoulder rolls get the baton from one hand to the other, and they're usually done with body facing either one-quarter right or one-quarter left.

For right-shoulder roll, follow same procedure, beginning with baton in left hand, ball leading behind back and over right shoulder into right hand.

4. Shoulder Passes. Shoulder passes also get the baton from one hand to the other. Execute from one-quarter right or left position. In the shoulder roll, you brought the baton behind your body and over to your opposite shoulder. In the shoulder pass, bring the baton over to the opposite shoulder in front of your body.

134   135

LEFT-SHOULDER PASS

134. Hold baton in right hand at tip end. Ball leads as baton travels down in front of your body and under left armpit.

135. Pass to left hand as ball leads over shoulder.

Follow the same procedure for right-shoulder pass, beginning with baton in left hand and ending in right.

Shoulder rolls and shoulder passes look good if you snap up on your toes or kick left as baton hits receiving hand (photos on page 49).

5. Vertical Loop Behind Head. Face front and imagine a gigantic wagon wheel in front of you, blocking your body. As you do this move, the baton follows the outline of the imaginary wheel, doing one complete circle.

As the baton does its circle, you'll be doing a complete turnaround to the left. The baton remains in the front plane the whole time, right where the imaginary wheel is. Entire maneuver is done with baton in the right hand. Be sure to turn your body and the baton at the same speed. Eventually, this maneuver goes very fast, at whip speed, taking no more than a single count to complete.

6. Two-hand Turning Spin. Facing front, execute a two-hand spin from right to left hand. Body then begins one full turn to the right. When your body is facing rear, pass baton behind back to right hand (both palms out). During the pass, the baton remains in front plane (facing audience), but your back is facing audience, so baton is behind you.

Keep moving your body to the right until you once again face front. After you've passed the baton behind your back to your right hand, make sure you keep it in the front plane until your body completes its turn.

Bodywork

Don't get so involved in learning the maneuvers that you forget about developing bodywork. Learning to move the baton goes hand in hand with learning to move your body. Good bodywork will enhance your baton work. Here are some basic principles to follow in developing bodywork for your routines. The photographs are on page 49.

1. Your free hand (the one that isn't holding the baton) should have definite positions. Usually, it's stretched out to the side. Never leave it hanging or dangling.

2. Add lunges at appropriate times, particularly when following through on aerials.

3. When facing front, don't forget that you can point a toe forward. This is especially effective during maneuvers like elbow rolls.

4. Turn on your toes during body spins.

5. Add kicks to give snap to moves like shoulder rolls and passes.

6. A "flash out" or leap while executing a simple figure eight or finger twirl makes the maneuver more interesting. Remember to start and finish in "cushion" position. Keep legs straight while you're in the air . . . and above all, point your toes.

136   137   138

7. Don't forget about your face. Look at the audience and smile. Eye contact and a natural smile make you look confident and professional. They contribute to an overall dynamic projection and super showmanship.

8. Remember, your bodywork sells you as a performer.

143. **KICK:** Keep leg straight and toe pointed. With practice, you'll be able to get your leg higher and higher. But better to keep leg low than to bend knee. So don't kick any higher than you can while keeping your leg straight.

144. **LUNGE:** Put weight on bent leg and point the other toe.

48

139

140

141

142

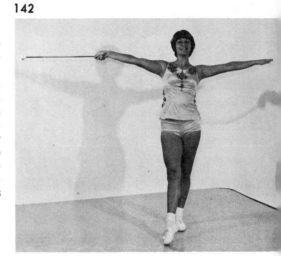

VERTICAL LOOP BEHIND HEAD

136, 137, 138, 139, 140, 141, 142. Begin facing front with baton in right hand. Hold thumb to ball at tip end at your right side, with ball pointing down. As you begin turning to left, bring ball up (136). Continue lifting arm as your body continues turning (137). As you face rear, baton continues making outline of wheel (138, 139), staying in front plane as you face rear. Baton should not come behind your head before your body is facing rear, or it will be out of plane. Turning body and baton at same speed helps keep baton in correct plane. By the time baton has finished loop behind head (140), body has finished three fourths of its turn (141) and returns to front as baton completes circle (142).

145. **TOE POINT:** Be sure to keep the other leg straight.

146   147

146, 147. **FLASH-OUT LEAP:** A good crouch (146) gives the best spring. Stretch for maximum effect while you're in the air (147). Make sure legs are straight, toes pointed.

Routines

We've included two sample routines that you can use, in competitions or in performances—or just for practice. One routine is a bit more difficult than the other, but both are one minute long—regulation length for USTA beginners.

You can order the official solo competition record from the USTA, or practice to a one-minute music selection of your choice. (If you compete, you'll perform to the official record, so if you're planning to enter a contest, it's a good idea to order the record.)

Don't limit yourself to these routines. You can certainly change them or make up your own. Here are some tips that will help you put together a good routine and improve your performance.

1. Open and close with a bang.
2. Keep flat sections together, building up to more difficulty.
3. Keep roll section together.
4. Avoid repetitions.
5. Vary body positions to make your moves more exciting.
6. Construct the routine so all your body turns aren't in the same direction.
7. Keep body and baton in fluid motion at all times.
8. Make sure footwork is planned and exact.
9. Don't let free hand dangle. Plan poses and stick to the plan.

10. Know where ball and tip of baton are at all times. This helps you avoid drops, fumbles, or breaks.

11. Keep facial expression pleasant and natural. Relax and enjoy what you're doing. Plenty of eye contact with the judge helps sell the routine.

12. Execute tricks with snap and pizazz to make your performance interesting to watch.

SIMPLE BEGINNER ROUTINE

1. Salute.
2. High aerial, catch right. Follow through with lunge to left and do reverse figure 8 at left side.
3. Figure-8 turnaround to the right, end facing ¼ left. (Up on toes during turnaround.)
4. Right-hand reverse-cartwheel flip toss. Catch in left hand. Right leg points forward toward left side as you toss.
5. Left-hand reverse-cartwheel flip toss. Catch under left leg in deep lunge still facing ¼ left. (Bring right leg back so you can lunge to the left.)
6. Bring baton out from under leg with a circle swing over the head (vertical) as you turn to the left.
7. Right-hand whip.
8. Horizontal neck wrap with right hand, catch in left.
9. Left-hand horizontal toss. Catch thumb to ball in right hand.
10. Right-hand horizontal wrist twirl into . . .
11. . . . horizontal four-finger, with body turn on toes to the left.
12. Horizontal pass to left hand. Both hands palm down on pass. Left hand takes baton thumb to tip.
13. Horizontal four-finger overhead. Continue turning to left on toes.
14. Waist wrap from left to right hand, with left leg pointed forward.
15. Two-hand spin flat overhead while body turns left on toes.
16. Wrap around both legs from left to right hand.
17. Bring baton out into horizontal wrist twirl; bring immediately to chest and turn around to the left.
18. Two-finger flat down in right hand. Keep feet together and bend from waist.
19. Two-finger overhead. Come up on toes.
20. Two-finger down. Bend both knees in crouch position.
21. Baton overhead in two-finger and flash-out leap to right side.
22. Horizontal pass from left to right hand. Turn to the left as you bring baton up overhead in flat circle.
23. Pass to right hand around left leg, from behind leg, as you lunge left.

24. Right figure 8 at right side and slide to tip.
25. Pass over left shoulder facing ¼ right.
26. Continue on around to the back and pass baton in back from left to right hand.
27. Continue turning to face front. Right figure 8 at right side.
28. Left elbow, catch right.
29. Vertical loop behind head as you turn to the left.
30. Double-elbow roll and catch left behind back.
31. Reverse figure 8.
32. Pass left to right behind both knees, knees bent.
33. High aerial.
34. Catch thumb to tip and bow.
35. Final salute.

MORE DIFFICULT BEGINNER ROUTINE

1. Salute.
2. Left-hand flip into reverse figure 8 and pass behind the back, turning left.
3. High right-handed aerial, as in previous routine ⁂1.
4. Figure 8 at right side.
5. Right-hand whip. Cushion for leap.
6. Flash out to right-side leap with figure 8.
7. Face ¼ left. Reverse-cartwheel flip from right hand. Catch under and outside right leg in left hand.
8. Bring baton out and turn left to face back.
9. Left-hand thumb flip to right hand and continue turn to face front.
10. Two-hand turning spin.
11. Two-hand spin and left- and right-leg passes.
12. Two-hand spin, feet together.
13. Split jump and back pass.
14. Flat circle overhead and turn to the left.
15. Flat neck wrap from right to left hand.
16. Flat throw from left hand to right. Catch thumb to ball.
17. Right flat two-finger down.
18. Right flat two-finger overhead.
19. Right flat two-finger down. Bend both knees in crouch.
20. Right flat two-finger overhead with flash-out leap to right.
21. Flat neck wrap from right hand to left. Body turns to the left.
23. Pass behind back and keep turning to the left.
24. Split jump and pass baton between legs.
25. Figure 8 at right side.
26. Double-elbow roll and catch behind back in left hand.

27. Left-hand thumb flip back and catch with right hand. Turn left to face ¼ right.
28. Figure 8 slide to the tip and pass over left shoulder as you kick left leg facing to right side, and then bring it back into lunge to right.
29. Baton over right shoulder, passing from the front. Snap up on toes.
30. Two-hand spin and pass around both knees from behind.
31. High steeple throw.
32. Catch thumb to tip in right hand and bow. Then come up in pose, arms extended in a Y.
33. Final salute.

If you're going to compete, start as soon as possible. If you wait until you can do the routines perfectly, you'll be waiting too long. There's nothing like competition to hasten improvement. So take your chances, make mistakes, learn from them, and eventually, you'll come home with a medal or a trophy.

A sample competition score sheet for soloists is included below. You'll notice that the routine is judged for its variety and difficulty. The speed and smoothness with which you perform are evaluated, as is your showmanship.

Look at the penalty area. You'll see that you'll get deductions for drops, breaks, and slips (unplanned interruption in the routine), and getting out of pattern (plane).

OFFICIAL USTA SCORE SHEET
SOLO, TWO BATON, THREE BATON AND DUET

PLACE_____
CLASS_____
EVENT_____

Name_____
Age_____

THIS SCORE SHEET IS DESIGNED FOR USE IN SOLO, TWO BATON, THREE BATON AND DUET CONTESTS WITHOUT CHANGES. Do not erase; cross out mistakes and initial. Please avoid personal comments.

		COMMENTS	SCORE
VARIETY	20		
DIFFICULTY	20		
SPEED	20		
SMOOTHNESS	20		
SHOWMANSHIP	20		

GROSS SCORE

PENALTIES (Deduct from total)												
DROPS	.5	1.0	1.5	2.0	2.5	3.0	3.5	4.0	4.5	5.0		
BREAKS OR SLIPS	.1	.2	.3	.4	.5	.6	.7	.8	.9	1.0		
PATTERN	.1	.2	.3	.4	.5	.6	.7	.8	.9	1.0		
	1.1	1.2	1.3	1.4	1.5	1.6	1.7	1.8	1.9	2.0		
LOSS OF BALANCE	.1	.2	.3	.4	.5	.6	.7	.8	.9	1.0		
OUT OF POSITION	.1	.2	.3	.4	.5	.6	.7	.8	.9	1.0		
UNISON (DUETS ONLY)	.1	.2	.3	.4	.5	.6	.7	.8	.9	1.0		

OUT OF STEP – ENTRANCE .5   EXIT .5
FAILURE TO EXIT WITH DRUMS .5
PERSONAL APPEARANCE .5 to 5.0
FALLING DOWN 2.0   PARTIAL FALL .5
INCORRECT SALUTE – OPENING .1   CLOSING .1
FAILURE TO SALUTE – OPENING 1.0   CLOSING 1.0
OTHER PENALTIES
UNSPORTSMANLIKE CONDUCT – UP TO 5 POINTS
OVERTIME .5
UNDERTIME .5

TOTAL PENALTIES

TOTAL SCORE

Date_____ Judge's Signature_____

THIS SCORE SHEET MAY NOT BE REPRODUCED IN ANY FORM WITHOUT EXPRESS PERMISSION OF THE UNITED STATES TWIRLING ASSOCIATION.

Don't be frightened by the score sheet. We've included it to help you plan your performance, and so you'll know what to expect from the judge.

When you compete, you'll receive your score sheet after you've been judged. The judge's comments will help you see your strengths and weaknesses. The best evaluations can be a good guide as to where you need the most practice and work.

There's more about competitive twirling in Chapter Three, so read on. If you've been practicing regularly for ten weeks, working on all the tricks in this chapter, then you're ready.

If you're interested in becoming a majorette, then Chapter Four will have special appeal to you. Anyone who has completed Chapter Two is a good majorette candidate.

Whatever you do, don't stop learning. Intermediate baton maneuvers are taught in Chapter Five, and you should start them fairly soon.

Don't wait until you've mastered every beginning maneuver before going on. Work on beginning and intermediate tricks simultaneously now. You may find that you can do some intermediate maneuvers more easily than you can do the most difficult beginning moves.

THREE

Competitive Solo Twirling

Whether you're a beginner, intermediate, or advanced twirler, you can twirl competitively if you want to. Some of you may be wondering why we've put the chapter on competitive twirling so early in the book—before we've covered all the skill levels and twirling specialties.

The reason is simple. We want to encourage beginners to compete, to make sure that twirlers understand from the start what competitive twirling is all about. We want beginners to be aware that in competitive twirling, there are as many opportunities for them to enter and win as there are for more experienced twirlers.

Whatever your skill level, competitive twirling gives you an opportunity to test yourself against other twirlers of your sex and age. And it gives beginners an evaluation of their technique and performance and helps them understand areas that most need improvement.

In competitive twirling, there are three skill levels—beginner, intermediate, and advanced. How do you know where you fit? It's easy.

148. **1976 USTA GRAND NATIONAL CHAMPION:** Holly Mayer, 18, from Novelty, Ohio.

The labels are easily defined. They're technical. If you've won fewer than three first-place awards, you're a beginner. If you've won more than three firsts, but fewer than eight, you're an intermediate. And if you've won eight or more first-place awards, you're an advanced.

The skills we're describing in this book are also labeled beginner, intermediate, and advanced. They correspond to those skills you'll need to have if you're planning to compete. For example, by the time you've mastered the beginning skills in the previous chapter, you'll be quite capable of winning enough first-place awards to take you out of the beginner category. You'll then have to compete as an intermediate, and to win awards as an intermediate, you'll need to work on and perfect the maneuvers classified in this book as intermediate.

In competition, beginners compete against other beginners, intermediates against other intermediates, advanced against advanced. This makes competitive twirling very fair and gives all twirlers an equal chance to get the recognition they deserve for all the hard work they've done.

Twirling contests are held often—in some areas as frequently as once a week. Twirlers who compete regularly may enter more than two hundred contests in the course of their twirling careers. Chances are you'll have plenty of opportunities to win the necessary awards to advance.

Of course, winning isn't the only important thing about competing. It's not even the most important. Self-improvement is the most valuable thing you can get out of competitive twirling.

In one contest you may place second. In the next, you may place fifth. That doesn't necessarily mean you're not improving. You'll have to compare your scores and the judges' comments from one competition to the next. You may find you've come a long way—regardless of how you placed in relationship to the other twirlers.

It's more meaningful to rate your progress against your own past performances than to compare yourself to others in your group.

In addition to giving you the joy of recognition, competitive twirling also provides you with a great deal of incentive to practice and improve. Over the Christmas holidays, for example, we find that a lot of students slack off. They come back to their classes in January and they look awful. Gloria sometimes wonders whether she's really taught them anything at all. Fred often has doubts about whether they really even want to be there.

Then, all of a sudden, there'll be a contest coming up in February. Everybody perks up. By the end of January their batons aren't dragging anymore. The twirling has sharpened up, the kids are enthusiastic, they're working hard and raring to go.

Whenever you compete, regardless of your skill level, chances are you'll be seeing twirlers who are more experienced and more advanced than you are. You can learn from them, be inspired by them, and increase your own determination to develop your skill even further.

Fred remembers very well the first time he was inspired by another twirler. He was a teen-ager, at his first contest. There was a wonderful twirler doing incredible things with his baton. Fred's eyes nearly popped out of his head. He couldn't believe how good the other fellow was.

After he got over his initial shock, he began to watch the other twirler very carefully. Then he said to himself, "Maybe I can learn that. Maybe if I really work at it, I can get to be as good as he is. Maybe someday I can even beat him."

Eventually, he did. Fred never felt any malice toward him, or any thrill of winning for winning's sake. He didn't feel great because he beat someone else, but because he had set himself a goal and had accomplished it.

Fred really admired the other guy. Because of seeing his tricks, Fred had stretched his own imagination, rethought what was possible to do with a baton. He'd been challenged, excited, and motivated, just like kids today are when they go to their first competition.

Since we've been teaching, we've found that most children and teen-agers are positive and optimistic by nature. They're not flattened by defeat, and they're not discouraged when they see someone else doing something better than they can. (We find that when a kid is negative and pessimistic, it's often the parents' attitude that's being reflected in the child.)

Instead of saying, "Gee, I might as well quit, I'll never be able to do that," young people will more often say, "If she can do it, maybe I can too. So I'll give it a try." Or, when they see a really superfantastic twirler, they'll say, "Wow, isn't that terrific. Now if I just change it slightly, add thus and so, I'll come out with a whole new trick." These kids are really getting their creative juices flowing, just like Fred did that first time years ago.

Now let's be realistic about this. Just because you think you can do better than the person you admire doesn't always turn out to be true. Maybe you're not going to beat the other girl, ever, no matter how hard you try. But one thing's for certain. If you don't think you can do it, you haven't got a chance in the world. And if you don't try, you'll never know. And if you don't try, you'll never improve. Even if you don't improve as much as you'd like to, you've stretched your ability just by putting forth the effort.

One of the things we all have to accept in life is that we're not all going to be the best at everything. We may not even be the best in anything. But that doesn't have to be a tragedy.

Competitive twirling not only helps you develop your abilities, it also helps you to accept your limitations. It helps you realize that you don't have to be "best" or "first" to enjoy what you're doing. This holds true for twirling and for everything else.

Winning and losing. It's always easier to deal with winning than losing. So let's talk a little about losing. There's probably nothing we or anyone else can do to make losing pleasant. And it's not supposed to be pleasant. It's disappointing, but it's not the worst thing that can happen to you. The sooner you realize that, the better off you're going to be.

Losing a competition often ignites a spark and helps you to give the extra push that's needed. There's always another chance, and besides, if you've improved from one contest to the next, you're a winner no matter what anyone says.

One of our hopes is that more and more twirling teachers will instill this philosophy in their students from the beginning. It can make competitions much less painful and far more meaningful.

All twirlers must have the ability to accept a judge's decision. And you must accept it gracefully, without anger or hostility or hatred—not toward the judge, not toward another competitor, not toward yourself.

One of the first things we tell our students is that the scoring is simply a matter of judges' opinions. Judges are human beings. Usually they know what they're doing, but sometimes they make mistakes. Sometimes they're too easily impressed; sometimes they're not as aware as we'd like them to be. Sometimes they blink or become distracted. Sometimes they're not experienced enough.

Whenever Fred spots a sore loser, he handles it this way. He says to the girl, "Maybe you shouldn't have lost this time. But just remember, you've won sometimes when you didn't deserve it. The score is probably pretty even."

How do you handle wins you don't really deserve? When one of Gloria's students wins with a performance that's not up to her true level, she says, "I'm happy for you that you won, but I'd be much happier, and you would be too, if you'd done a top-notch job. I'd rather see you come in third doing your best than getting first by 'lucking out' with a poor job."

If winning isn't the point, what is? We think it's to improve. And winning—or even increasing your score from one performance to another—is no real proof of improvement. Judges are fallible, remember. Just as winning isn't always proof of anything, neither is losing. Losing may not always mean you haven't improved. It may only mean that the judge thought someone else twirled better than you did that time. But sometimes losing is a sign you haven't worked hard enough. You have to face up to this and practice more.

Only you and your teacher can determine whether you're really improving. The most important thing competitive twirlers must learn is to be objective about their own work. Don't be unduly influenced by a score sheet or a judge—especially if you're getting lots of compliments. Think over what other people say about your performance. Maybe you'll agree; maybe not. Be honest with yourself. You know how good you are and how hard you've worked. You know how you stack up against the competition, and whether or not you performed up to par at any given time. Nothing anyone else says can change what you know.

This is true whether you win or lose. Of course, it's always a blow to lose when you know you deserved to win. But whatever the reason for not winning, there'll always be a next time. So consider yourself lucky and be sure you make the most of it.

And if you do win, don't get a swelled head. Someone will beat you sometime. Maybe next time, or the time after that. There's nothing more unattractive than an "I'm better than everyone else" attitude. Fortunately, this doesn't happen much in twirling.

Experience has taught us that most children and teen-agers can take both winning and losing in stride. If they can't, we suggest they get out of competition. Usually they change their attitudes rather than quit.

Sometimes, adults have more problems in this area than kids have. It's no secret that a twirling student usually adopts or develops the same attitude as the teacher. Today, there are a few too many teachers who overemphasize the importance of winning rather than the importance of continual improvement and helpful self-criticism.

We like our students to win, don't get us wrong. And our students do win —very often. We want them to win, but not at all costs. If all we're doing is teaching our students how to twirl a baton well enough to win, then we aren't doing much of a job.

We want to help our students develop grace, poise, fitness, maturity, self-confidence, self-knowledge, discipline—things that will ultimately be far more valuable to them than a thousand trophies.

It's important that parents aren't shortsighted about the ultimate goals of twirling. Sometimes it's difficult for parents to accept the fact that their children don't come in first. And it's also hard for them to sit back when they feel a child isn't adequately rewarded for a job well done. Sometimes parents identify too closely with their children. They take it as a personal insult if their kids don't win—and they consider it their personal glory if they do.

Look at it this way, whether or not you or your child win a trophy today has very little to do with the future. Not everyone can be the national championship twirler. Twirling is such a refined art today that it takes incredible motivation and drive to go all the way to the top. And it isn't necessary to reach the top before you reap the benefits of twirling.

Today, there are more twirlers than ever before, but fewer and fewer are putting forth the intense effort needed to become national champions. To become a champion, you've got to be better than advanced. It takes a rare talent—and often total dedication.

You don't have to be a champion to enjoy the fringe benefits of twirling. For example, a good twirler who doesn't hold top twirling honors can be just as appealing to a college band director or a college admission board— and she is just as likely to get a scholarship as the girl with a roomful of trophies.

Time after time, band directors have said to one or the other of us, "Well, I know Alice was national champion, and she sure does twirl better than Dotty, but Dotty has some special sparkle, and she's the one I'm choosing."

When to begin? If you've never competed before and think you'd like to try, then there's no time like the present to start. If you're a novice, you should enter just as soon as you can smoothly execute enough of the basic maneuvers to put together a routine, following the principles of routine construction in Chapter Two.

Your age doesn't matter either. You can't be too young—or too old. Maybe you're a teen-ager who's just learning to twirl. Don't be frightened off by all those little tots in the competitions. Of course, you'd feel a little silly competing against someone eight or nine years younger than you, but in competitive twirling each event has separate divisions for every age.

What are the events? Well, there's solo twirling, of course. And there's also strut, dance twirl, and two- and three-baton twirling. Teams and corps also compete. But we'll get to all those other events later on.

As a beginner, you will probably be unable to enter any event except beginning solo, and perhaps dance twirl. If you win first place in your age division, then you'll compete in a "twirl-off"—against first-place winners from all the other beginner divisions. Twirl-off first-place winners are called grand champions of the entire competition.

In a twirl-off it's impossible to predict by age who will win. Winning usually has nothing to do with how old you are. Whether you're the youngest, oldest, or in between means very little. A winner can come from any age group.

One story illustrates this point very well. Fred calls it the saga of Gayle and Joan because it went on over a period of several years. One of his students, Gayle, became grand national champion when she was ten. That's very unusual, but Gayle was exceptionally talented. Her friend Joan, who was the same age, hadn't even started to twirl when Gayle won her highest honor. But several years later, she started taking lessons.

Joan also had a lot of natural ability, but she worked like the dickens. She began to compete, won the first-place awards she needed to advance through the ranks, and she became an advanced twirler. At that point, she and Gayle began to compete against each other.

Joan was dying to become grand national champion, but she didn't really think she could ever beat Gayle, although other girls had done it. But Joan kept saying, "Gayle's been twirling six years longer than I have. How can I ever beat her?"

"Do you think everyone who's been grand national champion since Gayle has been twirling since age six? Not on your life," Fred told Joan. "You can do it, but you'll never make it if you think about how important those extra years are. Believe me, they don't matter—except in your head."

Well, finally, when they were both fifteen, Joan did it. And the following year, Gayle, for the second time, became grand national champion again. (Winning this honor twice is very unusual.)

How to do it. Contests throughout the country are sanctioned by one of the baton-twirling associations. A USTA-sanctioned contest, for example, must be cleared through and approved by USTA headquarters. All events will be judged by USTA-certified judges, and contest procedures will follow USTA rules. Although the group that sponsors the contest (usually a corps from one area or another) pays a sanction fee to the association, it also earns money by being a sponsor.

Your teacher may be a member of one or both twirling associations. She (or he) will be able to tell you about contests coming up in your area. If you're a member of one of the associations, then you'll probably automatically receive word in the mail. If you don't have a teacher who can supply you with information, then write to the associations for a calendar of competitive events, as well as for membership information.

Both associations hold contests on local, state, regional, and national levels. If you've never competed before, a local contest is the best way to get your feet wet. Local contests provide the best opportunities because they are held frequently. State, regional, and national contests are once-a-year events. Frequent participation in local contests will give you plenty of valuable competition experience and help you build confidence. This is the level at which most people win the first-place awards they need to advance from beginners to intermediate and so on.

If you're unsure about entering, why not visit a local association competition and watch. You'll get some idea of how a twirling contest operates and feel more comfortable about competing yourself the next time around.

Events. You can enter more than one event in a contest. If you've just started to twirl, then beginning solo may be the only event you're qualified to enter. But if you're also learning strutting or dance twirl, you can enter them as well.

Furthermore, your skill level might be different for different events. An intermediate twirler might be a beginning strutter, for example. Or an advanced one-baton twirler might be an intermediate in two-baton. Remember, you'll be categorized according to the number of first-place awards you've previously won in each event.

You can enter a state or national contest regardless of what competitions you have or haven't entered previously, and regardless of whether you've been a winner before. Let's assume, for example, you've never won a state championship, but you want to enter the nationals. That's allowed.

On the other hand, you may be a state champion in twirling or strutting or whatever. That doesn't automatically give you entry into the national finals. You've got to enter qualifying rounds at the national competition in order to become eligible for the national finals.

What does it cost to compete? In competitive twirling, each event has a separate entry fee, usually about three dollars for solo events. Fifty cents of this is usually refundable to members of the association that sanctions the contest. To get the $.50 refund, take each of your score sheets to the association officials and show your membership card. This way, each event costs you $2.50.

The sponsoring group uses the entry fees, plus general-admission fees paid by parents and other people in the audience, to meet the contest expenses, such as judges' salaries, trophy costs, food, publicity, rental of the school gym where the contest is held, etc. What's left is profit for the sponsoring group (usually a corps), which needs funds to compete and perform.

If you're entering a lot of events, or if you're in a contest far from home, then you'll have to pay more. If you're traveling, then you've got bus or train or plane fare to consider. State, regional, and national contests may last several days or even longer, so if you've traveled far to attend, you'll probably have to stay in a hotel. Reduced group-travel fares and hotel rates are frequently available through the twirling association.

Miscellaneous events. If you send away for a competition entry blank, you'll probably notice some events we haven't mentioned so far. Events such as "fancy strut," "military strut," etc. These events will be marked with an asterisk, which signifies that they're "non-sanctioned." That is, the

USTA has no such official category—although they will judge these events at official competitions.

You won't find non-sanctioned events at state or national contests, but they are very popular at local competitions. The sponsors of the contests like to include them because they give twirlers an opportunity to get good experience in preparation for later entering related sanctioned events. For example, the fancy-strut event helps give a girl the confidence she needs to go into the much more involved beginner strut event.

Since non-sanctioned events are so popular, they are also a good source of income for the sponsor of the competition. If you see some non-sanctioned events in the program for a contest you're thinking of entering, ask your teacher about them. If you feel nervous or not quite ready to compete, the non-sanctioned events are easier and would probably be a good place for you to start.

Sometimes, non-sanctioned events include a beauty contest, where twirlers simply parade across the floor. Quite frankly, if there is to be an event of this kind, we'd like to see some twirling required and have the contestant evaluated according to her showmanship and projection, rather than just looks and costume.

There is a sanctioned beauty-pageant type of contest that is held at the state level—but it does include twirling talent, as well as poise, personality, and appearance. This "Miss America" category is the only event that you must win on a state level to be eligible for nationals.

Another sanctioned miscellaneous event that you'll find at local contests, but not at state or national contests, is the *duet*. This is a novelty type of event that's a lot of fun to enter with a best friend.

The most important thing about being in a duet is to twirl perfectly in unison with your partner. Age divisions for duets are determined by the combined ages of you and your partner. If you and your partner add up your ages and the sum is twenty-one or under, you're a junior duet. Anything over twenty-one is a senior duet.

Costumes. If you're going to twirl competitively, you'll have to turn in your practice shorts for a genuine costume. While some twirlers, especially the very advanced girls, may have costumes costing nearly $200, you can have a lovely, more-than-adequate costume for around twenty dollars. When figuring your costume budget, keep in mind that you may want something different for every event you're entering, although you can wear the same costume for all solo events if your budget doesn't allow for more than one.

You can either make or buy a costume. Making your own costume has two big advantages. It's usually much cheaper than a ready-made, and more original too.

There's a list of costume suppliers in the Appendix. Send for their catalogues even if you're planning to sew your own. You'll get some ideas for designs and trims, but even better, you'll also know exactly how much you're saving by doing it yourself.

If you don't know how to sew, then the easiest and least expensive thing to do is buy a basic leotard and trim it yourself. Leotard companies will often give a substantial discount to teachers who order in large quantities. Ask your teacher if she has such an arrangement. She may very well—especially if most of her students are using leotards as the basis of a costume.

If you're making the leotard from scratch, you'll need a stretch material—one that stretches lengthwise. Light- or heavyweight Jumbo spandex is good. So are double knits, super-stretch florescents, and lamés. Quiana is also becoming popular now.

You can alter a basic bodysuit, leotard, or bathing suit pattern in any number of ways: boat neck, V neck, deep V in back with straps crossing over your back, cut-out ovals at sides of the waist, empire waist, etc.

The trim is the most expensive part of the costume, but if you sew it on carefully, you can take it off and reuse it on another costume. That's what most girls who use very costly trim do.

There are four types of trim commonly used. Rhinestones come in single or double strands, which makes sewing easier. Use strands to outline a decorative area on the costume. You can also use single rhinestones to dot the costume. You can sew on the singles or staple them on with a special hand gun made for this purpose. It's not terribly expensive, and a great time-saver if you're planning on using single rhinestones often.

You can also sew rhinestone designs on net. It's not difficult to do, but net costumes usually turn out to be quite expensive.

Sequins are another popular trim. They're attractive—though not as sparkly as rhinestones—and they're less expensive. They also come in strands or in single sequins.

You can also consider lace or eyelet trimmed with satin or velvet strands. Beaded embroidery is also very beautiful, but expensive. Unless you're quite advanced in twirling, you probably shouldn't consider it.

Beginners are really better off investing as little as possible until they know for sure they're going to stick with competitive twirling.

Don't wear a hat—unless you're entering a military strut event. Solo twirlers find tiaras most suitable. You can get them with rhinestones, beads, or sequins. Make sure your tiara is well-secured. You want it to hold up under vigorous activity.

Now what about footwear? Not much choice here. White socks and gym shoes, unless you're strutting. While most strutters are still choosing white sneakers, lots of girls are turning to gymnastic slippers instead. Ballet slippers are also acceptable for strutting, but aren't very popular.

Future of competitive twirling. There have been a lot of changes in competitive twirling over the years. Twirlers have gotten better, for one thing. There's been a tremendous increase in the difficulty of tricks over the past fifteen years.

The art of twirling has become much more refined. The number of events in competitive twirling has increased, the judging has become more sophisticated, the costumes more elegant. Also, the number of people who twirl in competitions is increasing every year.

What does the future hold? More changes along the same lines, or something drastically different?

There are two major changes we predict. First, cash awards will begin to replace trophies and medals. Prize money could help defray the cost of competing, or it could go toward further education. While most universities and colleges offer some type of scholarship to twirlers, there's no reason the twirling associations couldn't eventually offer them as well. We'd like to see the national championship twirlers receive full scholarships as prizes.

Second, we believe competitive twirling should and will become an Olympic event. More and more countries are becoming interested in twirling, and more and more twirlers from the United States are traveling throughout all parts of the world to perform. In Japan and France, twirling is a national passion. Once it catches on in the Soviet Union, twirling will begin to appeal to Olympic officials.

Twirling has already gained considerable international status. There is a four-member international team on tour, teaching, performing, and promoting twirling in Europe.

As an Olympic event, twirling will offer even more exciting opportunities to young women than it presently does. In addition, it will also become a richer source of entertainment, given the same TV coverage as other Olympic events.

66

FOUR

Majorettes

Whenever most people think of baton twirling, they think of the high school majorette marching down the football field, twirling to music provided by the school's marching band. Twirling owes much of its current popularity to majorettes. It's through majorette performances that the general public— and most new twirlers as well—first become aware of baton twirling.

Being a majorette is an attractive and popular alternative to being a competitive twirler. In fact, it has some decided advantages. More girls can become majorettes than can become competitive twirlers, because less talent, skill, and dedication are required. But even girls with superior twirling talent find greater appeal in being a majorette. First of all, it requires less practice time, leaving more room for other activities. Becoming a majorette gives you an instant opportunity to get involved in school activities, and brings you wide recognition within your school.

Majoretting started in the early 1940s, when band directors here and there decided to increase the audience appeal of the marching band by add-

149. **MAJORETTE** Karen Rodberg, featured twirler at the University of Alabama, wears eye-catching stretch costume that allows freedom of movement.

ing a baton twirler or two. This exposure got more and more teen-age girls interested in twirling, and soon more and more band directors began to use majorettes. The number of majorettes kept increasing, and today, many high schools have not just one or two majorettes, but whole teams consisting of as many as sixteen (or more). A majorette who has exceptional twirling skill may have a featured role. But just as often the band also uses a featured twirler who is not on the majorette squad, but who is a competitive twirler who attends that school.

150. **MAJORETTE** Jackie Mays (now Jackie Mays Miller) wore a loose-fitting military-style uniform in the early 1950s.

Should You Become a Majorette?

If you like twirling and have the time to become involved in extra-curricular activities, there's no reason not to try out. Tryouts are usually held once a year, and you'll have to find out when. If it isn't publicized, ask the director of your school band.

We feel that everyone who wants to should be eligible to try out—either for the majorette team or for the featured twirler role. Furthermore, we don't think seniority should be a factor. Even girls who previously twirled with the band should be required to try out each year.

We also suggest that the band director and teacher-adviser use non-local judges for tryouts. If there's a college nearby, perhaps the band director there would cooperate and evaluate each girl's performance. Or maybe you can work out a reciprocal arrangement with high school band directors in neighboring communities.

What Do Majorettes Do?

Majorettes usually perform at half-time shows, of course. But there's more to it than just marching out on the field when the time comes. Getting the show together takes a lot of work and discipline—more so than most audiences realize.

Majorette teams usually have a head captain or team captain. She often makes up the routines (with or without the help of a teacher-adviser), and she may also be in charge of rehearsals and discipline of the other team members. If the team is large, there may be assistant captains or squad captains to whom the head captain delegates various tasks.

A good captain must make sure all members are on time for practices and performances. She must also continually check up on the team members, to be sure they learn the routine and can perform in perfect unison with the rest of the group. She may have to help girls who learn more slowly or who are having trouble with certain parts of the routine.

The captain should also check to see that uniformity of knee levels and strutting technique prevails. She also has to help each member project throughout the entire routine. Everyone is responsible for the "sell"—but the captain may have to remind the girls frequently.

The captain must make the team rules clear to all members and enforce discipline. Sometimes the captain must even suspend or "bench" a girl who has been detrimental to the unit as a whole.

Being captain isn't easy. So if the job is offered to you, think twice. You not only need the organizing and choreographing skills, but also the strength to suspend even your best friend, if necessary.

Team captains must also learn to meet the requirements of the band director. Remember, the purpose of the majorette is to enhance the band's performance. The majorette team is the icing on the cake—not the cake. Sometimes the band director will want to highlight the majorettes—but sometimes not. No grumping and groaning from you in this event.

The band director chooses the music and mood and theme of the performance. Don't argue with him. Don't attempt to upstage the band. It's not appropriate and will only cause friction. You, as a majorette, are performing because the band director decided to include majorettes. He can just as easily decide not to include them.

Every majorette, captain or otherwise, must be willing to practice alone and with the rest of the team. You have to learn the marching drills and twirling maneuvers until they become automatic. You can't rely on the captains or other team members to compensate for your sloppy job. When you're out on the field, you've got to be in top form. So work until you can do the routine perfectly.

Then concentrate on projecting yourself. Remember, the show has to have oomph. If your performance is lackluster, the audience will head for the hot dog stand during half time. Your job is to keep the people in the stands.

You should do anything extra that you can to help the team. For example, if you know the material better than some of the other girls, don't skip practice. Instead, help others who aren't up to your level. Don't wait for someone to ask, and don't wait for the captain to direct you. Just offer. If you do this in the spirit of friendship and not as a way of showing off your superior ability, your teammates will be grateful.

Remember, one poor performance can ruin the reputation of the whole squad. Adequate preparation, as individuals and as a team, will make your group interesting to watch. You can be as big a draw as the football team itself—an even better draw if the team isn't so hot. So don't slack off in your practice. Keep rehearsing right up to show time if you need to.

As we mentioned, a solo performer or featured twirler may be one of the majorettes or a competitive twirler who isn't on the team. The most important aspect of the soloist's performance is her projection, sparkle, and pizazz. Showmanship and an extraordinary display of self-confidence, along with a polished, smooth execution, are crucial.

If the featured twirler is very experienced or especially skilled with the baton, she might do a two-baton or three-baton routine. But it isn't really necessary for the solo routine to be terribly difficult. It must be exciting to watch, and the excitement can come from the twirler's enthusiasm for what she's doing rather than from the difficulty of her tricks.

The featured twirler must always remember that she's only a part of the whole show. So she shouldn't hog the spotlight. If you're a featured twirler, your routine should be no longer than the routine the entire squad is doing. Ideally, it should be a little shorter.

Costumes

Majorette costumes have changed over the years. Modern costumes usually consist of a one-piece leotard type of uniform—stretchy and colorful. Usually the school colors and nickname or theme are carried out in the uniform.

You can add a matching jacket, possibly with tails and lapels. This varies the look you can achieve, and also gives you protection against the cold. When you're not wearing the jacket, you can use mitts or wear fingerless gloves that come up to your elbows.

Some majorette squads choose shorts or brief skirts instead of stretch uniforms. It's true that overweight girls look better in the looser costumes, but frankly, we'd prefer to see these girls reduce and have the team stick to the tight-fitting leotards. They're much flashier looking and also easier to twirl in.

Some type of headgear like tiaras or crowns are acceptable for majorettes but not mandatory. If you decide to wear a headpiece, make sure it's fastened securely.

Each majorette is responsible for keeping her uniform and footwear in good repair, clean, and fitting properly.

Principles of Half-time Twirling

Team captains and teacher-advisers should keep certain things in mind when planning majorette routines. First, go up into the stands and watch someone twirling on the field. You'll notice that some things are far more effective at long-distance range than others.

Use plenty of large or exaggerated motions and avoid delicate twirls. They'll be nearly invisible anyway. Use super-high aerials, which look best out of doors. Avoid extensive horizontal work. Keep the routine moving quickly, and up the twirling speed and bodywork. Most marching-band music moves along at a quick tempo, and you'll want your choreography to correspond.

Half-time shows present great opportunities for specialty work—using hoops, fire batons, flags, sabers, knives, etc. Make sure your choice of props and routine materials fits the theme set by the band director.

Remember that *unison* is the one thing that makes group twirling look good. Twirling maneuvers shouldn't be so difficult that unison is sacrificed. Keeping twirling tricks relatively simple helps the team to avoid drops and keeps the performance smooth.

In addition to marching and meneuvering, majorettes should be able to execute twirling and dance-twirl routines. Very often one of the band's songs will highlight the majorettes during one of these sections of the routine—hopefully, all three.

Entrances and exits are usually with the band. Sometimes the majorette squad will be incorporated into the band's formations—the wheels of a train, the clapper of a bell, the points of a star, etc.

Routines can be varied from week to week by changes in the formation, changes in the order of the tricks, changes in props, etc. It's not simple to learn a completely different routine every week, but it is possible to change an old routine enough so that it seems completely different to the audience.

Several types of routines for majorettes follow. If you're interested in having your majorettes or featured twirler use fire batons, you'll find instructions and sample routines in Chapter Ten.

Guide to Abbreviations Used in Routine Notations

L—left	LL—left leg
R—right	RL—right leg
LA—left arm	LK—left knee
RA—right arm	RK—right knee
LS—left side	LH—left hand
RS—right side	RH—right hand

Under footwork column, terms such as cross L over R, means cross left foot over right foot (word foot or "F," meaning foot, are not included, since the column indicates it is footwork).

MAJORETTE–DANCE-TWIRL ROUTINE

Music: *"Don't Rain on My Parade"*

SET	COUNTS	FOOTWORK	ARMWORK
Introduction:			
Face RS, R toe out, baton at R toe			LH behind back
	1–2		Bring baton up shoulder level
	3–4	Step turn to LS	Rev. fig. 8—overhead
	5–6	Face front	Arms straight out
1	1–2	Cross L over R	Swing LA to RS, RA back to LS
	3–4	Step ball change	Arms straight out
	5–6	Cross R over L	Swing RA to LS
	7–8	Face front	Arms straight out
2	1–2	Step turn to back	Hold baton on both ends—twist up
	3–4	Hold	Slide hand to end overhead
	5–6	Step turn to front	Collapse baton to elbows
	7–8	Point L toe	Thrust arms straight out
3	1–2	Go toward LS, point L toe	Rev. in RH low
	3–4	Point R toe	Fig. 8 high
	5–8	Turn slowly to RS	Rev. fig.-8 whip
4	1–2	Kick LL to RS	Hands to LS
	3–4	Lunge	Baton up, LH to RS
5	1–2	Step L, step ball change	Fwd. fig. 8 on RS
	3–4	Step R, step ball change	Rev. behind
	5–6		Fwd. fig. 8
	7–8	Turn R to LS—R toe up	Point LS

73

SET	COUNTS	FOOTWORK	ARMWORK
6	1–2	Cross R over L to back	Bring arms straight out to back
	3–4	Turn R, fan, kick R	Hold ends of baton—down
	5–6	Pull LK up	Hold ends of baton—down
	7–8	Face front	Push arms up
7	1–2	Lunge L	Hold baton both H, LH on hip
	3–4	Lunge R	RH on hip
	5–6		Circle and cross arms
	7–8	Bend knees	Arms straight out, loop
8	1–2	Turn L	Loop baton under RA
	3–4	Pull up LK	Circle overhead
	5–6		Neck wrap
	7–8	Pose L toe pointed	LH and baton up, RA out
9	1–2	Bend down	Grab baton RH down
	3–4	Come up	Grab LH palm up
	5–6		Pass from LH to RH
	7–8	Turn R	Flag swing
10	1–2	Step L, kick R	Circle, pass under RL
	3–4	Turn to RS	Rev. in LH, pass to RH
	5–6	Face RS—bend knees	Arms to S
	7–8	Face LS—bend knees	Arms to S
11	1–2	Lunge R	Bend down—arms down
	3–4	Lunge L	Push arms up
	5–6	Lunge R	Bend down—arms down
	7–8	Lunge L	Push
12	1–2	Face LS, back step	Rev. in RH
	3–4	Face front	Arms straight out
	5–6	Pick up LK	Pass to LH
	7–8	Feet together	Pass to RH overhead
13	1–2	Face LS, back step	Rev. in RH
	3–4	Face LS, point R toe	Hold baton in front of body
	5	Lunge L to back	Pass baton to LH in back
	6	Return to 3–4	Pass baton to RH
	7	Bend knees	Bring RH down to LS
	8	Straighten	Return RH to RS
14	1–2	Hop R	Rev. loop in RH
	3–4	Lunge R	Arms straight out
	5–6	Cross L	Cross arms in front
	7–8	Pull L to R, point R toe	Arms straight out, Rev. loop
15	1–6	Step turns from sides	Swing baton overhead
	7–8	Face front	Arms straight out

74

SET	COUNTS	FOOTWORK	ARMWORK
16	1–2	Step L to LS	Front 2 hand
	3–4	Step L, pull RK up, turn L to back	Back pass
	5–6	Step R together	Front 2 hand
	7–8	Step R, point L	Back pass
17	1–2	Point L	Turn shoulders L
	3–4	Point R	Turn shoulders R
	5–8	Turn L to front with fan, kick, point R toe	Flat wrist twirl
18	1–2	Lunge L	Flat wrist twirl to L
	3–4	Lunge R	Flat wrist
	5–6	Turn L	Flat twirl, pass to LH
	7		Release LH flat throw
	8		
19	1–2	Deep knee bend	Catch, cross arms in front
	3–4	Back steps	Circle arms in front
	5	Step L (at R diag.)	Swing baton fwd.
	6	Step R	Swing baton back
	7	Kick L, bring L to knee	Swing baton fwd.
	8	Kick L back out	Hold, count 7

REPEAT Sets 1, 2, 3, 4, 5, 6, 7, and 8. Then REPEAT Set 19, counts 5–8.

MAJORETTE–DOWN-THE-FIELD STRUT

MUSIC: *"This Land Is Your Land"*

SET	COUNTS	ARMWORK	FOOTWORK
1	1–4	Dip baton, point tip up L arm in front of face	Step on RF—kick LL and pull back into a lunge
	5–8	(2nd set repeat count 1–4)	
2	1–2	Circle R arm	Lunge L
	3–4	Windmill arms	Turn
	5–6	Both arms down and bow	Point L toe fwd.
	7–8	Both arms up	
3	1–2	L arm out, circle R arm	March
	3–4	Wave baton	
	5–6	Pass baton over R shoulder, grab with L arm behind back	
	7–8	L hard rev.—back pass	

SET	COUNTS	ARMWORK	FOOTWORK
4	1–2	R arm point to side	
	3–4	L arm point to side	
	5–6	Wave arms above head	
	7–8	Arms down at side	Turnaround
5	1–2		Hitch-kick
	3	Pass baton and circle both arms on LS	March
	4	Baton up on R shoulder	
	5–6	Push baton down	
	7	L hand on L shoulder	
	8	Push L arm up	
6	1	Point baton in front	
	2	Pull baton back on R shoulder —L arm out	
	3	Push tip fwd.	
	4	Push ball bkwd.	
	5–6	Flat rev. fig. 8 and set on R shoulder	
	7	½ revolution flip	
	8	Arms down at side	
7	1–2	Arms wave	Step—turn
	3–4	Repeat	Repeat
*	5–6	Dip baton down	Step—knee
	7–8	Rev. baton up	Step—kick
8	1–2	Fig. 8, baton in front	Step–step–step
	3–4	Rev. baton in back	Step–step–step
	5–6	Repeat counts 1–2	Repeat
	7–8	Repeat counts 3–4	Repeat
9	1	Pass to LH	
	2	Pull shaft	
	3–4	Shift to RS	
	5–6	Flat twirl	Step–step–step
	7–8	Flat twirl	Step–step–step
10	1–2	Pass	Step–kick
	3–4	Flip	Step–kick
	5–8	Repeat flat series	
11	1–4	Repeat flat series	
	5–6	Cradle baton and push	March
	7–8	Slowly lower arms	
12	1–2	Slap	
	3–4	Attention	

Repeat from Set 2 through 3–4 of Set 7—go to ending

SET	COUNTS	ARMWORK	FOOTWORK
Ending			
*	5–6	Point baton fwd.	Step–step–step
	7–8	Point baton back	Step–step–step
	1–2	Circle baton	Lunge to L
	3–4	Windmill arms	Spin around
	5–6	Dip baton, point baton up	Step—kick L leg
	7–8	L arm fwd.	Kick back and lunge—drop head

MAJORETTE–TWIRLING ROUTINE

MUSIC: *"That's Entertainment"*

SET	COUNTS	ARMWORK	FOOTWORK
1	1–4	Circle arms up and around, end arms out to side	Feet together
	5–6	Hands touch overhead	LF up by RK—
	7–8	Arms out to side	Feet together
2	1–4	Airplane turn	Turn R
	5–8	Cross arms in front Back out to side	Lunge on LF—RF back
3	1–2	Circle, slide baton in RH	Feet together
	3–4	Neck wrap	Lunge on RF
	5–8	Rev. windmill turn in LH	Turn R
4	1–2	Fig. 8	Facing RS—lunge on RF
	3–4	4-finger in LH	Point L toe
	5–6	Pass over R shoulder to RH	
	7–8	Turn R to front	Turn R to front
5	1–2	Fig. 8 to RS	Feet together
	3–8	Windmill	Lunge on LL—lunge on RL
6	1–6	Windmill turn	Lunge on LL—turn R
	7–8	Pull baton behind back	Stop facing LS
7	1–4	Thumb-flip baton to LH	Step on LF—point R toe
	5–8	Thumb-flip baton to RH	Step on RF—point L toe
8	1–2	Fig. 8 to side	Face front
	3–4	Pass baton under LK to LH	Lift LF
	5–6	Rev. in LH	Feet together
	7–8	Pass baton under L to RH	Kick LL out to side
9	1–2	Circle arms	Feet together
	3–6	Head swing	Turn L
	7–8	Circle arms opposite directions	Face LS—bend knee

77

SET	COUNTS	ARMWORK	FOOTWORK
10	1–2	Arms straight in front	Lunge on LL
	3–4	Left arm in front—pull baton to R shoulder	Feet together
	5–8	Flat twirl in RH	Step with LL—turn to front
11	1–6	Flat twirls	Step turns with RF—turn L
	7–8	Pass baton to LH	Step—ball—change
12	1–6	Flat twirls	Step turns with lift—turn R
	7–8	Pass baton to RH overhead	Up on toes—LF in front
13	1–2	Flat twirl	Step on LL—cross
	3–4	2-finger down	Lunge on LL
	5–6	Pull baton up	Step on RL—cross
	7–8	2-finger up	Lunge on RL
14	1–6	4-finger	Turn L—lift RK
	7–8	Upside-down pass to LH	
15	1–8	Flat dip—throw baton to partner on count 3	Turn facing partner
16	1–8	Flat dip and repeat Set 15	
17	1–2	Flat circle slide overhead in RH	Face front
	3–4	1-handed back wrap	Feet together
	5–8	Fig. 8 to side	Feet together
18	1–8	Windmill—push LH on 5	1st group—lunge L—lunge R
19	1–8	Windmill—push LH on 5	Everybody—lunge L—lunge R
20	1–4	Push baton with LH on inside of arm	Turn facing LS
	5–6	Airplane turn	Turn L
	7–8	Cross arms in front	Point L toe
21	1–2	Arm out to side	Point L toe
	3–4	Circle arms behind head End with arms in V	Point L toe

FIVE

Intermediate Twirling

How do you know if you're ready to learn the maneuvers in this chapter? What makes you an intermediate twirler? If you've been competing, then you've got a good idea of where you belong. You know that for competition purposes, you're a beginner with fewer than three first-place awards.

But that doesn't mean you shouldn't start learning intermediate twirls now. You'll want to be ready to compete as an intermediate as soon as you qualify. So once you're reasonably comfortable with most of the tricks from Chapter Two, you should begin on the harder maneuvers.

If you're already competing as an intermediate, you're probably fairly familiar with many of the tricks we're going to teach you here. But there may be some new things that will help you beef up your routines. And there may be some new variations you never thought of, even though the basic maneuver is one that you already know. So study this chapter. It may help you progress to the advanced class. (Remember, after your eighth first-place award, you don't compete as an intermediate any more.)

79

As an intermediate twirler, you have a wider choice of twirling activities to partake of. You can start twirling in a group—either on a dance-twirl team or in a corps. You can become a corps captain or featured twirler with a majorette squad. You can learn to strut and try your hand at two-baton twirling.

Increasing the difficulty of your repertoire adds a new dimension to your life as a twirler. That, plus the thrill of continued improvement and constant challenge are good reasons for working hard to learn everything in this chapter.

Be sure to keep working on your beginner tricks. Your progress may seem a little uneven, with mastery of *some* of the intermediate meneuvers coming before mastery of *all* the beginning ones.

But keep working, and by the time you've practiced every lesson in this chapter, adding a new lesson every week or two, you'll be a solid intermediate. You'll be ready to work on the intermediate routines at the end of the chapter and, what's more, you'll be able to start your move into the advanced class.

LESSON ONE
FINGERWORK

In intermediate fingerwork, one of the things you're going to do is add something to the four-finger twirl you learned in Chapter Two. And the regular four-finger twirl, plus the new addition, is called an eight-finger twirl.

The first half is identical to the regular four-finger. When the baton gets to your pinky, keep it moving, over the back of your ring finger, and then between each finger until it returns to your thumb, or start position.

You should learn eight-finger twirls in both hands, in all the planes.

Flat Eight-finger Twirl

The easiest plane to learn an eight-finger in is the left overhead flat.

Most twirlers have a tendency to let the baton slant on the flats. Watch it! If you keep your fingers loose and relaxed, it helps keep the baton horizontal.

Flat Eight-finger Variations

1. Two body spins to the left, baton in right hand, fingers pointing down. Keep right arm extended to right side, and left arm out to left side.

151

152

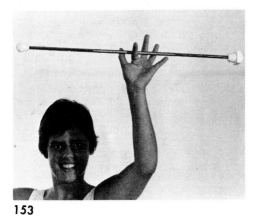

153

154

LEFT FLAT OVERHEAD EIGHT-FINGER TWIRL

151. Baton comes over back of ring finger after finish of regular flat four-finger.
152. Half a revolution to second finger of eight-finger twirl.
153. Third finger of eight-finger twirl.
154. Finish with roll into full hand.

FLAT OVERHEAD EIGHT-FINGER VARIATION

155. Arm above head during first four-finger.
156. Straighten arm on second four-finger, or eight-finger.

155 156

Complete one body spin as you finish the first four-finger, and complete the last four-finger (or eight-finger) on your second body spin.

2. Arm overhead on first four-finger, elbow bent slightly. Snap arm straight up on second four-finger.

Vertical Eight-finger Twirl

Be sure to practice this with both hands, and start with a regular vertical four-finger.

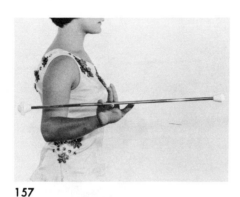

157

RIGHT VERTICAL EIGHT-FINGER TWIRL

157. Start of eight-finger, as baton continues over back of ring finger after completing regular four-finger.

158. Half a revolution over back of middle finger . . .

159. . . . . and onto index finger, ready to finish by rolling back to start position of regular four-finger.

158

159

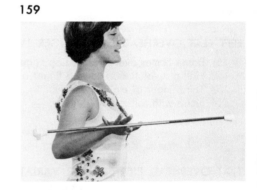

Vertical Eight-finger Variations

1. At side planes, arm lifted high during four-finger and lowered for eight-finger.

2. Turn twice to the right. Be sure to keep baton vertical on the turns. Spin your body at the same speed as the baton. If you turn your body too fast or too slow, the baton will go out of plane. Practice will give you the proper coordination and timing.

160

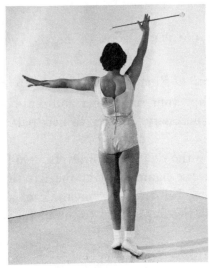

161

162

163

VERTICAL EIGHT-FINGER TURN TWICE

164

160. Keep right hand high and begin spin as you start regular four-finger.

161. Be sure to spin on your toes for faster turn and more graceful look.

162. Left arm stays stretched out to left side. Complete the first spin as you finish regular four-finger.

163. Complete eight-finger during second spin.

164. Bring baton into full hand as you finish second body turn.

Vertical Reverse Two-finger Twirl

Tape your ring finger and pinky together for the two-finger twirls if it's still necessary. But try to get that "hook" down, so you can give up your tape.

Do the right vertical reverse two-finger, facing one-quarter left. Start with a reverse figure eight at the left side, as baton proceeds through first two fingers, ball traveling on inside of arm. Bring baton over to right side and finish two fingers back to thumb on outside of arm.

165

166

167

168

169

170

RIGHT VERTICAL REVERSE TWO-FINGER

165. Bring baton to left side and start it through your first finger.
166. Baton proceeds through next finger and is locked in "hook."
167. Supported by "hook," baton begins to come back to right side.
168. Ready to start back through two-finger.
169. Baton goes over middle finger . . .
170. . . . and ends up in index finger, ready to move to left side and begin again. Repeat for continuous side-to-side motion of arm.

| 172 | 173 | 174 |

VERTICAL REVERSE TWO-FINGER VARIATION

171. Raise figure-eight two-finger on right side.
172. Two-finger facing rear as you turn to left.
173. Complete turnaround, do a two-finger under left leg, and toss off thumb.
174. Catch.

Continuous Four-finger Twirl

Practice these with both hands. Hold baton horizontal with ball to left for left hand and ball to right for right hand. Thumb is to ball, palm is up, baton between thumb and index finger.

Tip proceeds downward as shaft moves through each finger to pinky. Then baton rolls over the backs of your three middle fingers, returning to thumb and index for a repeat.

As baton rolls back to start position, ball willl lead each set.

Practice with both hands, and strive for an even rhythm. Count "And one, two; and one, two." Say the "and" as baton rolls over fingers back to thumb and index finger. Take counts one and two to get the baton through fingers to the pinky.

LESSON TWO
AERIALS

You've already learned how to do basic throws in Chapter Two. Here are some new ways to release the baton into the air.

1. Open-hand release and follow-through. Release is just like the throw

175

176

177

178

OPEN-HAND RELEASE AND FOLLOW-THROUGH

175, 176, 177, 178. Just before release (175); open hand with palm out to release (176); ready to catch (177); catch with follow-through, arm extending out to side (178).

you already know, except palm faces out (instead of up, as in the beginner's throw).

2. Thumb release. This is a thumb flip of more than one revolution, done in the 12-o'clock position.

3. Full-hand release. This is an open-hand release combined with a wrist rotation, so palm faces up, rather than out, just prior to release.

4. Backhand, or reverse thumb pinch. Begin with a left reverse figure eight just before the release.

Thumb-flip Back Catch

This is the same one-revolution thumb flip you learned in Chapter Two, with a turn to the right and catch behind the back added.

179

180

181

182

BACKHAND OR REVERSE THUMB PINCH

179. Begin palm up and start ball traveling up . . .

180. . . . using thumb to propel it on down . . .

181. . . . so ball will travel under arm in preparation for left, using thumb. (Keep baton pinched in thumb, as shown in 180.)

182. Catch right while you're learning. Later you'll learn other ways to recover this release.

THUMB-FLIP BACK CATCH

183. Flip for one revolution only and begin body turn to right as right hand goes behind back for recovery.

184. Catch right, thumb to ball. Keep catch away from your back, so you can continue turning evenly until you face front.

184

Toss Turnaround

In this maneuver, you toss the baton, turn your body completely around, and catch the baton as it descends.

First work on a turn to the left. Practice without the baton in the beginning. Mastering the footwork is crucial.

Step forward with your right foot, then push off with it to pivot left on the ball of your left (back) foot.

Turning toward the rear on your back foot gives your body a good fast spin. But most important—it gets you out from under the descending baton so you can see where to catch it—and so you won't be a target.

When you toss, be sure to spot the place in the air you want the baton to go. Then spin your body and grab right as you come back around to face front.

Intermediates should master a two-toss turnaround (two body spins to the left) and, hopefully, a three-toss turnaround as well.

You should also begin to practice turning to the right on this aerial in preparation for some of the advanced maneuvers we'll teach in the next chapter. Be sure to reverse footwork for right body spin.

Toss-turnaround Variations

You can make your toss turnarounds especially effective and graceful if you make use of one of the following arm positions as you turn your body.

TOSS-TURNAROUND VARIATION

185. Praying hands.
186. Hands on shoulders.
187. Arms outstretched to sides.
188. Arms extended upward.
189. Arms up, hands locked overhead.
190. Hindu dancer effect, arms bent.

185   186   187   188   189   190

LESSON THREE
MORE AERIALS

Blind Catch

Blind catches are done with your hand behind your head. Learn it this way: As your body turns left to face rear, do a right reverse at your left side. When baton is on outside revolution, raise your arm up toward the back of your head, roll the baton over your thumb, flip it one revolution, and catch left (palm up) from the left side of your head.

Since you can't see the baton as you're recovering, keep eyes on execution point, with head to the right. Thumb-to-ball recovery assures a full revolution.

191. **BLIND CATCH:** Behind-the-head recovery with left hand. Keep eyes right, on execution point of aerial released from right hand.

Blind-catch Variation

Follow the same procedure, using a toss for more revolutions. Or use a toss turnaround instead of a thumb flip.

Vertical Backhand Catch

This recovery should be done after a toss from the right hand or a reverse thumb-pinch release from left hand. Body turns one-quarter left as you catch in right hand (palm up and fingers pointing back) backhanded. See photographs on page 90.

Vertical Flashback

This is an especially pretty aerial with lots of dazzle. Begin facing rear. Toss right at right side of body. Execute the toss so that baton keeps in line

192   193

VERTICAL BACKHAND CATCH

192, 193. It's effective to circle right arm just prior to catch. Follow through upon recovery with a left kick back (192); or a bow with left toe pointing forward (193).

with back of body. You want it to come down directly behind your back. As baton is going up, keep head and eyes right. Before you complete the trick, you'll switch your head to the left, and back to the right again, as in the photos that follow.

All these aerials take lots of practice. Stick with it, and you'll notice some improvement every day.

VERTICAL FLASHBACK

194. When baton begins descending, twist at waist and switch head left, looking over your left shoulder at the baton as it comes down.

195. Bring right hand behind your back to catch.

196. Quickly switch, head back to the right on the catch. Then turn body to the right until you're facing front.

194   195   196

LESSON FOUR
STILL MORE AERIALS

Horizontal-toss Turnaround

Do a horizontal wrist twirl (ball coming over arm, as in Chapter Two), and then, keeping the baton horizontal, let it circle with ball coming under arm for more accurate lift. Toss to left using same footwork as in vertical-toss turnaround. Toss from your left hand, turn left, and catch right. Practice a turn to the right in preparation for advanced work.

Horizontal Back Catch

Face front. Do a horizontal toss from right or left hand. Turn halfway around to the right, to face rear, springing into a deep lunge at the last second, before catching with your right hand on your back.

HORIZONTAL BACK CATCH

197   198

197. Twirler has done horizontal toss and is turning right to face rear. Looking over left shoulder at baton descending helps determine exact lunge position for catch.

198. Go into lunge as body comes around to face rear. Catch right with baton horizontal.

Horizontal One-and-a-half

Horizontal toss from left hand. Then turn to the right, one complete turn, plus another half turn to face rear. Catch in back catch, as in above photo.

Horizontal Backhand Catch

From a left horizontal aerial or a horizontal-toss turnaround, step on right foot and kick left leg as you catch right, in backhand, recovering baton with palm up from under shaft as it descends.

199. **HORIZONTAL BACKHAND CATCH:** Body should be in graceful horizontal line for this catch. Be sure baton is horizontal through aerial and upon recovery.

LESSON FIVE

MORE WAYS TO RECOVER

Here are two very impressive recoveries—the *straddle floor catch* and the *leg-fan floor catch*—that audiences usually applaud. It's not easy to do them well, but keep practicing until you can make these catches look graceful and effortless.

200. **STRADDLE FLOOR CATCH:** From an aerial, face one-quarter right and catch right, inside right leg. Extend left leg and arm fully, toes and fingertips pointed for graceful line. Reverse the position for straddle floor catch in left hand. One-quarter left for catch, inside left leg with right leg and arm extended.

201. **LEG-FAN FLOOR CATCH:** Face one-quarter right. Catch right, outside left leg, as right leg fans up and to the right as body completes a full turn. Reverse position to catch in left hand.

200

201

LESSON SIX
ROLLS

We hope you've continued working on your beginner rolls as you've been practicing the first five intermediate lessons. None of the intermediate rolls is simple, but if you've been practicing the other rolls consistently, you'll be able to handle these fairly comfortably after a few weeks of daily practice.

Left Elbow, Right Elbow, with Fishtail

In your beginning left-elbow-right-elbow combination, the baton went directly from the left arm to a roll over the right arm. Now it's going to roll over both wrists in fishtail fashion before rolling over the right arm. So the pattern is roll over bent left arm, to left wrist, to right wrist, to right arm, and catch behind the back. The photographs below will help you.

HINT: During "sandwich" resist all temptation to help baton along with either thumb. Instead, rely solely on the baton's momentum. If you refrain from handling rolls from the start, you'll learn them much more easily, without suffering penalties on your rolls during competitions.

LEFT ELBOW, RIGHT ELBOW, WITH FISHTAIL

202. Left-elbow roll, as you learned it in Chapter Two.
203. Ball drops as tip leads over left wrist.
204. Right palm on top of shaft, sandwiching baton between right and left hands, both palms down. Ball starts traveling up so shaft rolls with ball leading over right wrist (palm down).
205. Tip comes up and leads as shaft rolls over right elbow. Left hand moves behind back to prepare for catch.
206. Baton drops off elbow and does one revolution in the air before the catch. Catch is palm up, thumb to tip.

202   203   204   205   206

Left-hand Fishtail

This is a very difficult roll, and you'll have to really work every day without fail to learn it. First, we'll take you through each step, giving you an assist, so you can fix the pattern firmly in your mind. The next three steps are all things you've already learned to do in Chapter Two.

1. Face one-quarter right throughout. With left arm at right side, do inside revolution of left figure eight.

2. Go directly into a left-wrist roll and grab left.

3. Bring arm over to left side of body and do a left-hand flip and grab. Then carry arm back to your right side and repeat all steps.

Not hard yet, right? Right! Now comes the difficult part. Do everything you just did—all three steps—but without the grabs. You'll find that you can't do it—not yet, without the assist.

Now you're going to try the maneuver without the grabs, but using another assist to keep the baton from dropping. This is a walkthrough, using your right hand to guide the baton. Follow the instructions with the photos below.

LEFT-HAND FISHTAIL WALKTHROUGH WITH RIGHT-HAND GUIDING ASSIST

207. Left figure eight, inside revolution, at right side.
208. Left-wrist roll. Don't grab. Keep baton on back of hand during whole maneuver, guiding with right hand.
209. Bring left arm to left side, and once there . . .

207

208

209

After you've done the walkthrough, practice without the right-hand assist. Aim for a continuous side-to-side motion of your left arm, with baton resting on back of left hand throughout the maneuver. Your left palm should be facing down the whole time, and your fingers should stretch up as far as possible to form a cradle for the baton on the back of your hand.

Whatever you do, don't get discouraged. We said this wasn't easy, but it will suddenly click if you keep practicing every day.

To do a right-hand fishtail, start with baton in right hand, face one-quarter left, and follow same procedure.

Right-elbow Layout

This is another difficult roll to master, but you've already learned part of it. You begin with the last half of the left-elbow-right-elbow fishtail and continue as in the photos on page 96.

Right-elbow Layup

Begin with the right-elbow layout, exactly as you learned it above. After finishing the layout, fishtail one time in your right hand, at the right side, and then follow the photos on page 96 to finish the layup.

210. . . . do left-hand flip, no grab, leaving baton on back of hand . . .
211. . . . guiding baton back over to right side for repeat.

211

   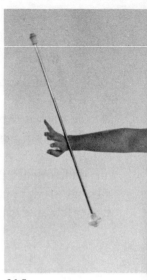

212　　**213**　　**214**　　**215**

216

RIGHT-ELBOW LAYOUT

212. Baton is ready to roll over right wrist, ball leading. Begin with a push from the left hand, as shown.

213. As shaft continues over right elbow, raise right arm up . . .

214. . . . and out to one-quarter right, as shaft contacts with upper arm.

215. Ball sinks down front of arm . . .

216. . . . shaft rolling into right palm (thumb to tip) as right arm fully extends to right side.

RIGHT-ELBOW LAYUP

217. After right-elbow layout and one right-hand fishtail at right side, bring elbow forward and let baton roll over arm as shown . . .

218. . . . to catch as in layout, but with thumb to ball.

217　　　　　　　　**218**

 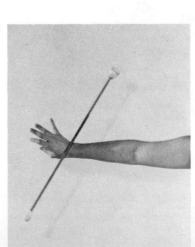

LESSON SEVEN
MORE ROLLS

Multiple Elbow Rolls

Multiple elbow rolls are repeated elbow rolls during which time the baton rolls over the left elbow, then the right, then across your back to the left again, to the right, etc.

You've already done the left-elbow-to-right-elbow roll in Chapter Two. So the new part of this trick is getting the baton over your back after it completes the right-elbow roll so it can begin the roll over left elbow.

To practice this "connector" for the multiple elbow rolls, start with a regular right-elbow roll, and continue as shown in the photos below.

CONNECTOR FOR MULTIPLE ELBOW ROLLS

219. As baton rolls over forearm of bent right arm, pivot to your left (turning *into* the baton). Make sure elbow is level with shoulder. In this photo, twirler is just about to pivot left, into baton as tip leads . . .

220. . . . over right elbow. Let the baton come across your back and raise left elbow. Keep on turning left, into the baton, as ball leads roll over left elbow. By the time left-elbow roll is completed you'll be ready to pivot left again into the baton as it comes over the right elbow starting repeat of entire procedure.

219   220

Once you've learned the connector, set your baton down and work without it until you master the footwork for the multiple elbows.

Imagine yourself standing on a clock face on the floor. (If you can practice outdoors, draw a clock face with chalk on your driveway if no one objects.) Don't put any hands on the clock; just the numbers for every hour. You should space the numbers evenly in such a way that you can walk comfortably around the clock, left foot hitting floor on odd numbers, right foot hitting floor on even numbers.

As you do multiple elbow rolls, you're going to go around the clock, clockwise, pivoting once to the left between each hour, setting down alternate feet at each number.

Start on the 6. Pivot to the left on your right foot and land with left foot on the 7. Then pivot left on your left foot and land with right foot on the 8. Pivot left on your right foot and land left on the 9. Continue around the clock this way, always landing with right foot on even numbers and left foot on odd.

This sounds more complicated than it really is. Practice a few times and you'll get the hang of it. You're really just turning your body in a little circle between each number on the clock face.

After you've got the footwork firmly fixed in your mind, start working with the baton again.

Start with left foot for right-elbow roll. Pivot into baton as it comes over right arm. Keep turning as tail sinks down center of back and land on right foot as ball picks up roll over left shoulder. Keep pivoting into baton, landing left on odd number of clock as baton begins rolling over right elbow again.

East set will be done to a count of "one-two." "One" is the right-elbow roll with connector, and "two" is roll over left elbow. Left foot hits floor on count of "one," right on count of "two."

Keep the roll close to your shoulders for better control, in vertical plane.

Be sure to practice every day, aiming to get all the way around the clock as you do the multiple elbows. Once mastered, this trick is very impressive and most appreciated by audiences when it's done well.

Preparation for Continuous Neck Rolls

This isn't actually a trick you'll use in your routine, but it is something that you should begin working on now, to prepare for the continuous neck rolls you'll learn in the next chapter.

Start from a horizontal neck roll, ball leading to right elbow. When ball reaches forward, raise right elbow to push shaft back over shoulder and catch back.

FULL ANGEL

224, 225. (rear view) Do half angel, but don't catch on back. Keep baton on back . . .

224   **225**   **226**

221   222   223

HALF ANGEL

 221. Starting position after reverse figure eight.
 222. Baton starts a backward fishtail over left hand, as shown, tip leading.
 223. Ball leads as shaft rolls over upper arm, onto back. Baton does half a revolution in the air, and you catch in back with right hand, palm up, thumb to ball.

Now, take it out of flat plane into vertical by repeating above from vertical neck roll, using straight arm instead of bent right elbow, pushing shaft back with shoulder as tip drops down in back, turn body, using multiple-elbow footwork, to catch left behind head, thumb to tip.

Half Angel (or Reverse Layout)

In this roll, baton begins in left hand, does a roll over the upper left arm and ends in a right-hand catch behind the back. The photos will give you more details. Start with a left reverse figure eight at your left side.

Full Angel

Start with a half angel, but instead of catching the baton let it continue across your back and into a roll over your right arm and wrist. See photographs below for front and rear views of this maneuver.

 226, 227. (rear view) . . . and turn shoulders slightly to right so right arm picks up baton, as tip leads shaft over right upper arm.
 228. Ball leads shaft out over right wrist.
 229. Catch right thumb to ball.

     228   229

HINTS: Keep baton in perfect rear plane throughout whole maneuver. Be sure to look from left to right so you can track it. Many learners for some reason duck their heads so their eyes can't follow the baton as it comes over the right shoulder, and therefore they can't catch it.

Lunge slightly to left when starting the half angel and travel with the baton into a slight right lunge. This bodywork helps keep your body in line with the baton, making the catch easier.

LESSON EIGHT
CONNECTING MOVES

Vertical Taffy Pull

Start with both arms stretched out to sides. Hold baton at tip, thumb to ball, in right hand.

Swing baton down to horizontal position in front of body. Grab the shaft with left hand, palm down, next to right hand.

Then, do three things simultaneously. Begin turning body left to face rear *and* slide left hand up shaft to ball *and* turn baton vertical, ball up.

Then do three more things simultaneously: finish body turn back to facing front *and* bring baton to vertical tip-up position *and* slide right hand down shaft (thumb facing you) to meet left hand at the ball.

As you face front on completion of turn, let go of baton with left hand and stretch both arms out to sides as in start position. Baton is in right hand at ball end, thumb to tip.

230. **VERTICAL TAFFY PULL:** As right hand slides down shaft to meet left hand at ball, right thumb must be on inside of shaft.

100

Neck Choke

Hold baton at tip end, thumb to ball, in right hand. Place ball on left shoulder and begin a complete body turn to the left. Raise shaft overhead, keeping ball touching body until shaft rests on right shoulder, tip forward.

Hitch-kick Pass

Master the footwork first. It should be quick, with lots of snap. Kick forward with right leg, as high as you can. (Aim toe to reach to eye-level in air.) Then kick left to same height. Point toes and keep legs straight on kicks. Avoid bending over during kicks, so back stays straight.

Hold baton in right hand, thumb to tip, near ball end. On right kick, stretch arm to circle baton in vertical front plane. Time it so that you start your circle slightly before kicking right.

On left kick, baton is passed under raised left leg to left hand, which takes it palm down.

The timing on this maneuver takes practice. Remember, you want to complete a circle with right hand just as you end the right kick and begin the left. The second your left leg is in the air, you should be ready to pass the baton.

INTERMEDIATE ROUTINES

Now it's time to try the intermediate routines that follow. If you're not already competing as an intermediate, work on the simpler routine first and move on to the more difficult one as soon as you feel comfortable with the modified routine. Both are a minute and a half long—official competition length.

At first you may not be able to finish the routines within the allotted time, but keep working, remembering never to sacrifice smoothness to increase your speed. (Better to shorten the routine or make up a shorter one of your own if you haven't worked up to speed yet.)

If you're not officially in the intermediate class, you'll probably qualify soon if you keep competing and keep practicing. (Nearly every twirler who wants to become an intermediate can do it.)

There are three intermediate levels, really, although there's no official distinction. But you'll know yourself where you fall. Beginning intermediates can do some intermediate tricks, but they still need work on beginning maneuvers as well. Medium intermediates have mastered all the beginner's tricks and are well on their way to mastering all the intermediate maneuvers. High intermediates have mastered all intermediate maneuvers, and possibly some advanced.

It can take a year or more to become a high intermediate, so don't be discouraged if all the intermediate maneuvers don't come easily. Just keep practicing and realize that it will take time.

SIMPLE INTERMEDIATE ROUTINE

1. Salute. (Do a Y pose with ball up. Bring baton down with a circle and point ball to floor. Reverse figure 8 into salute position.)
2. Toss turnaround with right hand. (Turn to left.)
3. Catch baton in right hand. Reverse figure 8 with lunge to left side.
4. Bring baton back to right side in a figure 8. Do a right-hand whip.
5. Flash-out leap to the right side, with a figure 8.
6. Blind catch (throw from right to left hand), turning to the left and facing front just after completing catch.
7. Left reverse figure 8 and thumb-pinch flip. Catch behind back in right hand, while turning to the right.
8. Figure 8 at right side into . . .
9. . . . 1-toss turnaround to the left. Catch in left hand, in index finger, and continue into . . .
10. . . . 8-finger twirl overhead, turning twice to the left.
11. Left reverse figure 8 cartwheel flip on outside of left leg. Catch in deep lunge at ¼ left, in left hand.
12. Face ¼ right for 2-finger in right hand. Kick left leg forward.
13. Right-hand vertical 2-finger in front, then turn to the left.
14. Vertical 2-finger in the rear and continue on around to front.
15. Vertical 2-finger in front.
16. Vertical 2-finger overhead as you turn left and continue around to front.
17. Bring baton across the front of body to left side. Do a 2-finger bringing baton up overhead from the back. Baton should end up in middle two fingers.
18. Two-finger under left leg and toss off thumb. Catch in left hand in first finger and go into . . .
19. . . . left-hand 8-finger vertical overhead, turning twice to the left.
20. Reverse left-hand thumb-pinch-toss turnaround to the left. Catch in right hand. Reverse figure 8 lunge across to the left side. Bring baton back to right side with a figure 8 and into a right-hand whip.
21. Neck choke, by bringing baton horizontally up on left shoulder. Leave ball on left shoulder and raise tip first overhead to back.
22. Horizontal neck roll, letting baton turn just once as you turn to the left.

23. Grab in right hand. Horizontal wrist twirl. Turnaround to the left.
24. Flat-toss turnaround to left. Catch in right hand.
25. Continue turning after catch as you do a horizontal wrist twirl into . . .
26. . . . 8-finger in right hand (underhand fingers), turning twice to the left and up on toes. Palm should be facing down.
27. Two-finger down with knees bent in crouch position.
28. Two-finger up overhead with flash-out leap to right side.
29. Horizontal taffy pull (1 turn to front) to left hand on center of baton.
30. Baton is now in left hand. Left horizontal toss in the rear, and turnaround to front.
31. Pass to left hand under right leg, as right leg kicks high forward. (Continue on toes around to the left.)
32. High flat toss and right-hand back catch in deep lunge.
33. Bring baton out with reverse figure 8 to get it back into vertical plane.
34. Turnaround to the left, catch under left leg with left hand, in floor catch.
35. Left reverse figure 8 and cushion.
36. Pass overhead plain to right hand with high split-jump leap.
37. Right-hand figure 8 at right side.
38. One left-elbow roll, carry over to right side in fishtail.
39. Left-hand fishtails facing ¼ right.
40. Two-hand fishtail "sandwich" in front of body.
41. Baton comes up over right elbow into continuous elbow rolls. Catch behind back with left hand as baton rolls over last right elbow. Face ¼ left on catch.
42. Reverse figure 8 in left hand.
43. Half or full angel roll from left arm up over to right hand.
44. Right-elbow roll with layout to right side. Kick front with right leg.
45. Right-elbow roll, turnaround to the right. Come up on toes and only turn as far as you need to face rear.
46. Facing rear, bring baton up over right elbow—as though you're going to start multiple rolls—but just let it roll on across to the left elbow and then catch in left hand.
47. Left reverse figure 8, toss turnaround to the left.
48. Follow through with reverse figure 8, lunge to left, and bring baton back to right side with figure 8.
49. One-revolution thumb toss out of right hand. Catch under right leg on floor in illusion catch with right hand—as you continue turning around to right.
50. Continue on around to face front and do right-side figure 8.

51. Blind toss from right hand to left hand in front.
52. Pass behind back.
53. Two-toss turnaround to the left. Catch in right hand.
54. Bow.
55. Salute.

MORE DIFFICULT INTERMEDIATE ROUTINE

1. Salute.
2. One- or 2-toss turnaround and catch right.
3. Immediately into vertical head loop overhead as you turn to the left.
4. When facing front again, do a high hitch-kick pass from right to left hand.
5. Split-jump leap. Pass baton through legs from front to right hand.
6. One-toss turnaround to the left. Catch in index finger of left hand.
7. Four-finger overhead and turn to the left.
8. Four-finger in front of right knee. Left leg kicks back high. Turn to rear and toss from left to right hand, vertically.
9. Come around to face front. One-toss turnaround. Catch left under left leg in straddle catch. Right leg should extend into air.
10. Left-to-right rear-flip toss on the left side—in a lunge facing ¼ left.
11. Right-hand-to-left-hand throw, blind catch.
12. Flat platter or flat dip into . . .
13. . . . flat 1- or 2-toss turnaround.
14. Two-finger down.
15. Two-finger up overhead and turn to the left.
16. Two-finger down and cushion knees.
17. Two-finger up overhead and flash-out leap to right. Pass baton to left hand.
18. Flat 2-finger overhead and turn to left.
19. Flat 2-finger down, continue turning to left.
20. Eight-finger overhead and continue turning twice around to left.
21. Platter flat-toss turnaround. Straddle catch inside right leg with right hand, facing ¼ right.
22. Pass to left hand. Four-finger overhead, turn once to the left.
23. Flat 2-toss turnaround. Catch flat right in backhand catch, facing ¼ left and kicking left leg out to the side.
24. Bring baton up on left shoulder. Do flash neck wrap by bringing ball up overhead as you turn around to the left. Pass baton directly in front of neck, with palms facing in toward each other. Bring baton out in left hand directly overhead and do a complete twist of baton as you turn around to the left.

25. Flat thumb flip and catch right behind the back in deep lunge.
26. Come out with vertical reverse figure 8.
27. Vertical 1- or 2-toss turnaround. Catch left.
28. Left-hand fishtail into left-elbow layup, turning to the right until you face ¼ right.
29. Reverse and bring baton back to front.
30. Left-hand fishtail and out over right elbow in layout.
31. Bring back to the front and do a layout, turning to the right.
32. Figure 8 at right side.
33. Facing ¼ right. Pass baton to left hand in left-shoulder pass.
34. Deep lunge left. Fishtails. On last fishtail turn right to face front.
35. Full angel from left to right side.
36. Vertical taffy pull. Turn to left and continue around to front.
37. Continuous elbows, as many as possible. Catch left behind back.
38. Left reverse thumb-pinch flip and catch right behind back.
39. Two-hand spin and pass around both legs.
40. Two-toss turnaround to the left and catch backhanded in bow, facing ¼ left.
41. Salute.

SIX

Advanced Twirling

By the time you're edging over from medium to high intermediate, you should begin learning advanced twirling tricks. Start these after you feel comfortable with the intermediate moves. But don't wait too long. You'll be able to do some of the advanced moves fairly soon, but others will take awhile, and you'll still be working on intermediate moves at the same time.

If you're competing and have begun to win first-place awards in intermediates, then you should be preparing to enter the advanced category—after you win your eighth first prize. You can also become a member of a twirling team when your skills become advanced. Perhaps you've already begun some teaching at this point in your twirling career. If not, you can certainly think seriously about it. (You can read more about a teaching career in Chapter Fourteen.) You might also consider three-baton twirling to expand your horizons. Also, there are a large number of twirling scholarships available. Read more about those in the Appendix.

Becoming an advanced twirler is not something everyone can do or wants to do. It takes a lot of dedication and practice, but it's also very rewarding and challenging, with unlimited opportunities to stretch your imagination and your skills.

Twirling, from this point on, is very individualized. It gives you a good chance to be creative, and we urge you to invent your own original tricks to include in your routines.

Advanced work relies heavily on things you've already learned, combining tricks in ways that are more difficult, or varying previous maneuvers in ways that increase the difficulty factor.

LESSON ONE
FINGERWORK

Advanced fingerwork doesn't consist of any different individual finger twirls than those you already know. Advanced twirlers do series of finger twirls, combined with definite bodywork.

Vertical Finger Series

Right two-finger at right-rear plane, with arm held high, body facing front. Snap up on your toes and repeat the right two-finger behind your head, keeping baton in front plane as you do a body spin to the left.

Then turn right to face rear, and do a two-finger behind your head with another body spin to the right, ending facing the rear again. Then do another two-finger in the rear vertical plane at knee level.

Next comes a four-finger, arching around to the front as body spins left. Then a right-side whip, thumb flip to left index finger, catching under left leg. Pull the baton out as it's going through your fingers to your pinky.

Toss off pinky and catch in left index finger down under right leg in a deep lunge. Left your leg as baton proceeds through to pinky. Toss from pinky, catch blind (behind head) in left index finger.

Then do a left eight-finger behind the head, turning twice. Turn right to rear and do a left thumb flip backhand at rear. Turn left back to the front and do a left reverse whip. Finish series with a left aerial two-turnaround flashback.

Horizontal Finger Series

Start with a left two-finger overhead, then a two-finger down (with a body spin to the left). An eight-finger overhead, with a spin left during the first four-finger, and switching to a spin to the right to finish the eight-finger. Switch directions making a zigzag motion with your body. (This is called a "switch-switch.")

Then do a horizontal platter (two horizontal wrist twirls, one with ball over arm and one with ball under arm), with a rear flip from left to right hand.

Overhead whip, turn left. Horizontal two-finger down as you cushion, releasing baton at low point and execute a split jump (legs spread-eagled), pulling baton out with right hand.

Plain pass on chest to left hand, with body spin to left. Left-hand horizontal throw from inside of left leg, one turnaround, catch right outside of left leg in leg fan catch, facing one-quarter right.

231

232

233

234

SPLIT JUMP AND PULL OUT

231. Start with horizontal four-finger or eight-finger overhead. Then two-finger down with cushion to prepare for jump. Note horizontal baton, ball to right.

232. Jump, keeping legs spread-eagled and straight, toes pointed. Tip leads baton through legs.

233. Catch in right hand and pull baton from under right leg.

234. Stretch both arms out to sides as you land. Be sure to bend knees into deep cushion.

LESSON TWO
ROLLS

Elbow Lift

Begin with a left-elbow-right-elbow-left-elbow. As baton comes onto right elbow for another roll, lift it into the air with your right elbow, and then let it land there after one revolution in the air.

Elbow-lift Variation

Add one or two turnarounds between the lift and recovery on right elbow.

Turnaround Aerial with Right-to-left Full Angel

Start with a throw under the leg. Reach up with right arm so shaft lands on right forearm and continues into full right-to-left angel.

Left-to-right Angel, Lift Up, Right-to-left Angel

Start with baton in left hand, thumb to ball, palm up. Do a wrist roll over left wrist as you raise arm up to the left. Baton makes the following pattern: After the wrist roll, it slides down your arm to the forearm. Ball will drop to the back, then tip will come on over to right forearm. Pull right arm to the back as baton comes over. Let baton fishtail out to the right and lift baton up into the air off the wrist. As baton falls, catch on right forearm and go into reverse of what you did with the left arm. Then let baton fall onto right arm and then slide up to forearm and drop in back. Then bring left arm to the back and catch baton on forearm of left arm and out into figure-eight fishtail.

DROP ANGEL ROLL

235. Baton is caught on right arm between elbow and wrist with palm up. Baton then drops . . .

236. . . . down the back as shown, and continues into a roll out over the left arm. You can do this from a straight aerial or from turnaround aerial.

235   236

Neck Roll

This is the maneuver you prepared for in the intermediate chapter. Review it if necessary. To make the neck roll continuous, simply let your head drop down to the front, and let tip of baton come over left shoulder as you make your turn to the right.

Make sure your head is always under the baton. Lots of practice will enable you to continue this move as many times as you like. Just remember to get your head under the baton so that when it drops you can pick it up with your shoulder.

Left Fishtail Turns

Start with left fishtails at right side. Start turning to the left, keeping fishtail on back of hand. Do one, two, or three turns, ending with a left-to-right layup.

LESSON THREE
AERIALS

Overhead Throws

Face rear, do a left overhead throw to front vertical plane. Keep eyes looking over your left shoulder as you turn left to face front, grabbing baton with right hand.

Illusion Catch (Horizontal Floor Catch)

Start with a right-thumb toss under your left leg. Turn body completely around to the right and catch right inside of right leg in floor straddle catch, with left leg extending high in the air as it circles around with body completing full turn to the front.

237. **ILLUSION CATCH:** Be sure head is down toward floor to give your body a graceful line.

Split-jump Pull Out

Start with baton in right hand, behind your back. Whip to front into a right reverse. Right figure eight, then right-thumb flip, as you cushion and leap into spread-eagled jump. Left hand reaches in from behind left leg for catch.

Scissor-jump Pull Out

The scissor-jump pull out follows the same procedure as the split-jump pull out, only with body facing one-quarter left. During leap, right leg is forward and left leg is back in mid-air, as left hand reaches from inside right leg to catch on outside of right leg.

Jump-pull-out Variation

Bat or push up baton without catching after the first split jump and follow immediately with a scissor-jump pull out. Practice double jumps with deep cushion in between. Perfect timing is essential, and it will come with plenty of practice.

Horizontal Back Catch

Start with baton thumb to ball in right hand. Ball travels flat under arm as baton is released with slight upward thrust. Spin on your toes to the left. Left hand reaches around left side for grab behind back. Keep eyes over right shoulder.

One-and-a-half Turnaround (or More)

You can do this in vertical or flat plane. Body spins to the right, and you catch in the right hand behind your back. For a smooth and continuous flow of body motion, be sure to keep baton away from your body as you catch.

Switch Toss

Do a two-toss turnaround to the left, then switch direction of your body, spin to the right for a two-and-a-half-toss turnaround.

Blind Catches

Two-and-a-half- or three-and-a-half-toss turnaround, catch blind in left index finger. Follow with a four-finger twirl behind head, toss up from pinky into a one-and-a-half turnaround. Catch blind in stop lunge at one-quarter left.

238   239   240   241

SPLIT JUMP WITH BLIND CATCH

238. On the turnaround, cushion for leap . . .

239. . . . and catch blind as you execute the split jump.

HORIZONTAL BLIND CATCH WITH BACKBEND

240. Start with an aerial from either hand, plain or with turnarounds, and bend backward as baton descends . . .

241. . . . for blind catch with back bent.

Or, from the four-finger, go into a two-toss turnaround and catch blind in split jump.

CONNECTING MOVE

Right Kick and Neck Wrap

Start with baton in right hand, held out to your right side near tip end, thumb to ball. Kick right leg up as high as possible and bring baton under leg, ball leading into a neck wrap. Grab with left hand near ball end (left hand stays under right leg), as baton comes around neck, ball leading.

242. **RIGHT KICK AND NECK WRAP:** Twirler is just about to release baton from right hand. Left hand stays put to recover as baton comes around neck.

ADVANCED ROUTINE—2 minutes long

1. Two-toss turnaround, catch blind.
2. Back-pass turn.
3. Three-and-a-half-toss turnaround into right flash out with 2-finger at right side, proceeding into advanced finger series (vertical).
4. Right whip into split-jump pull out with "baton up" variation in scissor pull out.
5. Left 2-toss turnaround at rear, catch right at rear, pull around to front right. Blind catch left.
6. Platter into 3-horizontal-toss turnaround, catch in right index finger.
7. Right 2-finger down. Left baton in aerial from hook fingers, 2 body turns left, catch horizontal right underhand, body in horizontal position, left leg extended back.
8. Horizontal 2-hand spin overhead to left hand.
9. Two-and-a-half horizontal blind catch left.
10. Proceed to horizontal finger series.
11. Pass to left. Turn left.
12. Three-and-a-half horizontal catch back, deep lunge to right rear, right hand.
13. Two-toss turnaround, catch split jump, pull out in left hand.
14. Left reverse, left thumb-pinch toss, catch back right hand.
15. Right figure 8 into . . .
16. . . . continuous elbow rolls, 3 or 4 complete sets.
17. Elbow left.
18. Right layout, turn right to face rear.
19. Right wrist, right elbow onto left elbow. Body turns left to face front.
20. Left fishtails at right side.
21. Two fishtail turns.
22. Left-to-right angel lift up. Right-to-left angel.
23. Two-hand loop whip (vertical) behind head to right hand.
24. Continuous neck spin. Let baton drop off left side (¼ left), catch in lunge outside of left leg, in right hand.
25. Body turn to left. Right whip.
26. Switch toss. Right figure 8.
27. Illusion catch.
28. Four- or 5-toss turnaround.
29. Catch underhand right in low ¼ left.
30. Salute.

SEVEN

Strutting

What Is Strutting?

If you've read this far, chances are you've already become involved enough in twirling to know what strutting looks like, and many of you may have begun strutting already.

It used to be that strutters had only one place to perform—in front of the band in a parade. Strutting contests developed, in fact, as a means for parade strutters to improve their skills. Now, of course, competitive strutting is an event in its own right, and a very popular one at that.

A competition strutter's performance in many ways resembles the floor exercises you see in a gymnastics competition. In doing floor exercises, the gymnast must combine gymnastic and ballet moves into a graceful routine that shows off her skills in both areas.

In strutting, the twirler combines batonwork with both gymnastic and ballet moves. So strutting really is a whole different aspect of twirling. And it's not for every twirler.

Who Should Strut?

If you've studied ballet and/or gymnastics, then strutting will probably appeal to you. Twirlers with a dance background take the most easily to strutting.

But that doesn't mean you shouldn't try it if you haven't had dancing lessons before. We strongly recommend, however, that you begin ballet or gymnastic lessons when you start your strutting lessons. You'll need to do ballet or gymnastic exercises regularly (*every* day) if you expect to develop the form and control you'll need as a strutter.

Since learning to strut may mean considerable investment of additional time and money, you'll want to think it over pretty carefully before you begin.

If you're limber and supple, if you've been scoring high on bodywork and showmanship during your twirling performances, then you're a good candidate for strutting.

There's no perfect age to begin strutting lessons. Once you feel comfortable with the beginning twirling skills is a good time to start. In twirling contests, strutters compete with others their own age, and progress from beginning strut, to intermediate, to advanced according to the number of first-place awards.

Strutting Definitions

Here are the body moves you should be able to do—or should be learning—if you expect to become a strutter.

1. *Lunge.* Extending leg should be straight, with foot turned outward. Make your lunge at least two-feet wide, with a deep bend of the forward knee. Keep body erect, with weight over front knee. Extended leg can be to rear or out to the side.

2. *Split leap, or grand jeté.* Weight should be on forward leg upon take off. Strive for complete extension of legs, body, and arms. Work for height and distance. End with a bent knee landing on ball of foot before heel hits floor. Extending leg should be stretched out to the back upon landing.

3. *Hitch-kick.* (See photos on page 116.) Lift left leg straight forward on count of "one." Jump from the right foot to the left foot and lift right leg forward on count of "two." You can also begin with right leg lift and jump to the left.

4. *Arabesque.* This is a one-leg balance with the right (or left) leg raised backward, as high as it will go. Keep your back straight.

5. *Attitude leg hold.* Hold on right foot with left knee bent forward or

243, 244. **HITCH-KICK**

toward the rear and turned out. You can also hold on the left leg and bend right knee.

6. *Stag leap*. This leap is the same as a split leap except that the front leg is bent and the back leg is straight. Land on slightly bent front leg.

7. *Cabriole*. On count of "one," lift right leg forward. On count of "two," jump off the left leg, and close the left leg to the right leg. Land on left leg slightly bent and extend right leg forward. You can also do this starting on the opposite leg. You can begin with a leg lift to the back instead of to the front if you like.

8. *Tour jeté*. Swing right leg forward into the air and jump off left foot on count of "one." Make half turn to the left, so the right leg is in back while your body is still in the air, on count of "two." Land on slightly bent right leg with left leg extended back on count of "three."

TOUR JETE

245. Right leg comes up as you turn to rear.   246. Leap . . .   247. . . . land on right foot and end in pose.

9. *Backward hitch-kick*. Lift right leg to the rear, jump off left leg, and scissor legs in the air. Land on right leg with left leg raised behind you.

10. *Skater's spin*. Step left to the left side and step up on your right foot. Step back with left foot. Step on right foot and spin on it until you've made a complete turn with your body. Bend body so that your upper body is parallel to the floor, with left leg extended into the air behind you, arms out to sides.

248. Starting position. 249. Preparation to push off. 250. Turn.

SKATER'S SPIN

251. Ending pose.

252   253   254

ILLUSION TURN TO RIGHT

252. On count of "one," push with left foot to take off on right.
253. Push off, dropping upper body, on count of "two."
254. Keep turning, continuing to drop body lower, on count of "three."
255. Circle left leg down and bring body up as you complete turn on count of "four."

ILLUSION TURN TO LEFT

256. Face right. Kick left leg forward at count of "one."
257. Push left leg back to upright position and drop upper body on count of "two."
258. Turn left, on left foot (leg stays up), on count of "three."
259. Raise body and drop leg as you complete turn on count of "four."

256

5

11. *Illusion turn to the right.* Facing left, push with left foot to take off on right. As you push off, drop your upper body toward the right, aiming for below the waist. Lift left leg straight up. As you continue turning to the right, drop your upper body even lower, as far toward the floor as you can. Continue your turn, and as you complete it, left leg circles down and body comes upright. To do a double: push off onto right foot and repeat.

12. *Illusion turn to the left.* Facing right, kick left leg forward on count of "one." Push left leg back to upright position to left side and drop upper part of body below waist on count of "two." Turn on left foot to left, keeping leg up on turn, on count of "three." Raise body and drop leg to front as turn is completed on count of "four."

13. *Butterfly.* On count of "one," take off from right foot and drop upper body below waist with arms reaching outward toward the right. On count of

258   259

260   261   262

BUTTERFLY

"two," lift legs, keeping them straddled in air. Arms are lifted upward and to the sides. On count of "three," left foot lands, and on count of "four," you raise your body as you continue pivoting to the right on your left foot. On count of "five," right foot hits floor, your body having completed half a turn.

14. *Fouette.* Whip, most associated with a series of whipping turns.

15. *Pirouette.* A turn executed on one leg.

16. *Ronds de jambes.* Circular movement of leg from hip joint. Use with a high or low kick.

17. *Ballet turn.* A turn executed on one leg, with the other leg extended to the back in a relaxed-attitude position. Back is bent into shallow back-bend position. Head is relaxed back and arms are relaxed.

264. **BALLET TURN**

Learning to Strut

Assuming you have the basic knowledge of dance and body movement necessary for strutting, you can begin a routine right away.

Most strutting routines aren't difficult to learn, but perfecting your technique and form is not a simple matter. It takes lots of practice and daily exercise, just like dance or gymnastics.

The exercises help prepare your body. They help improve your form and your technique. Eventually, good execution of routine moves is automatic. You can then concentrate more on style—the creative interpretation of the various body moves included in your routine.

Your ultimate aim as a strutter is to develop good form, create your own style, perform your routines with confidence, and enjoy what you're doing—so much so that your inner pleasure in performing is evident to the judges and audience.

Strutting Routines

Each twirling association has slightly different routine requirements for strutting, but the emphasis in all strutting is on body lines, fluidity of motion, and precision.

In the USTA, strutting routines are divided into three separate sections. Together, these sections allow a strutter to fully express her art.

If you're learning to strut, you should send for the official USTA strutting record, which is used in competitions. It's a good idea to use it for practicing.

1. *Military Section.* All strutting routines begin with a military march. You begin immediately following the music introduction (usually 8 counts) and continue your march for 32 counts, making an L formation, as shown below.

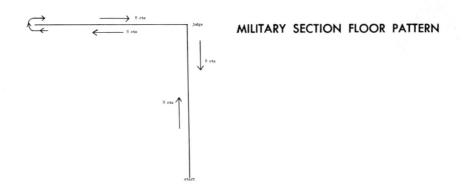

MILITARY SECTION FLOOR PATTERN

During the music introduction, you should acknowledge the judge in some way from an at-ease position. The acknowledgment can be a simple swing up with both arms, hold, and return to attention position before marching.

During the march, use the following arm movement: Hold baton close to ball end. Pull up above head and execute beat as left foot hits floor. Bring baton down when right foot hits floor.

The overhead beat can be done in several ways. We suggest a figure nine or a figure seven above the head, with a snappy, quick motion.

While marching, bring knee up to the upper thigh level. Step forward with your foot, stretching your instep, and hit floor toes first. Step as if you are stepping into a shoe.

Avoid bicycling (circling legs under body), and don't kick when stepping forward.

Be sure to keep your body erect by holding your diaphragm up and keeping chin parallel to shoulders.

Left hand stays at left hip bone, with fingers together and pointing toward right toes. Elbow stays directly to side. The line from your left wrist to your left elbow should be straight, as should the line from elbow to shoulder and from shoulder to ear.

All your movements should be sharp and precise. Exactness will come with practice. It may sound easy, but it takes lots of work.

2. *Presentation.* Following the military section comes a 32-count section that gives the strutter complete freedom to show off her skills and person-

ality. Steps, poses, leaps, illusions, arabesques, attitudes—all these can be used here, along with various types of baton handling.

Strutting routines, from this point on, should be choreographed and learned in sets of 8 counts, called *combinations*. Since the presentation section has 32 counts, it will consist of four combinations.

When you're practicing, work on one combination at a time, until you can do it relatively well and feel ready to start learning the next combination. Practice combinations separately, and after you've learned the first two, start stringing them together until you've got all four combinations flowing smoothly.

BASIC PRESENTATION ROUTINE (SAMPLE)

SET	COUNTS	ARMWORK	LEGWORK
1	1–2	Circle both arms up into position	Step forward with LF. Bring RF up behind. Up on toes, LF ahead of R
	3–4	Swing arms down in front and out to sides at shoulder level	Step to L with LF, point R toe fwd., backbend in lunge
	5–6– 7–8	Swing LH in graceful movement to RS and back to L, shoulder level	Remain in above pose holding head up, pulling in diaphragm
2	1–2	Pass baton to LH	Step fwd. with RL, turn L, and step L
	3–4	Pass baton to RH above head	Step fwd. with RL
	5–6	Bring both arms out to side, shoulder level	Kick LL to R angle and backbend
	7–8	Bring both arms up into V	Step fwd. with LL and up on toes to pose
3	1–2	Swing baton down	Step L. Kick RL to LS
	3–4	Loop behind head	Turn to L on ball of LF
	5–6	Swing baton down in front and out to LS. Hold L arm up straight	Step L, step R to LS and up on R toe to prepare for spin
	7–8	Push R arm (with baton) to RS. L arm follows across front at shoulder level	Step L, step R (still preparing for spin)
4	1–2– 3–4	R arm continues to a straight-up position on RS of head. Hold L arm at shoulder level to side	Spin on RF, arch back and hold LL back in ballet turn
	5–6– 7–8	Swing arms down	Step L. Point RL back and lunge fwd.

3. *Forward Motion*. This is the last and longest part of the strutting routine. It consists of thirteen combinations, plus an ending pose or trick.

Each combination (set of 8 counts, remember?) in the forward motion must move the strutter forward. However, turns, marching backward, jumps, leaps, lunges, ballet movements, and any other type of movement that can be done in time with the music—hitting each beat—is permitted.

The floor pattern of the routine is very important, because it adds a lot to the general effect. So you'll want to incorporate plenty of directional changes, interesting turns on corners, and good floor coverage. The following is an example of a good strutting floor pattern, with plenty of variety and excellent coverage.

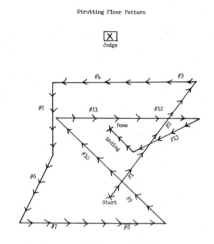

FORWARD MOTION FLOOR PATTERN

Don't forget the batonwork. The more baton maneuvers you can include, the more challenging and impressive this part of your routine will be.

Learn the forward-motion segment, combination by combination. String the combinations together and learn the directional changes and floor pattern at the same time until you can do all thirteen combinations together smoothly. Then polish each section of the routine.

BASIC FORWARD MOTION ROUTINE (SAMPLE)

SET	COUNTS	ARMWORK	LEGWORK
		Start forward motion to right angle.	
1	1	Loop from end of baton in motion of fig. 8 to LS	Bend into L step by bending RK when stepping L
	2	Loop high on RS	Step R
	3–4	Swing baton down to floor and up straight (hold up by RS of head). LH out in front from shoulder	Turn on LF to R

SET	COUNTS	ARMWORK	LEGWORK
	5–6	Circle R arm fwd. and back (arms are at angle with L arm, high)	March bkwd.—L, R—and bend fwd. into R step
	7–8	Hold above	March bkwd., turn R with LF on 8
2	1–2	Swing both arms down in front to cross then back up (on 2)	March L, R
	3–4	Pass over R shoulder to LH	March L, R
	5–6	Rev. fig. 8 in LH	March L, R
	7–8	Pass behind back to RH. Bend back into R corner	March L Turn on RF with twist
3	1–2	Circle R arm fwd. and up straight	Step L and lift (hold RL back) Step R
	3–4	Swing arms in march motion (fwd. and back)	Run L Run R
	5–6	Throw baton high (open-hand vert. toss)	Leap L, step R
	7–8	Catch baton in RH at RS	Leap L, step R
4	1–2	Airplane turn L (hold arms out to side while turning)	Turn LF on L March on R
	3–4	Hands under chin, elbows up. Push arms fwd. and out to side	March bkwd. L–R and turn to L
	5–6	Circle R arm in front. Hold at shoulder height	Leap L Leap R
	7–8	Arms to sides. Look over R shoulder in turn	Step L Step R, turn L on RF
5	1–2	Swing arms up in V in front, turn L	Turn on LF to L Step R
	3–4	Cross arms to center and then out to sides	March bkwd. L–R
	5–6	Hold arms to sides	Step L and kick back R Step R
	7–8	Pass baton to LH on 7 Flat toss to RH on 8	March bkwd. L–R
6	1–2	Hold baton on each end and swing to L	March bkwd. L–R, bend to RS
	3	Holding same pattern, swing to R	March L–R
	4	Place tip into RS of waist	Bend to LS
	5–6	Take LH off baton, swing straight up overhead. Hold baton in RH on RS in position	Turn on LF to L angle. Step R
	7	Grab baton backhanded with LH in center of shaft (keep holding with RH)	Step bkwd. with LF
	8	With RH, push baton (ball leads) around both legs	Step back with RL in bend. Hold LL fwd.

SET	COUNTS	ARMWORK	LEGWORK
7	1–2– 3–4	Both arms overhead in V	L–R, L–R, turning full turn to L
	5–6	Roll over L elbow, catch R	March L–R
	7	Circle in front	March L
	8	Loop high on RS	Lunge fwd. on R
8	1	Circle fwd. on LS	Step L
	2	Hold up on RS	Step R
	3–4	Flag swing in back	Step L turning R March bkwd. on L
	5–6	R throw (on 5) baton fwd., high	March bkwd. L–R
	7	Catch L	Step L with slide kick back, RL
	8	Hold in position after catch	Step R
9	1–4	Bring arms up in V	Full L turn, L–R, L–R
	5–6	Pass to LH and hold in front	March L–R
	7–8	Flat throw to RH	Hitch-kick (step L, kick R and down on R, kick L)
10	1–2	Circle flat overhead	Step L. Turn L, march bkwd. R
	3–4	From front, wrap baton around back of waist L–R, catch R backhand at RS	Step bkwd. L
	5–6	Baton on L shoulder, bring back of head and down on R shoulder	March bkwd. L–R
	7	Flat pass to LH in front	Turn L
	8	Flat overhead pass to RH	On L–R face corner
11	1–2	RH holds baton center, straight-up position	Step L, jump on RL, stretch LL back, lunge fwd.
	3	Push ball up in air, baton stays upright, no revolution	Step L–R, turn L
	4	Catch backhand in R	
	5–6	Hold in catch position, R arm to side	Continue turn L–R until marching bkwd.
	7–8	Push tip up straight in front with both hands	March bkwd. L–R
12	1–2	Pull R arm down, hold	Step back L, step fwd. R. Stretch RL and step into lunge, facing fwd.
	3–4	Fig. 8. Loop from end of baton from L to RS	Run L, run R
	5–6	Push baton into a throw from fig. 8. Loop on RS	5—Leap L; 6—Leap R
	7–8	Catch RH	7—Leap L; 8—Leap R
13	1–2	Swing baton down and into R angle. End in flat position, both arms to sides, shoulder level	Turn on LL to R angle Step R

SET	COUNTS	ARMWORK	LEGWORK
	3–4	Pass to LH	March L–R
	5–8	Throw high flat, turn L, catch RH	March with a fwd. motion, turning L–R, L–R
Ending	1	Pass to LH	Step L–L angle
Pose	2	Pass above head to R	R–L angle
	3–4	Open both arms wide in flat position	Kick LL and backbend, hold position
	5–6	Raise both arms up	Come up on toes
	7–8	Swing arms down to center and pose out to side	Step LL–LS Bring RL in back, bend LK, point RL back, and hold pose

265. **STRUTTING POSE:** Leg pose.

266. **STRUTTING POSE:** Backbend lunge.

Strutting Score Sheet

Familiarity with the score sheet (page 128) can help develop an appropriate routine and serve as a guide to performing. Study it, and you'll see how strutting is evaluated and what the judges look for in a champion strutter.

Making Your Routine More Difficult

The best way to progress in strutting is to build onto your basic routine, adding more and more new things until the routine becomes more difficult and more challenging.

You'll make your changes in the presentation and forward-motion segments. The military section stays basically the same, but your execution will improve as time goes on.

OFFICIAL USTA STRUTTING SCORE SHEET

Name_____

Age_____

PLACE_____
CLASS_____
EVENT_____

SCORE

MILITARY	15		
Beat		Definite 1-2 positions, consistency of baton style.	
Military Bearing		Erect posture, chin and head level, eye focus, sharp corners, left hand wrist straight fingers together.	
Knee Level			
PRESENTATION	**15**		
Variety		Diversity of body work (leaps, lunges, spins, kicks, poses).	
Difficulty		Challenging combinations of body and baton work, creating a degree of risk for perfect execution.	
Execution		Control, balance, timing, extensions of arm, leg and toe, graceful transitions between movements.	
FORWARD MOTION	**25**		
Arm Work Variety		Diversity of free arm movements and baton tricks.	
Leg Work Variety		Variation in method of hitting every beat of music (leaps, glides, kicks, etc.)	
Difficulty		Challenging combinations of baton and body work while maintaining rhythm of movement.	
Floor Pattern		Directional variation with interesting maintenance of forward motion.	
Knee Level			
CARRIAGE AND BODY LINE	**25**		
Posture		Head and back generally erect, stomach tucked in, shoulders in line with trunk.	
Knee Level		Upper leg perpendicular to body for military and other sections when a standard march step is used.	
Leg Lines and Toes		Leg extension during movements so designed (straight on kicks, leaps, lunges, etc.) Toes raised directly under knee or forward, correctly pointed to front on standard march step, extended on leg work.	
Body Control		Control of body for proper execution, smooth flowing transitions.	
Technique		Proper execution and discipline, skill and quality of execution, turn out, proper carriage.	
SHOWMANSHIP	**20**		
Appearance		Neat, attractive, well groomed.	
Poise and Grace		Confidence and control, use of head, smile and expression.	
Audience Appeal		Professionalism, dynamic projection and appeal, levels of expression and maintenance of eye contact, ability to maintain interest.	
Enthusiasm		Dynamic projection, snap, sparkle, spirit of performance.	
PENALTIES			
		Incorrect corner on military 1.0 per error	
		Loss of balance .1 per error	
		Partial fall .5 per error	
		Complete fall 2.0 per error	
		Failure to acknowledge end of presentation .1	
		Drop 1.0 per error	
		Break or slip .5 per error	
		Pattern .1 per error	
		Out of step — Minor 2.0 Major 5.0	
		Incorrect exit to drums .5	
		Interference 2.0	
		Personal appearance .5 to 5.0	
		Unsportsmanlike conduct — up to 5.0 or disqualification	
		Overtime .5 (No penalty 1:25 to 1:35) Undertime .5	

USTA

Clerk's Initials _____ Judge's Signature _____

Total Penalty [ ]

THIS SCORE SHEET MAY NOT BE REPRODUCED IN ANY FORM WITHOUT EXPRESS PERMISSION OF THE UNITED STATES TWIRLING ASSOCIATION   USTA 515A

TOTAL SCORE [ ]

By the time you're ready for a second routine, you can begin to think creatively. Work closely with your teacher to develop a style that suits you and uses your strong points to good advantage.

Below are two variations on the presentation and forward-motion routines already given. Variation Number 1 is simpler, and you should learn it after you've mastered the basic routine. Once you master variation Number 1, go on to learn the second variation.

PRESENTATION VARIATION 1

SET	COUNTS	ADDITIONS TO BASIC ROUTINE
1	3–4	Illusion to R
2	3–4	Add high flat throw
	5–6	Catch in backbend
3	1–2	Tour jeté
	3–4	Turn L on both toes, bend back
4	1–4	Skater's spin, then wrap around RL during spin (wrap from inside RL, catch R backhanded)

PRESENTATION VARIATION 2

SET	COUNTS	ADDITIONS TO VARIATION 1
1	3–4	Add R vert. throw to illusion, catch RH
2	3–4	Add cabriole
	5–6	Throw and catch in flat finger twirl in backbend
3	1–2	Add flat throw turnaround
	3–4	Catch in turn
4	1–4	Butterfly turn

FORWARD MOTION VARIATION 1

SET	COUNTS	ADDITION TO BASIC ROUTINE
1	3–4	Circle arm to back
	5–6	Bkwd. hitch-kick
	7–8	Fwd. with L, lunge fwd. on R
2	3–4	Tour jeté
	5–6	Vert. toss from L to RH
3	7–8	Catch blind with LH above head
4	1–4	Add illusion, turn on the move
5	3–4	Add ballet turn to left
	5–6	Pass to L and do higher flat throw
	7–8	Catch in ballet turn to L
6	1–4	Do all these in only 2 counts
	3–4	Do same turns as in Sets 5–6
	5	Step back with LF and prepare for lunge (pass baton to LH)
	6	Lunge to floor
	7–8	Turn L and step in complete turn L–R, arms overhead in V
7	1–2	Circle R arm
	3–4	L elbow roll
	5–6	R elbow roll into fishtail
8	5–8	Throw when coming out of flag swing, continue turning to R and catch in back with RH
9	1–2	Full turn
	3–4	Pass to LH
	5–6	Bkwd. hitch-kick
	7–8	Fwd. hitch-kick
10	3–4	Add bkwd. hitch-kick
	5–6	Circle overhead and turn L
11	3–6	Double turn (working for good form, throwing head back)
	7–8	Toss vert. from L to RH while marching L–R, up on toes in fwd. direction

SET	COUNTS	ADDITION TO BASIC ROUTINE
12	1–8	Same action, but work for higher leaps (grand jeté) and better form
13	5–8	Add tour jeté
End	1–4	Ronds de jambes into a fouette
Pose		Pirouette turn to L and into L illusion turn Continue with backbend

FORWARD MOTION VARIATION 2

SET	COUNTS	ADDITIONS TO VARIATION 1
1	5–6	Add vert. throw, catch on count 8 in lunge
2	3–4	Take baton in LH, add flat toss, catch under RL on tour jeté
	5–6	Pass flat to LH
	7–8	Step L–R into fwd. lunge while tossing flat in back from L–RH
3	7–8	Catch baton under LL with LH
4	1–4	Add throw under RL in illusion turn
5	3–4	Add finger twirl. Improve form to have more backbend on ballet turns
6	5–6	Add flat throw
7	1–2	Circle loop behind head and turn L
	3–6	Facing back, toss on RS and go into angel roll across shoulders to LS
	7	Take baton in RH and continue
8	5–8	Throw under RL when coming out of flag swing and continue turning to R and catch in back with RH. (Optional—go into illusion and catch under RL in illusion)
9	5–6	High flat throw
	7–8	Catch on 8 in RH in backbend
10	5–6	Add backbend ballet turn
	7–8	Step L, lunge fwd. on R while doing low flat toss in back from L to RH. Bend body back on lunge
11	3–6	Same as for Variation 1
	7–8	Same as for Variation 1
12	1–8	Same as for Variation 1
13	5–8	Use tour jeté and catch flat throw blind in LH
End Pose	1–4	Add flat throw. Continue with backbend, use same ending, or end in attitude LL or arabesque LL position

Non-sanctioned Strutting Events

These events are held at some USTA competitions, at the discretion of the contest director. They're judged as a courtesy by association judges. Prizes won in these events do not count toward awards needed to progress from beginner to intermediate and so on. Strutters in these events all compete at the same time.

Beginning strutters who aren't ready to perform solo with a complete three-part routine sometimes find these events useful preparation.

Basic Strut. Straight marching, making a square around the floor, using simple arm swing.

Military Strut. Marching around the floor in a square, using the military beat with the baton, as described in the military section of the competitive strut routine.

Fancy Strut. Strutter's choice of forward motion, incorporating any type of arm and leg movements she desires.

267. **USTA GRAND NATIONAL DANCE-TWIRL CHAMPION:** Lauren Ann Deery, 15, from Garden City, New York. Lauren is also Grand National Strutting Champion for 1976.

EIGHT

Dance Twirl

Dance twirl is the combination of dance steps and baton maneuvers. Routines are highly individualized and must be choreographed according to both your dancing and your twirling abilities. Some twirlers will be able to do complicated baton tricks, but if they haven't had much dance background, the dance steps will have to be relatively simple.

Other twirlers will have a more complete dance background, but might have less experience with the baton. In that case, the bodywork will be more intricate than the twirling.

But even if your dance and twirling levels aren't equal, dance steps and baton maneuvers must look well together—and everything must be coordinated to the music. Be especially careful not to choreograph very fast twirls with dance steps that are slow, and vice versa. If you've never studied dance, we recommend that you take some lessons if you want to try dance twirl. The simpler dance steps aren't too difficult to learn—especially if bodywork is something you're strong in.

Dance twirl is both a solo and a team event. (Four or more people constitute a dance-twirl team.)

Solo dance twirlers use a standard record, which you'll need to have in advance so you can choreograph to it. Order it from the USTA. Solo routines are between two and three minutes long. Solo dance twirl is a good event for intermediate twirlers, but difficult for beginners, especially since they're limited by preselected music.

Team dance twirl is another matter. Dance-twirl teams may choose their own music. Routines are between two and four minutes long and needn't be as complicated—neither the dancing nor the twirling—as a solo routine.

This makes dance twirl excellent for beginners. Gloria starts beginners on a dance-twirl team after just eight weeks of baton lessons. It gives beginners a chance to experience group twirling and gives them practice with those tricks they've already learned. Furthermore, it gives them an opportunity to compete before they may be ready with a solo routine.

Remember, dance-twirl routines must express personality and fit both twirling and dancing abilities. Two teams or two individuals can perform the same routine—yet it will look entirely different each time.

The best rule here is don't copy anyone else's style. Also, avoid overdoing anything that's cute, coy, or gushy. And don't put anything with sexy overtones into a routine.

Keep your facial expression natural, and use your body to best advantage by maintaining good posture and giving long stretch to arms and legs. Definite free-hand positions, a warm (not forced) smile and plenty of eye contact add sparkle to your performance.

When making up a dance-twirl routine, be sure to avoid dance steps you're not up to. You can use ballet steps, modern dance, or jazz steps—but keep in mind that any step looks ghastly if it isn't perfected. So keep it simple, unless you've studied dance and are already a fairly good dancer.

Aim for a good balance of baton and dance movements. Remember, the music is very important in dance twirl. Every step must enhance and accent the music. Batonwork, footwork, and music must be coordinated.

The score sheet that follows will give you an idea of how dance twirl is evaluated. Study the score sheet before you try planning a routine.

At the end of this chapter are two routines—one for solo dance twirl and another for team dance twirl. See if you can analyze the routines in terms of the score sheet. You can also use them to get ideas for combinations you might want to use in your own routines.

But be wary of using these routines as they are for yourself. Dance twirl is one area where individuality and self-expression are very important. It's un-

OFFICIAL USTA DANCE—TWIRL TEAM ☐ & SOLO ☐
SCORE SHEET

PLACE _____
CLASS _____

Name _____ EVENT _____

Division _____

THIS SCORE SHEET MAY NOT BE REPRODUCED IN ANY FORM WITHOUT
EXPRESS PERMISSION OF THE UNITED STATES TWIRLING ASSOCIATION.   SCORES

Category	Pts	Criteria
RHYTHM	20	Correlation of foot work to music
		Correlation of body work to music
		Combination of body and foot work set to music
		Baton and free hand coordination
		Change of pace
VARIETY	20	Dance steps with correlating baton moves
		Dance steps with correlating body moves
DIFFICULTY	20	DIFFICULTY CREATED THROUGH:
		Combination of dance steps
		Combination of twirls
		Combination of dance steps and twirls
		Timing and continuity
SHOWMANSHIP	20	Uniformity of style
		Facial Expression
		Effective use of hands and body
		Presentation of routine
		General effect
		Appearance
CHOREOGRAPHY	20	Interpretation of music through baton handling and body moves

DROPS	.5	1.0	1.5	2.0	2.5	3.0	3.5	4.0	4.5	5.0	5.5	6.0	6.5	7.0	7.5	8.0	8.5	9.0	9.5	10.0	
UNISON	.1	.2	.3	.4	.5	.6	.7	.8	.9	1.0	1.1	1.2	1.3	1.4	1.5	1.6	1.7	1.8	1.9	2.0	Gross Score
	2.1	2.2	2.3	2.4	2.5	2.6	2.7	2.8	2.9	3.0	3.1	3.2	3.3	3.4	3.5	3.6	3.7	3.8	3.9	4.0	
BREAKS	.1	.2	.3	.4	.5	.6	.7	.8	.9	1.0	1.1	1.2	1.3	1.4	1.5	1.6	1.7	1.8	1.9	2.0	Less Penalties
PATTERN	.1	.2	.3	.4	.5	.6	.7	.8	.9	1.0	1.1	1.2	1.3	1.4	1.5	1.6	1.7	1.8	1.9	2.0	

TEAM		SOLO		Total Score
UNDERTIME	2.0	UNDERTIME	0.5	
OVERTIME	2.0	OVERTIME	0.5	

Judge _____

likely that one of these routines would really suit you without any alteration at all.

Here are some dance terms and steps most dance twirlers use. If you don't already know these steps, you should work on them until you can do them well enough to include them in your routine.

1. *Attitude*. A pose. Up on one toe with the other leg stretched up behind you. Arms should also be in a pose, either up overhead, out to sides, or one arm in front and one behind—whatever looks graceful and best expresses what you want.

2. *Body bounce*. Your whole body bounces in time to the music.

3. *Brush*. Lightly brush against the floor with toe of one foot, next to the other foot. You can brush forward or back, with no weight on brushing foot. (See *Dig* and *Tap*.)

4. *Camel walk*. Using tiny (2 inch) steps and keeping feet side by side, place heel down first, then toe (while other foot places heel on floor).

5. *Charleston*. Kick forward, step back with same foot, step back with other foot, step forward with beginning foot.

6. *Charlie Chaplin*. Arms at sides, hands parallel to floor, fingers out to sides. Keep legs stiff and take very small steps. Heel touches floor first, to flat-foot position, toes pointing out. Drop shoulder, leaning toward foot you're stepping on.

135

THE COMPLETE BOOK OF BATON TWIRLING

7. *Chine turn* (Chain). A body turn on both toes, beginning with a step out on one foot. When turning right, start with right foot stepping out; left foot steps out for turn to left. A leap between each turn is very effective. Step and turn on counts "one" and "two"; leap and turn on "three" and "four."

8. *Dig.* Toe touches floor forcefully, as if you're digging it into the floor. (See *Tap.*)

9. *Hip bump.* Jolt your hip up or out to the side. (See *Step ball change.*) Combining a hip bump with a step ball change is effective. Take 8 counts to do it. Step left, ball change forward; step right. Left toe out to left side and slam left hip up on the next ball change.

10. *Knee-pop roll.* Knees together, up on toes, roll knees in clockwise direction and snap to legs-straight position.

11. *Pas de bourrée.* Step back with right foot, placing it behind left foot. Step to side with left foot. Step with right foot, crossing it over left foot. (You can also begin with left foot and reverse everything.)

12. *Pirouette.* A half turn or full body spin on one toe. Position of leg you're not spinning on is important. Keep leg bent, knee out to side, toe pointed and touching side of other knee.

13. *Preparation.* Feet together, knees bent, ready to spring up into leap or jump.

14. *Relevé.* Lift up onto toes from flat-foot position.

15. *Step ball change.* Two counts. Begin on either foot. Example: step on right (one count), shift weight to ball of left foot (half count), and then back to right foot (half count).

16. *Soussus.* Feet together, up on toes.

17. *Spinal twist.* Rotating body from waist up.

18. *Susie Q.* Cross one foot over the other, digging heel down first. Pivot on heel as you step to side, not changing your direction. Starting on left heel, you would travel to right, knees bent, shoulders twisted to face opposite of "heel" foot.

19. *Tap.* Touching toe to floor lightly, or tapping the floor with one toe. Tapping toe stays next to other foot. A tap carries more force than a brush and less than a dig.

20. *Trenches.* With knee bent, step in place and point other toe with leg stretched out to side. (Step and point all done in one count, with slight hopping motion.) Arm opposite the pointed foot touches the floor near the pointed foot, while other arm swings up straight.

21. *Twinkle.* Moving forward on toes. Each foot crosses in front of the other, picking knees up high as you pivot.

SOLO DANCE-TWIRL ROUTINE (Advanced)

(This routine was choreographed to the song "Dance Ten Looks Three" from the album *André Kostelanetz Plays* A *Chorus Line*—Columbia KC 33954.)

SET	COUNTS	TRICK	BODYWORK
1		Begin facing rear	Head down, feet apart, arms at sides, baton on arm
	1–2	Listen	
	3–4	Snap around R to front	R arm swings up and around facing front, arms at sides
	5–6	Cross arms R over L	Elbows out
	7–8	Push arms out to sides, tail off arm	L steps back into lunge. Throw head back
2	1–8	2-toss turnaround, catch L behind back at RS	Kick RL ¼ L and ½ backbend
3	1–4	L rev., pass to R high overhead	Preparation, jump to R diag., kick LL back, lunge to R. Hold (5–8)
	5–8	Hold	
4	1–4	Ice spin to L to front	
	5–6	RH roll at LS	R cross over L, as L arm swings behind. L toe behind RK, relevé, L step back. Hold (7–8)
	7–8	Hold	
5	1–6	R toss, illusion catch R inside of RL	Full body turn to R, face front
	7–8		Fan LL up and around
6	1–4	R flip catch back R	Turnaround to R, face front
	5–6	Baton on arm, push both hands fwd. and out in pose	Slight fwd. lunge with RF fwd., up on toes
	7–8		Pose
7	1–4	R rev. at LS	R cross over L, ball change
	5–8	R layout	L cross over R, ball change
8	1–4	R to L blind catch	R cross over L, ball change
	5–6	Tail to floor, arms at sides	Dig L toe next to R
	7–8	Body roll, face ¼ R	
9	1–2	Baton circles front of body. Cross arms front of knees	Step L, dig R at diag. L
	3–4	Both arms out to sides	Lunge to diag. R
	5–6	Baton at side	Spin turn to L, to face front
	7–8	L steps fwd., tail fwd., L arm out ¼ L	Bend both knees
10	1–4	Back roll (RH to RH)	Body bounce twice. L arm cross over L in front as if to recover baton. Both arms out to sides as R recovers

137

SET	COUNTS	TRICK	BODYWORK
	5–8	Horiz. taffy pull, both hands slide to ends	Step R rear, face ¼ R. LF drags to R. Up on toes
11	1–4	½ taffy pull to get thumb to tail, to baton up on R arm (1–2)	¼ R—hitch-kick (3–4), both arms out to sides
	5–6	Hands behind neck, elbows out	Twinkle (L to R)
	7–8	Leap ¼ R	Stretch arms out to sides. LL kicks back, R arm high, L arm low
12	1–4	Tail loops horiz. under R arm into horiz. wrist roll	Turn front, switch weight from R to L. Lunge. Kick R fwd. (1–2). Place R back in same lunge (3–4)
	5–6	Pass to LS, to LH against body, palm out	Step fwd. R
	7–8	R arm swings up, circles front of body out to RS	Snap up on toes
13	1–4	R horiz. 8-finger overhead during all 8 counts	1 body turn, L to front (LF, RF)
	5–6		Lunge to L
	7–8		Lunge to R
14	1–4	Flat L-to-R toss	On 3–4, step L, kick R facing ¼ L, as bending back on kick, head back
	5–8	Catch on 5	Fwd., kneel on 5, R kicking leg is front
15	1–4	R overhead loop	L arm out, bend back, still facing ¼ L
	5–8	Pass baton on chest to L, L arm. Ball out, diag. down, R arm diag. up pose	Switch knees as you turn L to L diag.
16	1–4	Pass to R by grabbing R over L, palm up so thumb is to tail. Bring out to RS. RH-to-RH flip counterclockwise at RS	Stand. Side step R, feet together, step R, step back L, circle both arms once in front of body
	5–8	RH-to-RH flip clockwise at L side	Side step L, feet together, step L, step back R
17	1–4	Preparation, leap ¼ R. Baton pass over R shoulder to L, grab behind back	LL kicks back
	5–6	Slap R hip up as LF up on toe	
	7–8	LH holds inside LK	L arm out to side, R hip pointing up, hold
18	1–4	L-to-R flip at rear	Body turns to front in L direction, up on toes
	5–8	¼ R, RS wrist roll, R fig. 8	L arm out to side

SET	COUNTS	TRICK	BODYWORK
19	1–4	R vert. 2-finger at L (inside arm) R vert. 2-finger at L (outside arm)	Deep lunge ¼ L. R kick (on 3) ¼ L
	5–8	R 2-finger pull back behind head	Lunge, pull up on toes, L arm out
20	1–4	R 4-finger behind head	Body turn on toes, L direction
	5–8	2-toss turnaround	Elbows out, hands behind back
21	1–4	R rev. at LS. R fig. 8 at RS	Lunge, then point L toe fwd.
	5–8	L-elbow fishtail turnaround	On toes
22	1–4	2 L fishtails, ¼ R	Lunge
	5–8	2 L fishtails, ¼ R	Kick LF back
23	1–4	Lift toss of back of LH	Pull up on toes
	5–8	R rev. at LS. R fig. 8 at RS	
24	1–4	Slide to tail end, loop behind back	Complete turn R to front on toes, release on 3 as LL kicks fwd.
	5–8	Throw R to L at rear, baton coming under L arm. Catch R behind head	Catch on 5, snap up on toes, hold facing front
25	1–8	Continuous elbows	Turn on toes, move feet with music
26	1–8	Catch L behind head, pass behind back, pull up to R fig. 8	Same as Set 25
27	1–8	2- or 3-toss turnaround, catch ¼ L underhand in RH	Preparation, jump, kick RL back ¼ L on catch. While body is in air, L arm circles once at rear
28	1–8	Arms at sides, down. RH holds ball close to leg while circling baton 8 times	Charlie Chaplin walk—R (1), L (2), R (3), hold (4), L (5–6), R (7–8)
29	1–4	Baton on arm	Charleston, start LF
	5–6	RF lunges back, ball touches floor	Bend over—head down, L arm back
	7–8	Step R fwd.	Natural swing to arms
30		Repeat Set 29	
31	1–2	Tail touches floor, both hands rest on ball	Feet together, diag. R., bend over
	3–8	Same	Knee pop roll, pop fanny back on 7, and hold on 8
32	1–8	L 2-finger up L 2-finger down L 2-finger up L 2-finger down R arm out to side	Step L, attitude Step R, step L
33	1–4	L 2- finger up, 2-finger down	Step R, kick L to ¼ L, turn in air to ¼ R into lunge

SET	COUNTS	TRICK	BODYWORK
	5–8	Flat 8-finger overhead, pass rear to R	Spin left
34	1–4	Baton on arm	Step L fwd., soussus
	5–8		Jazz lunge, both knees bent
35	1–4	Baton on arm	Pirouette R, arch back
	5–8	Same	Pirouette L, arch back
36	1–4	R 2-finger front at RS; R 2-finger front	Tap R, kick R, step back R, ball change
	5–8	R 2-finger front; R 2-finger pull behind head to LS	
37	1–2	Baton out to RS, slide to end	Step L fwd., pivot to ¼ R
	3–4	Pull back in air (no revolutions), catch L at RS rear	Step R tap
	5–8		Chinese leap
38	1–8		Chine turn to R, step R, step L. Leap on R, step L, face diag. R, R ball change. Face rear—hop feet apart, arms at sides.
39	1–4	Face rear, palms up, stretched to rear	Shoulder shake, lean back, head back
	5–8		Turn to R, RK up, feet apart facing front. Bend fwd., with LK bent. Tummy touches knee, head is down
40	1–8	Baton on arm	4 trenches
41		Repeat Set 40	
42	1–4		¾ split, RL fwd., rest weight on RH
	5		Flip body over R onto tummy, weight on both hands
	6–8		Come to sitting position, cross RL over L. Whole set is very fast
43	1–4		Stand up
	5–7		Face diag. L, step R, step L, tap R next to L
	8	Baton rev. loop outside R arm	Pushing both arms fwd., diag. L. L palm up, bend both knees

You can adapt the above routine for use by a team. On some sets have back line freeze while other line executes the set. Then have front line freeze as back line repeats the set.

TEAM DANCE-TWIRL ROUTINE (High Intermediate)

MUSIC: *"Hey, Pretty Pussy Cat,"* from Command Sampler, Com 14–S.D.

Team should be in 2 lines, and each line faces rear to begin.

SET	COUNTS	TRICK	BODYWORK
1	1–2	Hold, tail to floor	Feet together, head down, arms at sides
	3–4	Snap baton to R shoulder	Head snaps up, elbows up and out to sides. LF points to LS
	5–6 (Front line only; back freezes)	Baton snaps down to start position	L arm fwd. L arm snaps up and over to your rear to point toward audience. Place weight on L toe, knee bent, look at audience
	7–8	Baton on shoulder	
2	1–2	Do 3–4 from Set 1	
	3–4	Do 5–6 from Set 1	
	5–6 (Back line only; front freezes)	Do 7–8 from Set 1	
	7–8	Tail to floor	RF steps behind L, dip as you pivot on toes R to face front
3	(Back line)	Snakes to front line	
	1–4	R diag. run to R of girl in front of you	Zig to R (1–4), Zag to L (1–4). Toes pointed, natural swing to arms. Head to R, 4 counts; L, 4 counts
	5–8	L diag. run past front line (back line now front)	
	(Front line)		
	1–4	2-toss turnaround, recover	
	5–6	Baton on arm, arms straight	Step L, dig R, R arm up
	7–8	Baton on arm, arms straight	Step R, dig L, L arm up
4	Repeat Set 3, each line doing the other part, so original front line is again in front		
5	1–2	R circle fig. 8	L ball change
	3–4	Pass to rear, L rev.	R back step, step L
	5–6	Pass overhead, R fig. 8	R ball change
	7–8	Arms at side of hips	Spin to R 1½ times to face rear, elbows out, spin on toes
6	Repeat Set 5, facing opposite direction		
7	1–2	Baton swings to LS, perpendicular to floor	Hop L
	3	Baton swings down and over to RS, perpendicular to floor. Free hand follows baton each time	Brush R
	4	(On counts 2 and 4)	R step cross over L

SET	COUNTS	TRICK	BODYWORK
	5–8	Both hands hold ends of baton as it swings full circle clockwise	L ball change, back step. Stretched arms. Imperative for head to follow baton's movement
8	1–4	Repeat 1–4 from Set 7	R ball change, back step
	5–6	Baton on R arm crossed over L arm, elbows out	Turn L direction to face rear, feet together
	7–8	Tail off arm to Y position	Hop, feet apart, stretch arms, head back
9	1–2	Hold baton at ball end, tail loops under arm	L ball change
	3–4	Neck roll	Step R, fwd. Step L, turn L to face front
	5–6	L 8-finger overhead	R cross over L, point L toe to L side
	7–8	Finish 8-finger	L cross over R, point R toe to R side (Bend knee that's crossing)
10	1–2	L platter horiz. toss	Up on toes
	3–4	Catch flat on back (catch 3, hold 4)	Deep lunge, bend over, R diag. to rear
	5–7	Grab 2 hands center of baton, as tail leaps under arms, snap hands to ends of baton	Pull up on toes
	8	Hold	Arms stretch high overhead
11	1–2	L-elbow, R-elbow roll	Point L fwd.
	3–4	Catch L, palm up	Point R fwd.
	5–6	L fishtail turnaround	Spin to right on toes
	7–8	Thumb-pinch toss	Snap up on toes
12	1–2	R rev. at L side	Lunge ¼ L
	3–4	R 2-finger	Step R, ¼ R
	5–8	R 2-finger behind head	Spin on toes, a complete turn to left
13	1–4	R 2-finger inside arm R 2-finger outside arm	L ball change, ¼ L R ball change, ¼ R
	5–6	Facing rear, place baton on top of LH, dip tail to LS	Face rear by stepping L diag. and step R diag.
	7	Rev. direction to roll over wrist from under RS, grab R	Step L toward rear
	8	Both arms out to sides, front	Step R to front, turning R
14	1–2	Tail to floor, swing baton to L and R front of knees, L arm follows it	Feet together on toes, knees bent and together, point knees R and L
	3–4	R fig. 8 (big)	Cross L over R, kick R to side
	5–6	2-hand pass to L	Cross R over L, ball change
	7–8	Pass to L behind back	L steps fwd., turn R rear R steps fwd., face rear

SET	COUNTS	TRICK	BODYWORK
15		(Front line only, back freezes)	
	1–2	R toss	Deep lunge to R
	3–4	Catch L	Deep lunge to L (baton toward audience as you face rear)
	5–6	Toss turnaround	Turn L to face front
	7–8	L arm up straight, tip pointing ¼ L, R arm up straight	Pose lunge to L
16		Back line repeats Set 15. Front line freezes	
17	1–4	R arm up, baton on arm, L arm out to side	Ice spin—turn R, shift weight to RL
	5–6	Diag. R, backbend, both arms swing down and up rear	LL straight out, RK slightly bent, head back
	7	Baton continues up and over, tail touches floor	L arm out, still in diag. R. Bend over in fwd. lunge, LL back, head down
	8	Freeze	Freeze
18	1	Baton on arm	Step L, cross over R
	2	Baton touches floor	Bend over, R points to RS
	3	Elbows out, hands touching in front of chest	Step R, cross over L
	4	Arms out to sides, baton off arm	L points to LS
	5	Baton on chest, 2 hands	Step fwd. L
	6	Baton pushes up	Kick L fwd. and high
	7–8	Baton behind head, hold, 2 hands	Complete spin L to ¼ L for front line; ¼ R for back line
19	1–2	2 hands on ends of baton	Lunge away from other line
	3–4	Swing in direction of lunges	Lunge toward other line
	5–6	Lines go through each other, changing places	L ball change
	7–8		R ball change
20	1–2	Face each other	Arms down at sides
	3–4	Arms circle in opposite directions	Up on toes
	5–6	Throw exchange to partner	
	7–8	Catch L, pass rear	Turn: front line ¼ L, back line ¼ R
21	1–2	Stretch arms out to sides	
	3–4	Loop behind head	Turn on toes
	5–6	Throw exchange to partner	
	7–8	Turn for catch, baton coming to your rear	
22	1–2	R horiz. 2-finger down	Lunge, L arm up straight
	3–4	R horiz. 2-finger up	Pull up on toes as you spin to L, face front

SET	COUNTS	TRICK	BODYWORK
	5–6	R horiz. 2-finger down	Preparation
	7–8	R horiz. 2-finger up	Flash-out leap
23	1–2	Pass to L, L flat 2-finger up	1–8—spin 4 times, L direction, 2 counts per spin as team forms large circle
	3–4	L horiz. 2-finger up	
	5–8	Repeat 1–2 above	
24	1–4	Horiz. platter, horiz. toss turnaround	All face out from circle
	5	Catch R	
	6–7	Roll baton around back, from LS, catch R at RS	Up on toes, L arm up straight
	8	Hold	
25	1–4	L rev.; R fig. 8	L ball change, R ball change
	5–8	R fig. 8, R fig. 8 (circle, now traveling counterclockwise)	Move circle to maximum size
26	1–8	Repeat Set 25	Use maximum stretch, legs and arms—big leaps
27	1–4	Rev. circle to counterclockwise, with body turn to L. R horiz. wrist twirls, pass L on 4	L ball change R ball change
	5–6	L horiz., toss overhead and to rear	Hitch-kick, legs fwd.
	7–8	Catch from girl in front (circle travels clockwise)	Hitch-kick, legs back
28	Repeat Set 27		
29	1–4	Neck twist, neck roll	Spin L on toes 1½ turns to face out of circle
	5–8	Waist wrap	Step L, kick R as you do backbend
	7–8	R arm up, baton off arm, L down, still facing out	Up on toes
30	1–2	Loop behind head, spin to ¼ L	Use direction of spokes of wheel
	3–5	Throw exchange to girl opposite you in circle	
	6	Catch L, pass rear to R	
	7–8	Spin turn to L to face in	
31	Repeat Set 30		
32	1–6	Run to center of circle	Going out of circle, step L (turning right to go out of circle), step R
	7–8	Baton up and overhead as you turn out of circle, then baton down to RS	
33	(Use this set to go into a formation of a block of 2 lines)		
	1–4	Repeat 1 and 2 of Set 18	Keep coming out of center of circle

SET	COUNTS	TRICK	BODYWORK
	5	Arms at sides	Step L
	6	Arms at sides	Step R (face into circle as RF steps or dips back. Motion is still traveling away from center)
	7	Arms at sides	Step L—still moving out
	8	Arms at sides	Step R (head stays facing out 5–8)
34	1–4	2-toss turnaround (front line). Back line passes baton around waist of front girl and then passes to own rear	Arms high overhead in steeple position Lunge RL back
	5–8	Wrist-twirl turnaround	Back line travels to R of front girl, ending in one line
35		(All girls are now in company front)	
	1–8	Stagger from R end—2 counts per girl	
		2-toss turnaround	End in lunge pose ¼ L
36	1–8	Continue Set 35 to last girl on end	
37	1–8	Stagger ice spin turn from L girl to R girl, 2 counts per girl	
38	1–8	Continue Set 35 to end girl	
		Fade music	

268. **USTA GRAND NATIONAL TWO-BATON CHAMPION:** Robin Woodruff, 14, Castle Rock, Washington.

NINE

Two-baton Twirling

Twirling two batons at once is, as you can imagine, quite a bit more complicated and difficult than twirling just one. But it can be done, and it can be done well. It's a very popular event at competitions, and many twirlers enjoy the special challenge the two-baton offers.

If you're dedicated and willing to increase your current practice time to include working with two batons, you'll probably be able to learn this aspect of twirling.

When should you begin? You should have good mastery of the beginning single-baton skills and be well into intermediate maneuvers. Two-baton comes most quickly to solid intermediate twirlers.

To succeed at two-baton twirling, you need good baton control, superb body coordination, and the ability to move quickly and gracefully. Furthermore, you need excellent ambidexterity (ability to twirl equally well with either hand). All these things come with lots of practice, and if you've been twirling for a while, you've probably developed well in these areas.

Types of Two-baton Maneuvers

There are three kinds of two-baton maneuvers, and you'll have to be able to do all of them if you expect to put together a competitive two-baton routine.

1. Synchronization: Each hand does the same sequence or trick simultaneously. For example, right and left hands both do flat wrist twirls at the same time.

2. Coordination: Each hand does a different sequence or trick. For example, right hand does flat wrist twirl while left hand does flat four-finger overhead.

3. Toss-pass-catch: One baton gets tossed, the other gets passed, the tossed one gets caught in the empty hand. For example, throw the right-hand baton up, pass left-hand baton behind back to right hand, catch descending aerial in left hand.

BEGINNING TWO-BATON MANEUVERS

Don't attempt to learn all of these in one or two weeks. It's going to take you several months of practice before you can do most of these moves smoothly or without drops. As in single-baton twirling, mastery of fundamentals is crucial before going on to harder tricks. Work on these beginning moves until you have mastered most of them and are fairly comfortable with the rest, and keep practicing them as you start learning intermediate two-baton maneuvers.

HORIZONTALS OR FLATS

1. *Flat wrist twirls.* Both hands do horizontal wrist twirls. Remember to keep both batons moving counterclockwise.

2. *Flat wrist twirl, turnaround to the left.* Add a quick complete body spin to the left while doing flat wrist twirls in both hands.

3. *Flat showers.* Start with flat throw from left hand. Right-hand baton (held thumb to ball) is passed "dead stick" (no twirl) to left hand. Right hand is then empty, and can catch the aerial. Repeat with throw from left hand and continue the trick so that it becomes continuous, smooth, and fast, with both batons in constant motion.

Flat-shower variations. (1) When passing baton dead stick from right to left hand, pass under right leg on the first throw, then under the left leg on the second throw, and keep alternating legs as you continue the showers.

(2) Pass from right to left hand with a neck wrap and throw immediately from left hand.

269

270

271

269. FLAT SHOWERS

270. FLAT-SHOWERS-LEG-PASS VARIATION

271. FLAT-SHOWERS-NECK-WRAP VARIATION

4. *Flat two-finger series.* Right hand starts a two-finger flat down, while left hand does two-finger flat overhead. Then switch, bringing right hand up for flat two-finger overhead, and left hand down for a low flat two-finger.

Flat two-finger variation. Add a turnaround to the left, timing your body spin so that you face front each time left hand begins overhead two-finger.

VERTICALS OR SIDE MANEUVERS

1. *Side figure-eight turnaround.* Right hand starts with thumb to ball behind back. Bring baton out to front in vertical plane and do a figure eight to the side as you turn around on your toes. While you're turning, left hand does a reverse figure eight. Don't repeat, but go directly into your next trick.

 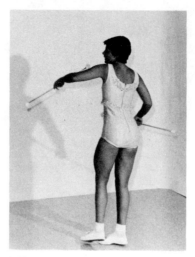 

272   273   274

WINDMILL SERIES

272. Lunge left and do reverse figure eights with both batons.

273. Turn to the right. Reverse figure eights become forward figure eights as your body moves to the right.

274. As you face front, figure eights become reversed again.

2. *Windmill series.* This is a series of figure eights and reverses, coupled with a turnaround and some lunges. The photos will guide you.

3. *Figure eight—four-finger series.* This is the same as you learned with one baton, only do it with both hands at the same time.

4. *Figure eight, back-pass series, with flip.* Hold both batons thumb to ball, one in each hand. Right baton is behind back to start, and left baton is directly in front of you.

Right hand begins with whip figure eight, back pass to left hand. Left hand does reverse figure eight, and flip.

Catch in right hand and go immediately into a figure-eight back pass to repeat the trick.

277. **FIGURE-EIGHT-BACK-PASS SERIES WITH FLIP:** Throw is out of left hand. Catch right after back pass of right baton to left hand.

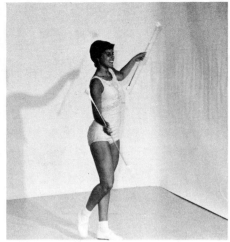

276

275. Lunge right. Right hand does forward figure eight, while left hand does reverse.
276. Begin reverses with both hands as you lunge left to complete series or repeat.

Variation. Instead of passing behind the back, pass under legs, alternating left and right leg passes each time you repeat the trick.

BASIC TOSS-PASS-CATCH SERIES

1. *Throw-and-pass-across-the-front series.* Right hand does right-side whip and two-revolution thumb toss to left hand, while left hand does reverse figure eight and passes in front to right hand. Ball should be down on pass. Grab in right hand, thumb to ball. Left hand goes directly from catch into reverse figure eight to repeat.

Variations. (1) Catch under right or left leg with left hand. (2) Catch behind back with left hand.

278. **THROW-AND-PASS-ACROSS-FRONT SERIES:** Be sure both thumbs are down as you pass in front from left to right hand.

279   **280**   **281**   **282**

SINGLE-TOSS SERIES

279. Start with right thumb to ball, left thumb to tip. Reverse figure eight with left hand while right hand does figure eight down to back pass.

280. Right hand keeps its baton and grabs baton from left hand behind back.

281. Right hand brings both batons out with a regular whip, ball leading . . .

282. . . . into a single (one baton) toss of one-and-a-half revolutions. After toss, right hand continues with right-side figure eight, as left hand catches thumb to tip. Finish right figure eight behind back and bring left baton into reverse behind back to repeat.

2. *Single-toss series.* This trick involves holding both batons in your right hand, but releasing only one of them. The photos above will help you do this maneuver.

3. *Double vertical toss.* Begins with both batons in right hand. Do right-side figure eight, and as baton comes toward front of body, release both batons simultaneously. As the batons descend, catch one in left hand, palm up, and grab the other in right hand, palm down. Follow through with reverse figure eights in both hands, lunging left.

283   **284**

DOUBLE VERTICAL TOSS

283. Releasing both batons from right hand.

284. Recover, palm up, in left hand; palm down, in right.

4. *Single-toss turnaround*. Right baton starts from behind back. Left baton starts in front. Both hands hold batons thumb to ball. Right hand does figure-eight whip to right side, while left hand does reverse-figure-eight whip on left side.

As right baton comes back to front, throw it and begin turning to the left. Left hand does a reverse figure eight during your turnaround. Catch aerial in right hand.

JUDGING AND SCORING TWO-BATON EVENTS

At twirling competitions, two-baton is evaluated according to the same factors as single-baton twirling. The score sheets are identical. Everything you've already learned about competing, performing, and composing a routine apply to this event.

Two-baton routines are a minute and a half long, and they're performed to an official association recording, which you can order from the USTA.

BEGINNING TWO-BATON ROUTINE

1. Salute. Use a normal right-hand salute. Your left hand has two options: Either put the left baton behind your back or place it under your left arm, thumb to tip, with ball facing toward audience. (This gives the appearance of left hand on hip.)
2. Start with a single-toss turnaround, with aerial coming directly out of the salute, eliminating whip figure 8 in back.
3. Side figure-8 turnaround.
4. Windmill series. Repeat twice.
5. Figure-8, back-pass series, with flips. Two times with behind-back passes, and two times with alternating leg passes.
6. Single-toss series. Do it twice.
7. Double vertical-toss series.
8. Throw-and-pass-across-the-front series. Do it twice.
9. Throw-and-pass-across-the-front series, with catch under left leg first and catch under right leg on the repeat.
10. Go immediately into flat wrist twirl, turnaround to the left.
11. Flat 2-finger series: one plain and one with turn to the left.
12. Flat showers. Do it plain, three times.
13. Flat showers with leg passes. Do it twice, one pass under each leg.
14. Flat showers with neck wrap. Do it twice.
15. Flat turnaround to the left and pass baton dead stick. (Throw flat from left hand, and on turnaround pass the dead stick from right to left hand. Catch flat aerial in right hand.)
16. Go into salute to finish.

285   286

FIGURE-EIGHT TURNAROUND WITH TIME-TOSS FLIPS

285. Right hand does thumb-flip toss as left hand does reverse figure eight.

286. Shift lunge position by shifting weight, not by moving feet. Right hand does forward figure eight while left does reverse backhand flip.

INTERMEDIATE TWO-BATON MANEUVERS

1. *Figure-eight turnarounds with time-toss flips.* Right hand and body-work: Right-hand baton is held thumb to ball, behind back. Do a figure-eight turnaround, halfway to the right, stepping out with left leg to right side. Do a stop lunge and a time-toss flip of one revolution. Upon catching, do a reverse figure eight, then a forward figure eight over to the opposite side. Don't move your feet, just shift your weight. Repeat the time toss.

Left hand: Left baton is held thumb to ball, out in front of you, ball to left. As you're turning, do left reverse figure eight at left side. Raise baton up as you turn to the right and drop ball so it's directly in front of your waist. Go into a left reverse at your right side, come back with a forward figure eight, do a backhand flip of one revolution, and go into reverse upon catching.

Time yourself, so that one hand does a flip as the other does figure eights.

2. *One-and-a-half turnaround to the left, and catch.* This maneuver has an aerial out of the right hand, back pass of left baton to right hand, quick figure eight with right hand, and catch under leg or behind back with left hand. The photographs on page 155 will explain further.

3. *Eight-finger raise and arm roll.* Left reverse figure eight and right-side figure eight. Left hand begins an eight-finger twirl, first four-finger with baton out in front and last four-finger with baton raised overhead. Right

154

7	288	289	290	291

ONE-AND-A-HALF TURNAROUND TO LEFT AND CATCH

287. Toss right-hand baton up into aerial and pass the other behind your back with reverse figure-eight back pass. Start turning body to the left.

288. Aerial is up as you keep turning, and pass behind your back.

289. As turn is completed, baton begins coming down. Do a quick raised figure-eight whip at your right side with right baton.

290. Prepare to catch aerial under right leg with left hand.

291. Raise right leg for catch.

EIGHT-FINGER RAISE AND ARM ROLL

292. Following left reverse, left hand does eight-finger raise, while right-hand baton rolls over upper left arm, following a side figure eight.

293. Ball drops down and then comes up over right wrist, as left hand continues the eight-finger.

294. Elbow roll completed, twirler is now ready for layout and turn to the right.

295. Baton is laid out in right arm. Turn to the right and catch layout in right hand, as left hand does a reverse figure eight.

92	293	294	295

baton simultaneously rolls over upper part of left arm, then goes into a right-elbow roll and layout. Turnaround to the right, while left hand, having completed the eight-finger twirl, does a reverse figure eight.

4. *Throw and double-elbow series.* Left hand throws a high aerial. Right baton does double-elbow roll. Catch elbow roll behind back in left hand, and catch aerial in right hand.

5. *Fishtail both hands with raised turn.* Face right. Figure eight in right hand while left hand does fishtail. Go into figure eight in left hand and fishtail in right. Keep repeating this for speed and smoothness. Once you've got it going nicely, start turning to the back (left), as you raise left hand into a reverse and let it roll over your left wrist as body comes around to the rear and continues to front. As you make the turn, right hand does reverse figure eight to left side and fishtail roll over right wrist.

6. *Right-elbow roll and time toss in back.* Turn to the left as right baton does right-elbow roll. Catch behind the head with left hand. During right-elbow roll, left hand does reverse and time toss behind the back, which is caught in the right hand. Keep turning and repeat trick when you come to face-front position.

7. *Neck-roll and back-pass series.* Right baton does a neck roll as left baton is passed behind the back. As the ball of the right baton comes over the left shoulder, grab with left hand, and pass it behind your back as right hand begins another neck roll.

8. *Left-hand quick-flat-toss series.* Throw high flat aerial from left hand to right. After left baton is released, quickly throw right baton up to left side. Catch first baton in right hand, pass it dead stick to left hand, then catch second aerial in right hand.

9. *Single and double flat-turnaround series.* Flat toss out of left hand, single turnaround, pass baton dead stick to left hand. Before first baton is down, throw the second baton flat out of left hand. Catch first baton in right hand, do two turnarounds, passing dead stick to left hand, freeing right hand to catch second baton.

10. *Back-catch-back-catch—one-and-a-half back-catch series.* Right baton starts behind back, left baton in front, thumb to ball, ball to right. Right hand does thumb-flip time toss directly in front. Catch behind you with right hand as you turn to the right.

Left hand does reverse flip, catching in back as you turn to the right.

Then turn to the left, as right hand does figure-eight and windmill series as you come around to face front. Then do a one-and-a-half back catch with a turn to the right. Left hand does a reverse figure eight while the one-and-a-half is in the air.

Make sure you've got the left-hand pattern correct, and that you're raising your left hand up to get full value out of the twirl.

11. *Back catch with shoulder pass.* Throw left baton up from a reverse figure eight, while right hand does a figure eight. Pivot a little to right and slide baton so you hold it at the end for a pass over your left shoulder. Leave your right hand behind your back after you do this, to catch the aerial. Follow through the shoulder pass with a left reverse figure eight.

12. *Reverse-throw and leg-pass and leg-catch series.* Throw left baton up while right hand does a figure eight and pass under left leg. (Pick up left leg for the pass, and turn body just a bit to the right.) Catch aerial under left leg with right hand, and continue turning to the right.

13. *Flat throw under leg and back-catch neck-wrap series.* Start with a left four-finger flat overhead and turn to the left as right hand does flat wrist twirl. Left hand then does an inside-leg throw flat under the left leg, while right hand does wrap around neck. When baton comes down, pivot right and catch flat behind the back with right hand, while left hand does reverse-side figure eight.

14. *Eight-finger—left-arm-balance series.* Left eight-finger flat out to left side, and turn twice, while right hand puts its baton dead stick in crevice of elbow and balances it there.

15. *Vertical single and double turnarounds.* Throw left baton up in reverse figure eight. Turnaround once to left while right hand does figure eight. Throw right baton up before first baton comes down. Catch first baton in right hand. Turnaround twice to the left, passing baton dead stick to left hand, freeing right hand to catch second aerial.

16. *Reverse dip—flat-throw and vertical-throw series.* Start with left-hand baton doing reverse flat dip up into flat throw, as right hand whips into a front high toss. Catch flat throw in right hand, pass dead stick under left leg, do left reverse figure eight with a turn to the right, and catch second baton in vertical back catch in right hand.

17. *Reverse-throw and blind-catch series.* Left throw from reverse figure eight, and time toss from right hand, while turning to the left. Catch the time toss blind behind the head with left hand, and catch the left aerial with the right hand.

18. *Vertical two-finger series overhead.* Both hands start with two-finger twirl as you turn around to right. Right hand should be in back when left hand is in front. Both hands are doing the two-finger simultaneously.

When you finish the two-finger and the one turn, bring right-hand two-finger down in front of you (dead stick), and then bring right hand up overhead in a two-finger. As you do this, left hand is doing two-finger in back. (Again, both hands doing the two-finger simultaneously.)

When you face front again, left hand comes up overhead doing a two-finger, while right hand does dead-stick turn to the back and into two-finger in back.

Continue on around to the left and complete the two-finger in each hand.

You can end this trick with both hands doing an inside two-finger directly in front. Kick left leg back in the air as you do this, continuing to complete the turn with both batons ending in full hand.

INTERMEDIATE TWO-BATON ROUTINE

1. Salute (same as beginners).
2. One-and-a-half turnaround to left, catch under leg (intermediate #2).
3. Side figure 8 turnaround series (beginners, vertical #1).
4. Windmill series (beginners, vertical #2).
5. Back-catch-back-catch—1½ back-catch series (intermediate #10).
6. Reverse-throw and leg-pass and leg-catch series (intermediate #12).
7. Figure-8 turnarounds with time-toss flips (intermediate #1).
8. Back catch with shoulder pass (intermediate #11).
9. Reverse dip—flat-throw and vertical-throw series (intermediate #16).
10. Left-hand quick-flat-toss series (intermediate #8).
11. Single and double flat-turnaround series (intermediate #9).
12. Flat 2-finger series with turns (beginners, horizontals #4).
13. Eight-finger—left-arm-balance series (intermediate #14).
14. Flat throw under leg and back-catch neck-wrap series (intermediate #13).
15. Neck-roll and back-pass series (intermediate #7).
16. Right-elbow roll and time toss in back (intermediate #6).
17. Eight-finger raise and arm roll (intermediate #3).
18. Throw and double-elbow series (intermediate #4).
19. Fishtails both hands with raised turn (intermediate #5).
20. Vertical single and double turnarounds (intermediate #15).
21. Vertical 2-finger series overhead (intermediate #18).
22. Reverse-throw and blind-catch series (intermediate #17).
23. Double turnaround with double vertical toss (beginners, toss-pass-catch #3, with another turnaround added before catching). Make sure to get the batons high.
24. Salute.

ADVANCED TWO-BATON MANEUVERS

1. *Four-elbow roll with double-turnaround aerial.* Do reverse figure eight in left hand followed by a very high aerial. After baton is in the air, do a four-elbow roll turning to the left, ending with behind-the-back catch in left hand. When aerial comes down, catch right in a lunge to the left, and follow through with reverse figure eight.

2. *Multiple elbows with flat hold.* Left reverse figure eight at left side. Then bring baton flat and tuck ball under right armpit. Right arm does right-side figure eight and then comes over the tip of the left arm into a flat-hold position. (Be sure left-hand baton is perfectly flat). Now start the multiple elbow rolls, turning to the left. When you finish, catch right baton backhanded with right hand. (Turn right hand to backhand position by turning wrist to the left, so thumb faces down.) Catch thumb to ball.

3. *Angel roll with aerial.* Start with right-side figure-eight whip, while left hand does reverse figure-eight whip. Throw right baton up into fairly high aerial. As it leaves your right hand, left baton does angel roll across shoulders and is caught in right hand. Catch aerial in left hand, and repeat the whole trick.

Variation. Instead of catching the aerial turn it into an angel roll. (Start with right arm, turn to the left, and catch baton on inside of arm to start the angel.) This is an extremely difficult maneuver and will take lots and lots of work.

4. *Two-and-a-half turnaround to the left and catch under left leg.* This is the same as intermediate trick ✻2, but doing an extra turn on the aerial.

5. *One-and-a-half or two-and-a-half back-catch series with quick throw and back catch.* Start a one-and-a-half turnaround to the right, with a right-hand throw, as left hand does reverse figure eight. Just before the baton comes down, throw left baton up. Catch first baton behind back, then figure-eight pass under left leg to left hand, freeing right behind to catch second aerial behind back. Practice in flat and vertical planes.

Variations. (1) Floor catch with right hand under right leg, kicking left leg high and continuing it down to the right. You'll need to pivot just a little to the right to make the catch. (2) Split-jump pull-out catch.

6. *High left-handed toss with one-and-a-half blind catch.* Throw left baton high with reverse figure eight. While it's in the air, do a one-and-a-half turn to the left, throwing right baton and catching it blind in left hand. Right hand catches high aerial to finish.

7. *Quick flat-throw series.* Begin with intermediate trick ✻13, but leave out the back catch. After the neck wrap, immediately throw baton in the air

159

and with the right hand catch the baton you threw under your leg. Go immediately into a waist wrap, by sliding your right hand to the tip of the baton as you catch it and throwing it around your waist. (Make sure baton touches your body the whole time.) Catch it *backhand* with right hand.

Upon catching, pass immediately to left hand. Then catch aerial in right hand, *backhanded*. Kick left leg up high and to the back for the catch.

8. *Double flat-throw turnaround.* Both batons in left hand to do reverse figure eight. Dip both batons and throw them into the air. When they come down, catch the one closest to you with your left hand, palm up; catch the other one in your right hand, palm up. Be sure you turn around completely to the left during the aerial—two or three turns, whichever you can manage.

9. *Vertical one-and-a-half or two-and-a-half back-catch series with double throw.* Both batons in right hand. Figure-eight whip on right side, and open (not off the thumb) toss into the air with both batons. Turn around one and a half or two and a half times to the right, then catch in the following way: closest baton caught in right hand behind the back, as left hand catches the other baton, palm up.

VERTICAL ONE-AND-A-HALF OR TWO-AND-A-HALF BACK-CATCH SERIES WITH DOUBLE THROW

296. Release from right hand in open-hand position.

297. Right hand catches closest baton, behind the back. Left hand takes other baton, palm up.

296   297

10. *Vertical or flat showers with single hands.* Start flat showers you learned in beginners. Once you get them going, throw and catch the baton in the same hand. Practice first in the right hand, then the left. And learn to do it both vertically and horizontally.

11. *Four-finger toss series from back with vertical showers.* Right-hand baton starts with figure eight four-finger to back. Make sure that when

baton reaches your pinky it's all the way to the back. Then toss off pinky from the back, so baton comes over right shoulder to front, for a right-hand catch.

While this is happening, left hand does reverse figure eight, turn to the right, then another reverse figure eight on the left side.

As right baton comes over your shoulder, toss left baton out of left hand to the back.

Once you catch the right baton in your right hand, pass it to the left hand, and catch the other aerial in your right hand, in back. Finish your turn and end facing front.

ADVANCED TWO-BATON ROUTINE

1. Salute (beginners and imtermediates).
2. Two-and-a-half turnaround under the left-leg catch (advanced ✳4, except throw right baton into the air after figure-8 raise).
3. Turnaround to the right with a reverse figure-8 turn, with the left hand. Then catch baton that's up in the air behind the back, turning to the right.
4. High left-hand toss with 1½ blind catch (advanced ✳6).
5. Vertical 2-finger series (intermediate ✳18).
6. Two-and-a-half-turn back-catch series to the right with quick throw and back catch. Use the first variation on the catch (advanced ✳5).
7. Four-finger toss series from back with vertical shower (advanced ✳11).
8. Angel roll with aerial (advanced ✳3).
9. Multiple elbow rolls with flat hold (advanced ✳2).
10. Eight-finger and arm raise (intermediate ✳3).
11. Four-elbow roll with double-turnaround aerial (advanced ✳1).
12. Right-elbow roll and time toss in back (intermediate ✳6).
13. Throw with double elbow catching in blind catch (intermediate ✳4, ending with blind catch behind head).
14. Quick flat-throw series (advanced ✳7).
15. Flat 2-finger series (beginners ✳4 with turns).
16. Eight-finger—left-arm balance (intermediate ✳14).
17. Pass both batons to left hand flat.
18. Double flat-throw turnaround (advanced ✳8).
19. Single flat showers in right hand (advanced ✳10).
20. Left-hand quick flat-toss series (intermediate ✳8, but insert turnarounds . . . first throw gets single turnaround to left, and second throw gets a double turnaround).
21. Come on around to the front and go into a right-handed high flat throw and pass left baton behind neck (tip leading to right hand), and then catch the aerial in flat blind catch in left hand.

22. Double and triple flat spin (intermediate #9, but make it a double turn and a triple turn, instead of a single and a double).
23. Neck-wrap and back-pass series (intermediate #7).
24. Pass both batons behind back to right hand.
25. Vertical 2½ back catch (advanced #9).
26. End routine with a double-baton vertical 3 turnarounds (advanced #9, but 3 turns instead of 2½).
27. Salute.

TEN

Three-baton and Novelty Twirling

Novelty twirling includes three-baton twirling, fire-baton twirling, saber twirling, flag twirling, pompon twirling—and anything else unusual or novel that you can think of.

The most popular types of novelty twirling are three-baton and fire-baton, so that's what we're going to cover in this chapter.

Three-baton twirling is open only to high advanced twirlers, but fire baton, contrary to what you might be thinking, is something that even good beginning twirlers can do. If you're not ready to try three-baton, at least skim over that section of the chapter. You'll get an idea of what it's all about and whether or not you might like to try it some day.

Then go on to the fire-baton section. There you'll find instructions and safety hints, as well as two routines—one if you're going to perform solo, and another you can use if you're in a majorette squad.

THREE-BATON TWIRLING

Unless you're a highly advanced solo twirler who is also proficient in two-baton, you shouldn't try to learn three-baton. Total baton control is a necessity if you expect to master three batons. So are body coordination, agility, and speed, as well as an extraordinary ability to concentrate.

There are three types of maneuvers in three-baton twirling:

1. Showers: Two batons in the air with the third being passed from one hand to the other. Showers can be done in flat or vertical planes.

2. Juggles: Throwing the batons from one hand to another so quickly that all appear to be in the air at the same time. The technique is identical to a circus juggler's technique and is used not only for batons, but apples, dishes, and what have you.

3. Two-baton tricks, altered somewhat to incorporate having the third baton in the air.

BASIC THREE-BATON MANEUVERS

1. *Flat showers.* Left hand will do the throwing. Right hand catches and passes. Remember this and you won't get confused.

Start with one baton in left hand and two in right. Throw left baton, pass one of the right batons to the empty left hand, and toss it. Pass the third baton to your left hand, catch first aerial in empty right hand, and toss the baton in your left hand. Pass right hand baton to left hand, freeing right hand to catch next descending baton.

Work on this until you can manage to keep two batons in the air while passing the third. Remember to keep all batons in horizontal plane at all times.

298. **FLAT SHOWERS**

299. USTA THREE-BATON GRAND NATIONAL CHAMPION, 1976: Ginnette Groome, 18, Syosset, New York.

300   301   302   303

VERTICAL SHOWERS

300. Practice with one baton first. To pass, hold baton in right hand, thumb to ball. Pass dead stick to left hand . . .

301. . . . which grasps it palm up.

302. Left hand throws with a reverse backhand flip.

303. Try it with two batons next. Left hand is just about ready to twist for the backhand toss.

304. Finally, try three batons. Left hand has just released baton. Right hand will pass its baton before catching baton that's in the air.

305. Right hand will catch as soon as pass-is completed. Left hand will then toss passed baton.

304   305

2. *Vertical showers*. Again, you'll throw with the left hand, catch and pass with the right. To keep the baton in the correct plane, you have to toss, pass, and catch properly. So first, just practice with one baton until you know how to do it. The photographs on page 166 will illustrate the correct hand and baton positions.

Now see if you can get three batons going. Start with one in the left hand and two in the right. Get left-hand baton in the air to begin.

3. *Basic juggle*. Both hands throw and catch. No passing in this maneuver. The left hand catches batons thrown with the right hand; right hand catches all batons thrown with the left hand. Throw all batons diagonally toward the opposite hand. Each baton should do one revolution in the air before it's caught.

Begin with two batons in your right hand (call them #1 and #3) and one baton in your left hand (call it #2).

Throw baton #1 from your right hand. Before catching it in your left hand, throw baton #2. Before catching #2 in your right hand, throw baton #3. Before catching #3 in your left hand, throw #1 (which you caught after releasing #2).

Keep the process going until it's smooth and exact. Remember, you always catch with a free hand, which means the catching hand must throw just prior to recovery.

Expect lots of drops when you first start working on showers and juggles. All these maneuvers take incredible coordination, fast reflexes, lots of baton control, and hours of practice.

306. **JUGGLE:** In a good fast juggle, all batons are in constant motion at the same time.

4. *Two-baton maneuvers incorporating third baton.* The two-baton moves to work with are intermediate #2, 3, 5, 6, 7, 14, 18, and advanced #2 and 8. Throw high (horizontally or vertically) from the right hand and do any of the above two-baton tricks under the high throw. After completion of the two-baton trick, be sure to get right baton into left hand, so that you can catch the high throw in the right hand.

MORE ADVANCED
THREE-BATON MANEUVERS

Three-baton twirling is highly individualized, and most twirlers, once they master the basics, have no trouble thinking of ways to elaborate upon them. Start by adding turnarounds to the showers. Take all the tricks as far as you dare. Anything goes here, so have a good time and pull out all the stops.

One of the most difficult things about three-baton is to get good showmanship into your performance. It's unbelievably hard to have lots of eye contact with the audience when you're concentrating so hard on where the batons are at every instant. It's also not easy to move gracefully while juggling three batons at once.

Not many twirlers are able to handle three batons. Those who can are very dedicated, but they also get special pleasure from one of the most challenging and difficult areas in twirling.

FIRE BATON

Most people think of fire twirling as being very beautiful, very difficult, and very dangerous. Actually, they're only right about the beauty. It's neither difficult nor dangerous, providing you take proper safety precautions.

If you're a high beginner or intermediate, you can twirl with fire. Save your fire routines for evening performances out of doors. If you do fire baton inside, it's less safe; if you do it outside, but during daylight, you lose the spectacular effect. Here's how to do a fire routine without any casualties.

Equipment

1. Be sure you have regulation fire batons. Order them from one of the supply houses listed in the Appendix. Don't try to jerry-build a fire baton, either from your regular baton or from anything else.

2. Use unleaded or white gasoline if available. It's less dangerous in the unlikely event of a burn. If not available, use regular gasoline.

307. **FIRE BATON:** A lovely nighttime spectacular.

3. Have on hand two ✳10 cans for soaking the ends of your fire baton.

4. Have on hand a clean dry cloth to wipe excess gasoline off the shaft.

5. You'll need an enclosed fireproof box, or a fire tube to put your baton in after the routine. If you have a tube, placing the baton inside it will automatically extinguish the fire. You can also extinguish the fire with a blanket. Then roll the baton in the blanket and put it in the box. (Be sure you close the box.)

Preparing the Baton

1. Be sure to have a soaking area far away from the performing area.

2. Never, never light your baton in or near the soaking area. Nearly every mishap that occurs in fire twirling is a result of ignoring this essential safety rule.

3. Soak each end of the baton for about five minutes, or until bubbles stop appearing in the gasoline. Give the first end a last-minute soak before going over to the performing area to light the baton.

4. Shake each end of the baton when you remove it from the gasoline, to avoid flying drops of gasoline.

5. Wipe off the shaft with a cloth to be sure there's no gasoline on it.

Costumes

1. Be sure your uniform is very fitted. Avoid skirts and sleeves.

2. Tuck your hair into a tightly fitted cap. You can decorate the cap with rhinestones or sequins to make it look fancy and festive. Long hair should be put into a secure bun, so there's no chance it can fall out of the cap.

How to Twirl with Fire

1. Stay alert. Fire twirling is really quite safe, but you must be prepared for the unexpected. Occasionally, one of the lighted ends of the baton may brush against your skin. The contact is very brief and normally does not result in a burn. At the most, a few hairs might get singed.

We're not telling you this to frighten you. We want you to know that even if the end of the baton does touch you, you aren't likely to get hurt. So don't panic if this happens.

2. Don't twirl with fire if you're afraid, or if you're not confident in handling the baton. Twirlers who are frightened and/or hesitant with the baton create danger for themselves and others.

3. Don't attempt a difficult routine. (Simple routines are not only safer, but they look better as well.) This is no time to experiment with twirling material you're not sure of. Your confidence with the baton is very important.

4. Keep the baton in constant motion. When the baton is stopped, the flame gets larger and is more apt to start a fire somewhere else. Keep your body moving too. The more motion, the safer. Prettier, too.

5. Don't do any tricks in which the baton is close to your body. Wraps, for example, can't be used. Whips are okay, as long as you don't have to hold the baton near the end. Keep this in mind when you're making up a fire routine.

6. The main effect of fire twirling comes from the circles of light the baton's revolution makes. Tricks in the vertical side planes don't make these circles very visible to the audience, so you might as well avoid them.

The larger your circles, the greater the visual impact. For this reason, make your baton and body movements broad and large.

Intricate or subtle tricks have little or no effect on a fire-baton audience. They can't see much except the circles of light the baton is making. Simple aerials are very beautiful and work very well in a fire routine.

Below are two fire-baton routines. You can certainly use these, but try to find your own combinations as well—remembering to keep it simple.

FIRE-BATON ROUTINE
FOR MAJORETTE SQUAD

SET	COUNTS	TRICK	FOOTWORK AND/OR BODYWORK
Intro.	1–2	2 hands center of baton stretched overhead. Spin turn to L	On toes
	3–4	Hold	Point LF front
	5–6	Bow fwd., baton down to LF, horiz. position	L arm out to side LF stays fwd.
	7	Baton pushes overhead	Same as above
	8	Hold pose	Same as above
1	1–8	2-hand full circle, ending with R fig. 8	Lunge to R, lunge to L, up on toes for overhead pass
2	1–8	2 RH circles	Lunge to L, L arm out to side
3	1–4	RH circle	Lunge and kick R to ¼ L position
	5–8	RH fig. 8 turnaround	Body spin to the R
4	1–4	Back pass	
	5–8	LL pass	Lunge to L
5	1–4	RL pass	Lunge to R
	5–8	Pass behind both knees	
6	1–4	Split jump while doing 2-hand pass behind knees	
	5–8	2 R fig. 8s	Pose with LF fwd., both arms to either side
7	1–4	Pass to rear from RS to L rev.	LF fwd.
	5–6	LL pass	Lunge L
	7–8	Whip baton out from behind LK, to flat R overhead whip	L arm out to side Spin to L
8	1–4	Face ¼ R, do R horiz. wrist twirls	RF pointing fwd.
	5–6	4 R horiz. wrist twirls as you turn	Spin to L on toes
	7–8	Pass to LH	LF fwd.
9	1–4	L to R horiz. toss (1 or 2 revolutions)	LF fwd.
	5–8	4 R flat wrist twirls	L arm out to side
10	1–2	Flat 2-finger down (R)	Lunge L, arm to side
	3–4	Flat 2-finger up (R)	Snap up on toes
	5–6	Repeat 1–2	Repeat 1–2
	7–8	Repeat 3–4	Repeat 3–4

SET	COUNTS	TRICK	FOOTWORK AND/OR BODYWORK
11	1–4	L flat 4-finger. Throw your head back so it looks like fire is on your nose	Spin to L, R arm out
	5–8	L horiz. toss to RH	LF pointing fwd.
12	1–4	Flat pass to LH overhead to behind back	Spin to L
	5–8	R aerial (2 revolutions)	
End	Tag or 9th beat	Freeze on catch for this beat	Face ¼ L. Raise up on toes, L arm fwd., R arm high overhead. Baton parallel to ground. Throw head back, eyes on audience

Suggested music for the band to play during this routine: "Light My Fire."

SOLO FIRE-BATON ROUTINE

Before starting routine, you can, if you want to, take some gasoline into the performing area. Pour the gasoline on the ground, in a circle about ten feet in diameter. While still outside the circle, light your baton. Step into the circle and light the ground, where you've poured the gasoline. Do your routine in the center of the circle, surrounded by fire. This makes a spectacular effect and leaves the audience gasping for breath. Don't use this effect unless you've done fire twirling before and have the confidence and alertness you need to perform safely with a fire baton.

1. Hold fire baton overhead with both hands.
2. Bring it down in the right hand with a figure 8.
3. High toss with right hand. Catch in right hand and go into a reverse figure 8 at your left side.
4. Figure-8 turnaround completely to the right.
5. Windmill series. (Figure 8 at right side in lunge to right. Bring arm behind the back and twist into a left lunge. Do a reverse figure 8, and face front again.)
6. Figure 8, turn around completely to the left.
7. Thumb flip and catch behind back with right hand.
8. Figure 8 and pass under right leg to left hand.
9. Reverse and pass behind the back.
10. Figure 8 and pass under left leg.
11. Reverse and pass behind the back.
12. Flat wrist twirl, with quick turnaround to the left.
13. Flat pass from right hand to left hand.
14. Flat throw from left hand to right hand.
15. Flat 2-finger down.

16. Flat 2-finger overhead with turn to left.
17. Flat 2-finger down.
18. Flat 2-finger overhead (no turn, remain facing front).
19. Pass to left hand.
20. Flat 8-finger overhead, with turn to the left.
21. Flat high toss from left hand to right hand.
22. Bring baton up overhead flat with right hand and grab with left hand. (Don't turn baton.) Just turn around twice to left while holding the baton still.
23. Come out to left side with a reverse figure 8. Then figure 8 at right side.
24. Two-hand spin and pass around left leg from behind, in left lunge.
25. Two-hand spin and pass through center of legs from front, in right lunge.
26. Two-hand spin and pass around both legs from behind.
27. Come out in a high toss with right hand . . .
28. . . . catch and go into a reverse figure 8, lunge to left side, then bring back to right side with a figure 8.
29. Thumb flip and catch behind the back with right hand. Do 3 times for a really spectacular effect.
30. Now start wrist twirl in right hand, facing ¼ right. As you do this, run forward about 8 steps, raising the baton up and down while you're running.
31. Pass baton behind the back to left hand.
32. Reverse figure 8 and reverse thumb-pinch toss from left hand. Toss to the left so you can move back into position.
33. Go into a figure-8 turnaround to the right.
34. Come out immediately with a high toss.
35. Upon catching, go into a dead stop with baton and raise baton over your head, holding with both hands.
36. Bring baton straight down in front and all the way to the ground in a bow. Then quickly snap back up to starting position over your head.

A solo routine like this is an effective number for a featured twirler during half-time shows, especially if the entire squad is not using fire batons. A fast, spirited band accompaniment is best. "Saber Dance," or something in that line, usually makes a good impression with audiences.

ELEVEN

Teams

A superadvanced solo twirler doing incredible tricks is very impressive to watch. She can awe an entire audience with her skill. But, oddly enough, it's not usually the solo work that drives an audience wild. Instead, it's the group competitive events, stunning performances by teams and corps, that wow audiences and give the biggest visual thrills. For sheer spectacle, you can't beat a large musical corps, but it's in the team performances that you'll generally see the sharpest twirling.

What is a team? Very simply, it's a group of four or more advanced twirlers, performing together as a unit. Team twirling is something nearly every twirler aspires to. It has its own special thrills. There's an excitement in twirling with a team, a unique pleasure different from solo twirling. As a team member, you have other people to share in your triumphs and disappointments, which makes the highs higher and the lows less low. Sharing experiences usually results in close friendships among team members.

Sharing the responsibility for the overall performance of the team fosters a sense of partnership with your teammates. On a team, you've got support.

Everyone is counting on you, as you are counting on everyone else. The knowledge that you're not alone calms you. Team twirlers are less likely than soloists to make mistakes caused by nervousness. When you're on a team you don't only want to do well for yourself, but for your teammates as well. There's added incentive to give your all. If you goof on your solo, it's too bad, but it's too bad only for you. But if you don't do a good job on your team routine, you've not only hurt yourself but a number of other people too.

Not everyone can twirl on a team, not even everyone with advanced skills. A good soloist doesn't necessarily make the best team twirler. Teamwork requires a high degree of twirling proficiency, plus a basic knowledge of marching fundamentals. You also need the willingness and ability to gear your own skills and timing to those of the others on the team. A team twirler must be versatile, patient, cooperative, hardworking, superalert, able to think on her feet. She must not only develop herself as an individual, but as a group member as well.

It's important to realize that a twirling team is not merely a bunch of soloists doing the same tricks at the same time. A team is a unit unto itself, finely tuned and well-practiced individuals who function as one during a performance or a competition. Being chosen for a team is an honor any twirler can be proud of.

For competitions, twirling teams are categorized according to the size of the team and the age of its members. Age divisions break down into *primary* (8 and under); juvenile (9–11); junior (12–14) and senior (15–21).

Teams come in two sizes. *Small* teams have from four to eight members. *Large* teams have nine or more. How large does a large team get? There's no official limit, but most have between twelve and sixteen—rarely more than twenty-four, because it's very difficult to find that many well-matched twirlers. If you try to put more than twenty-four on a team, you'll probably be limiting the range of difficulty and variety in the routine—and increase the likelihood of penalties.

In team competition, like competes against like. So large teams don't compete against small teams. According to USTA rules, you may not compete on both a large and a small team. Rely on the teacher's judgment for the best size team for you.

Putting together a top team isn't easy for any teacher, even if the whole school is filled with terrific advanced twirlers. Most teachers are in conflict when they're choosing a team. They want to give as many students as possible a chance to twirl on a team, yet they also want to build a team that will have a competitive edge.

Talent, intelligence, enthusiasm, and discipline are most important qualities to look for when selecting team members. A girl needn't be "pretty" or have a terrific figure—but her appearance must be clean and neat.

Watch out for careless or indifferent team members. Don't lower your standards to accommodate the weaker members of your team. Instead, see that they strive for improvement and make continual progress.

It's nearly impossible to set hard and fast rules about the best way to create a winning team because there are so many variables. If you're a teacher with capable students, but your teams aren't winning much, there might be several reasons. Maybe you need to change your routine or the music or the twirling style. Maybe you should juggle the girls around and re-arrange the team. Sometimes, finding a winning combination is a matter of trial and error. Don't be afraid to try new things. Look at it as a learning process.

Who goes on what team? Generally speaking, try to put the best techni-cians on a small team. Since the technically perfect girls are usually in the minority, this will probably be a natural division.

A large team is a better spot for a girl who can twirl well, with advanced skills, but whose showmanship, bodywork, projection, and strutting are just a bit stronger than her twirling. Since a large team does a longer routine, it has more of a chance to let its personality shine through. Take advantage of this by using "personality plus" types on your large teams whenever this is feasible.

Take a good look at your students and evaluate them keenly. You want to match the girls in as many ways as you can, from their technical twirling proficiency, to style of twirling, to even their appearance, if possible.

Let's say you've got ten advanced twirlers. Your first inclination would probably be to make one large team. But if their skills and styles aren't a good match, this might not be wise.

If you've got a large team that isn't doing well in competition, you might consider forming two small teams. Sure, they'd be competing against each other, but there's really no harm in that. Both teams will probably improve more as a result. We've both done this when it seemed the best way to use the talent available. And very often the team we thought was least skilled improved enough to beat the team that started off in first place.

If you're lucky, you'll be able to match the members of a team not only according to their skills and personalities, but with regard to their appear-ance as well. This gives your team a more unified look. If possible, choose girls of similar stature to be on one team and have them style their hair alike. (We aren't suggesting it, but we once knew a teacher who had all the girls on her team wear identical wigs.)

Work on the fine points. When readying a team for competition, most teachers do everything they can to make the twirling perfect. They use lots of fancy tricks and put in plenty of difficult exchanges (transferring batons from one twirler to another). But no matter how terrific the twirling is, your team will look shoddy if you forget the fine points.

Here are some questions to ask yourself. Are all the girls holding their heads at the same angle? Do they turn their heads in the same direction at the same time? Are all eyes on the same spot? Between various sections of the routine, do the girls fidget, or do they stand perfectly poised and still waiting to begin again? Do you have girls scratching their noses or pushing stray hairs back into place? You may not believe this, but we've even seen a girl tighten her shoelace or pull up a sock during a lull in a routine.

If you want your team to look good, you've got to think about the tiny details that may seem far removed from twirling but are crucial for a professional, prize-winning performance.

Choosing your music. Twirling teams select their own music. The final responsibility for the choice rests on the teacher's shoulders. If you're a teacher and want to offer your students some choice of music, that's fine. Just make sure you're letting them choose from two or more things *you've* previously selected. Once they understand the type of music needed to give a team a competitive edge, they can make suggestions. If you're so inclined, listen to the music they bring you, but don't give up your authority in this—or any other—area. If you abdicate, your chances of making a winning team are slight.

Choosing the music is one of the most interesting, enjoyable, and creative aspects of team twirling. It's also the most difficult. In competitions we see a surprisingly large number of teams using the worst possible music. They don't stand a chance of winning. We're not sure why they make such terrible decisions about music, but we can guess.

Most likely the teachers don't really know much about music. Or they're not familiar with many different kinds of music. Or they're trying to be too democratic and are giving the students too much power in this area. Or, possibly, they just don't know some of the basic principles of selecting music for a team.

Here are some general principles that will guide you in selecting music. And don't forget, it takes lots of listening.

1. Don't use vocal music. It distracts the twirlers, the audience, and the judges. It detracts from a routine.

2. Avoid country music, rock and roll, or anything that's a fad. One exception to this principle—rock and roll, instrumental versions *only*, can be

appropriate for the dance-twirl section of a twirling team's routine. It gives a good change of pace.

3. Use instrumental music only, preferably something strong on strings. The music should be pleasing to a large variety of people, have a catchy melody, and should be easy to follow and count to. Something with a strong beat and a melody that is easy to hum.

Stick to orchestrated pops music in the vein of Arthur Fiedler or Hugo Winterhalter. Show tunes are usually very good. We've used songs like "There's No Business Like Show Business," "Old Man River," "Send in the Clowns," "Singing in the Rain," and dozens of other favorites, old and new.

4. Overtures from stage or movie musicals are excellent choices because they contain change of pace (variations of mood and tempo), which is a requirement of team routines.

Some of the overtures we've used successfully include: *Roar of the Greasepaint* . . . , *Funny Girl, Company, Applause,* and *That's Entertainment* (the movie). You can also choose songs from older shows. Irving Berlin's music, for example, usually works very well. Don't be worried about your rock-and-roll-loving students not accepting this kind of music. Once they're exposed to it, and especially after they've twirled to it, they'll really like it.

5. Vary the dynamics of the music. Choose selections that have some loud parts and some soft parts. Contrast shows off your team's abilities. But don't let the loud sections get *too* loud. There's no need to blast your music at top volume. A judge who is wishing for an earplug isn't likely to appreciate your team. Music that's too loud is a common error.

6. Buy or borrow all the instrumental semi-pop records you can and listen a lot. When the right thing comes along, you'll recognize it. It will inspire you. You'll practically be visualizing the routine as you're listening. Nearly every successful team director says that once you choose the right music, the routine as much as choreographs itself. If you're having a really hard time making up a routine, you've probably made an unwise music decision. Choose something else and begin again.

7. Do not attempt to create a routine before you select the music. Did George Balanchine created a *Firebird* before Stravinsky did? No! Did Bob Fosse choreograph *Pippin* before Stephen Schwartz gave him the music? No! Did Michael Bennett make up the dances for A *Chorus Line* before Marvin Hamlisch composed it? No!

Do Fred Miller and Gloria Smith choreograph team routines before picking out the music? No! Are you going to create a routine without music? Only if you want to relinquish both your own sanity and your team's competitive edge.

It's absolutely futile to make up a routine and later try to find some music to which it can be performed. Chances are there's no recorded music anywhere that will be perfect. And even if there were, you could spend your life trying to find it.

What you'll do instead is take the first music you think *might* do. Only it doesn't *do* at all. We can almost always spot a team whose coach planned the routine first and music later. The choreography and music work together only sporadically, if at all. The girls have trouble keeping the beat because it was a terrible match from the start. Some sections of the routine seem out of character with the rest, having been altered or tacked on or added to because the original wasn't right.

Choreography. The first step is listening to the music you've selected. Tap out the beats, 8 counts at a time. You'll begin to notice that the music divides neatly into sections consisting of 8 beats or multiples of 8.

If you plan your routine in sections of 8 counts—or 16 or 32 or whatever multiple of 8 corresponds to the number of beats in each section of music— you're on your way.

Try to keep the mood of the routine consistent with the mood of the music. Of course, a single piece of music will have varying moods (and your routine needs this change of pace), yet everything fits together to make a unified whole. The routine you choreograph should also be unified, even though it will have several different moods within it.

Learn to be a critical observer. Don't ever stop evaluating your team's performance. But watch other teams, as well as your own, with a critical eye. When we say critical, we don't mean you should find something wrong with every other team, or even with the winning team. We mean evaluate and judge that other team sharply, with close attention to what's good as well as what's sloppy.

When something impresses you as good, study it. Figure out why it's good. Maybe it's the difficulty of the routine. Maybe not. A simple routine performed perfectly is more impressive than a difficult routine badly done.

Maybe the team looks good because all the knee levels are uniform. Maybe it looks good because the costumes are simple enough not to detract from the polished twirling. Maybe it looks good because the costumes and twirling style express the music well. Maybe it looks good because the precision is well-developed.

You can help your team a lot by deciding what makes other teams look terrific and by noticing the things that make them look shoddy. Until you've got your team able to score high on all the finer points, try to keep the routine as uncomplicated as possible without making it too easy or dull.

Take a USTA team score sheet (reprinted below) and study it. While your team is practicing, score the girls according to the way they'll be judged in competition. Be tough. Pretend your team is really a team that's competing against you, and judge it harshly—as if you didn't want the team to win. You're going to pick that team apart. Then, take those areas you scored low and have your team work on them.

Team Scoring

As you will see from the score sheets reprinted below, teams are judged in five separate areas by at least four different judges. You'll also see just how many points can be won or lost in each area.

Becoming familiar with the scoring method will help you coach your team and insure you're working to get a good score in each area. But don't rely too much on the score sheet when making up your routine. "Playing to the score sheet" can limit your creativity and make your routine mechanical. It's best to do the choreography first, then use the score sheet as a check list during rehearsals to see if the routine falls flat in one area or another.

The girls on the team should also understand scoring methods. Let's go over them.

1. *Marching and maneuvering.* A twirling team doesn't just get out on the floor and dazzle the judges with fancy baton tricks. There's more to it than that. Marching and maneuvering—or M and M—means that the team will be moving forward (marching or strutting) and will be forming various

---

A   OFFICIAL USTA TWIRLING TEAM SCORE SHEET

PLACE_____
CLASS_____
EVENT_____

Name of Team_____ Number of Team_____

Address_____ City & State_____

	POINTS POSSIBLE	SCORE	COMMENTS	SCORE
MARCHING AND MANEUVERING	40			
Variety of Maneuvers 10				
Originality of Maneuvers 10				
Difficulty of Maneuvers 10				
Effectiveness of Floor Coverage 10				
TOTAL				

PENALTIES (TO BE DEDUCTED)

	.5	1.0	1.5	2.0	2.5	3.0	3.5	4.0	4.5	5.0	
.5 Out of Step	.5	1.0	1.5	2.0	2.5	3.0	3.5	4.0	4.5	5.0	
.1 Alignment	.1	.2	.3	.4	.5	.6	.7	.8	.9	1.0	
.1 Interval	.1	.2	.3	.4	.5	.6	.7	.8	.9	1.0	
.1 Distance	.1	.2	.3	.4	.5	.6	.7	.8	.9	1.0	

Possible Penalty

Net

Clerk's Initials _____   Judge's Signature _____

GENERAL COMMENTS

TOTAL SCORE [   ]

B   OFFICIAL USTA TWIRLING TEAM SCORE SHEET

PLACE_____
CLASS_____
EVENT_____

Name of Team_____ Number of Team_____

Address_____ City & State_____

	Points Possible	Score	Comments	Sc
TWIRLING	90			
Difficulty	15			
Speed	10			
Variety	15			
Exchanges	10			
TOTAL	50			
Smoothness	10			
Team Work	15			
Baton Handling While Maneuvering	15			
TOTAL	40			

PENALTIES (TO BE DEDUCTED)

	.1	.2	.3	.4	.5	.6	.7	.8	.9	1.0	
.1 Unison	.1	.2	.3	.4	.5	.6	.7	.8	.9	1.0	
.5 Drops	1.1	1.2	1.3	1.4	1.5	1.6	1.7	1.8	1.9	2.0	
	.5	1.0	1.5	2.0	2.5	3.0	3.5	4.0	4.5	5.0	
.1 Break and Slips	.1	.2	.3	.4	.5	.6	.7	.8	.9	1.0	
.1 Pattern	.1	.2	.3	.4	.5	.6	.7	.8	.9	1.0	

Possible Penalty

Net

Clerk's Initials _____   Judge's Signature _____

GENERAL COMMENTS

TOTAL SCORE [   ]

patterns on the floor—all while twirling. M and M must be included in the team's entrance and exit, and should definitely be included in the main body of the routine.

As you can see from the score sheet, M and M is judged on four different counts.

VARIETY—how often the team changes formations and how many different formations are included in a routine. Naturally, you'll want to avoid repetition.

ORIGINALITY—how unusual the formations are. If the judges have seen your formations time and time again, then you'll score low on originality.

DIFFICULTY—giving the girls maneuvers that are hard for them to accomplish. Also, having the team risk making errors by performing maneuvers that are intricate and complicated.

EFFECTIVENESS OF FLOOR COVERAGE—how much of the floor area (size of a basketball court) your team uses during maneuvering. Judges will be making new evaluations of floor coverage every sixteen steps, or with every change in direction the team makes.

Penalties (M and M)

OUT OF STEP—wrong foot on beat. Remember, in marching, to start on left foot on count of "one." From then on, left foot hits the floor on all odd-numbered beats, right foot on even numbered.

OFFICIAL USTA TWIRLING TEAM SCORE SHEET

PLACE _____
CLASS _____
EVENT _____

Team _____ Number of Team _____

City & State _____

	POINTS POSSIBLE	SCORE	COMMENTS	SCORE
TWIRL	40			
r of Body Moves 5				
of Body Moves 5				
ty of Body Moves 5				
ion of Body Work				
ic 5				
ion of Baton				
ng to Music 5				
aphy				
retation of Music				
h Baton Handling				
dy Moves) 15				
	TOTAL			
EFFECT	30			
nship 5				
of Pace 5				
Performance 5				
Appearance 5				
ion to Music 5				
ty of Style 5				
	TOTAL			

Possible _____
Penalty _____
Net _____

Clerk's Initials _____   Judge's Signature _____

TOTAL SCORE _____

GENERAL COMMENTS

THIS SCORE SHEET MAY NOT BE REPRODUCED IN ANY FORM WITHOUT EXPRESS PERMISSION OF THE UNITED STATES TWIRLING ASSOCIATION.

D   OFFICIAL USTA TWIRLING TEAM SCORE SHEET

PLACE _____
CLASS _____
EVENT _____

Name of Team _____ Number of Team _____

Address _____ City & State _____

PENALTIES	PENALTY	COMMENTS	TOTAL
2.0 Improper Entrance			
2.0 Improper Exit			
Up to 5.0 Unsportsmanlike Conduct			
2.0 Overtime			
2.0 Undertime			
Up to 5.0 Personal Appearance			
2.0 Failure to Cross Exit Line			

(TOTAL PENALTIES ON THIS SHEET TO BE SUBTRACTED FROM OVERALL SCORE.)

Time _____

TOTAL ON PENALTY SHEET _____

Clerk's Initials _____   Judge's Signature _____

GENERAL COMMENTS

THIS SCORE SHEET MAY NOT BE REPRODUCED IN ANY FORM WITHOUT EXPRESS PERMISSION OF THE UNITED STATES TWIRLING ASSOCIATION.

ALIGNMENT—lines must be straight. Line your shoulders up with the shoulder of the girl on each side of you; line your nose up squarely in the center of the head of the girl in front of you.

INTERVAL—space between you and your neighbor on either side. Horizontal, or lateral, lines should have equal amount of space between each girl. Two ways to check and establish intervals: (1) Have each girl stretch out right arm to the side. Fingertips should just touch shoulder of right-hand neighbor; (2) For shorter intervals, have the girls hold both arms straight out to sides and bend at elbows. Each girl's elbows should be touching elbows of neighbors.

DISTANCE—space between you and the girl in front of you and behind you. Vertical lines, like horizontal lines, should have equal spacing between team members. Easiest way to establish and check distance is to hold one arm out straight in front of you. Your fingertips should come to the back of the person ahead of you.

On the score sheet, you'll notice that points are deducted each time a penalty occurs. If one of the members is out of step once, that's half a point off. Two members out of step once is one point, as is one member out of step twice.

Alignment, intervals, and distance are very sneaky. They change even though you're doing your best to maintain them. Team members must be highly observant and constantly on the alert, making corrections when necessary. If the girl next to you moves a bit to the side (because the girl next to her did), and you don't see her move and make the correction, then the whole line is off. So when you're performing, keep your eye on the person in front of you, and train your peripheral vision on the people on either side of you. Don't try to line yourself up with anyone other than those three people. (If this sounds simple, remember that you're also twirling, so you've got to have your head in many places at the same time.) Uniformity of stride helps reduce penalties.

2. *Twirling.* Judges will be evaluating your team's twirling abilities throughout the routine as well as during specific sections of the routine devoted primarily to showing off the team's twirling skills. Generally speaking, you'll want to use your flashiest tricks and exchanges during the twirling sections of the routine. The more skilled your twirlers, the more difficulty you can add during other parts of the routine.

Twirling is judged in seven different areas.

DIFFICULTY—how hard are the tricks you've chosen for your team? Limiting yourself to simple tricks, where the team is unlikely to make a mistake, eliminates the risk factor but lowers difficulty score. You have to find a happy medium.

SPEED—is the baton revolving at a speed consistent with the motion of the team as it proceeds through the routine? Is the speed of the routine itself appropriate to the type of twirling the team is doing? Does the twirling speed fit the tempo of the music? You can improve your speed score by using faster music during the twirling segments of the routine.

VARIETY—have you used various types of twirls and baton maneuvers through the routine? You should be sure the team twirls in each plane, and uses a good combination of finger twirls, rolls and wraps, aerials, etc.

EXCHANGES—transferring batons through the air among all the members of the group. Exchanges will be judged according to difficulty and variety. The more difficult exchanges your team completes successfully, the higher it will score.

SMOOTHNESS—is the baton work smooth and uninterrupted? Are the girls graceful? Does the baton seem like an extension of the girl, or does she look awkward twirling?

TEAMWORK—is every member of the team contributing? Has the team practiced to attain a team style, or is each member working in a style all her own? Is everyone doing the same number of turns on each aerial? Are all aerials the same height? Is everyone's footwork the same? Can the team stay together on fingerwork? Unison is crucial and must prevail from beginning to end.

BATON HANDLING WHILE MANEUVERING—the number of baton tricks your team does while moving from one area of the floor to another. The more use your team makes of the baton during the non-twirling sections, the better you'll score. The type of batonwork should blend nicely with the floor patterns and be appropriate to the section of the routine and the music.

Penalties (twirling)

UNISON—each girl should begin and end a trick at the same instant. All releases and catches should be timed precisely so that all take place at the same moment.

DROPS—it's nearly impossible to get through a performance with no drops. But practice hard and try to get close to perfection. A large team that completes a long routine with no more than half a dozen drops can congratulate itself. Small teams do well if they only have three drops.

Dropped batons not only hurt your routine and lower your score, but also can be dangerous. Some team member can easily trip over a baton that's lying on the floor.

If you drop your baton, recover it immediately unless it hurts the formation.

THE COMPLETE BOOK OF·BATON TWIRLING

This is one of those times when you'll have to make a split-second decision. Whether or not you retrieve the baton will have a lot to do with
whether or not you're doing floor patterns (constantly moving) or just
twirling more or less in place. Try to retrieve the baton without breaking
your rhythm.

Constructing a Routine

Large team routines are from four to seven minutes long. Small teams
have shorter competition times—from three to five minutes. Three different
musical selections are usually appropriate—although a large team doing a
longish routine might be able to slip in a fourth song. Most recordings will
have to be cut to reduce time and to eliminate unsatisfactory portions.

Routines are roughly divided into three or four sections, depending on
length. Twirling, exchanges, and marching and maneuvering are included in
each section and should be distributed throughout the routine.

1. *Entrance.* Start with some kind of acknowledgment or pose before you
march onto the performing area of the floor. Entrance should be flashy and
dramatic with regard to both music and choreography. It should include
some strutting and marching and maneuvering (a simple drill routine will
do nicely here). Once the team is on the floor and in position, a flashy
twirling section including exchanges should follow.

2. *Twirling.* If your routine is short, this section will probably use the
same music as section 1. In fact, it may be more an elaboration of the last
part of the entrance than a section unto itself.

Get plenty of exchanges in, as well as a complete variety of twirling maneuvers. Strutting or a kick line is always impressive here if done well. Small
teams should concentrate heavily on fancy twirling maneuvers, while large
teams may include more strutting. Remember that the routine difficulty is
limited by the skill level of the most inexperienced twirler.

The routine should build. Start flashy, then taper off, then build again
with exchanges to a climax, and finish with a salute.

3. *Dance twirl.* The dance-twirl section provides the best opportunity for
change of pace and mood. Be sure your music is dramatically different from
entrance and exit numbers.

Keep this section brief. A minute is the ideal time, and anything over a
minute and a half is too long. Small teams should incorporate more twirling
in this section, and the twirling should be more difficult.

Vary your floor pattern several times during this section. See Chapter
Eight for more hints on dance twirl.

4. *Exit.* Large teams can include some additional marching and maneu-

vering plus more exchanges just before the exit. Small teams, which devote a higher percentage of routine time to twirling, probably won't have time for much additional maneuvering, if any.

Exit, like entrance, must be dramatic and exciting. This is your last chance to create an impression, so use it wisely. Your exit should definitely say "good-bye" to the judges—and a loud, powerful finish that leaves them wanting more usually works best. When your team gets to the finish line, end with a final acknowledgment.

What follows is an *abbreviated* twirling-team routine. You won't be able to use it without adjusting and expanding it to fit the time limits and the precise counts of music. But if you study it, you'll begin to understand just how to go about choreographing a twirling-team routine of your own. This routine is meant for a small team of eight girls, but can be adjusted for any number.

SECTION 1. Entrance (introduction through Set 8) plus main twirling portion (Sets 9–20). Suggested music: "There's No Business Like Show Business" by Stanley Black.

SET	COUNTS	TRICK	BODYWORK
Intro	1–8	Tip rests on back of R calf, staggered spin turn to L	L arm out to side. From R lunge, shift weight to LF, spin on ball of LF
Intro	1–5	2- or 3-toss turnaround	Recover in Y position on 5
	6–7	Bend arms in and push out as baton loops once	Acknowledge with head to accent pose
	8		Hold
1	1–8	Use an exciting entrance strut (leaps, tour jetés, jazz runs) making sure movements accent and interpret music. Form 2 lines. Every other girl starts moving on count 1. Remaining 4 girls start on count 5	
2	1–8		
3	1–4	Back row: vert. toss overhead of front row, as front row tosses vert. at RS plane to back line	All toss on count of 1, catch on 5
	5–7	Catch R. Spin turn L to front, looping baton behind head	Pose on 7, both arms out to side, baton on arm
	8	Hold	
4	1–8	Strut to center	Vary arm movements and footwork, keep unison
5	9–16	Front line meets center floor line on 12. Back line meets on 16	March to R of front girl
6	1–8	Center pivot	Arms rigid at sides, knees high
7	1–8		

185

SET	COUNTS	TRICK	BODYWORK
8	1–6	Girls ☀1, 3, 5, 7 travel to front Girls ☀2, 4, 6, 8 travel to rear	Use leaps or runs
	7	Pose (rear line faces front for pose)	Bow or go up on toes. L arm up, tip to floor
	8	Hold	

Main twirling section begins here

SET	COUNTS	TRICK	BODYWORK
9	1–4	2- or 3-toss turnaround	Hands on hips
	5–8	R rev. at L. Leap to R as you do R 2-finger	L arm out
10	1–2	R 2-finger behind head	Body spin to L to front
	3–4	R 2-finger at rear	Body turns R to rear
	5–6	R 2-finger front	Up on toes, L arm up
	7–8	R 2-finger at ¼ R	Kick LL ¼ R
11	1–2	R 2-finger behind head	Jump turn L to front (1½ turn). Legs straight and together, toes pointed
	3–5	R-toss turnaround, catch L index finger	
	6–8	L 4-finger behind head	Body spins L to front
12	1–2	L toss from pinky	
	3–4	Catch R outside LL	LL steps over to ¼ R RL fans up and around
	5–6	Pull baton around to front	R direction body turn to front
	7–8	R fig. 8	
13	1–4	R to L blind catch	Turn L to face front
	5–8	L horiz. platter into horiz. toss to R	Toss on 5
14	1–4	L to R horiz. 2-toss turnaround	
	5–6	Horiz. taffy pull	
	7–8	Spin baton on chest	Spin on toes
15	1–2	R 2 horiz. finger down	Deep lunge L
	3–4	R 2 horiz. finger up	Up on toes
	5–8	Repeat 1–4 facing rear	Deep lunge R on 5–6 Up on toes for 7–8
16	1–8	8 horiz. finger underhand, pass to L	Spin on toes, 2 body turns to L
17	1–2	L 2-finger up	Do a third body spin to L,
	3–4	L 2-finger down	keeping both arms out to sides
	5–8	L to R horiz. flip rear of body	Lunge L (5–6) Lunge R (7–8)
18	1–4	2 taffy pulls	Change floor pattern to a circle
	5–8	L to R horiz. toss, catch on back	Deep lunge to R diag. rear
19	1–2	Head loop	Body turn to L
	3–6	Horiz. exchange	Vertical throw to opposite girl, catch L, back pass

SET	COUNTS	TRICK	BODYWORK
	7	Pose	Face out of circle on toes, L arm up, tip to floor
	8	Hold	Flip of L wrist for accent
20	1–4	RH to RH back catch	Body spin turn moving forward
	5–8	Repeat 1–4	On 8, baton remains behind back, L arm out—pose

SECTION 2. *Dance-twirl*. See Chapter Eight for dance-twirl routine suggestions. Music suggested to go with the routine here is "Evil Ways" by Santana. To move from your dance-twirl section into Section 3, which follows, end your dance-twirl portion in two lines facing front.

SECTION 3. *Exit*. Suggested music: "Look Sharp" by Arthur Fiedler.

SET	COUNTS	TRICK	BODYWORK
1	1–2	Listen to establish start	Keep eye contact with audience, back leg remains straight
	3–4	Leap R. diag. with R to L shoulder roll	
	5–8	L rev. thumb-pinch flip turnaround, recover ¼ L on toes, tail off arm	Both arms recover to ¼ L, L palm up, arch back
2	1–4	Backbend	Point R toe fwd., arms move down and to rear and up, complete circle to starting position. Head back, bend LL for deeper bend
	5–6	Baton snaps on arm	Snap up on toes facing front, both arms out to sides
	7	Nod head	
	8	Hold	
3	1–8	Back and front line march toward each other, meeting on 8	Apply fitting arm movements to music
4	1–8	End pivot from L end to form a V, point of V facing exit (135° turn)	Apply fitting arm movements. Knee level of each girl identical
5	1–8		
6	1–8	Vert. exchange (each girl throws to girl at R—girl at RF of V throws across to girl at LF of V)	Much practice for accuracy. Point twirler and partner toss higher than others
7	1–8	Cross through each other on running step forming 2 lines approx. 15′ apart.	
8	1–8	Kick legs fwd. as you run	
9	1–8	Horiz. exchange with girl catty-corner	
10	1–2	L elbow	Point L toe fwd.
	3–4	L fishtail turn	Turn R to front on toes
	5–8	L fishtails	¼ R

SET	COUNTS	TRICK	BODYWORK
11	1–4	L fishtail onto R elbow, catch R underhand	Face ¼ L, pull feet back on catch
	5–8	R layout	Step R, step L, cross over R, lunge R (5–6–7)
12	1–8	L elbow into continuous elbow rolls	
13	1–6	Continue Set 12	Change floor pattern to end in diag. line
	7–8	Catch L, back pass	
14	1–8	Staggered vert. 3-toss	Each girl kneels after catch, holding pose, R knee up
15	1–8	turnaround	
16	1–2	Point R toe fwd.	Arms out to side
	3–4	Squat in sitting position on back leg	Baton on arm
	5	Head touches RK	
	6–8	Hold	
17	1–4	Return to original kneel position	Arms at sides
	5–8	Stand LF meeting R	Arms fwd. and out to sides
18	1–8	Center pivot to face exit	
19	1–8	Runs or leaps toward exit	Use interesting arm movements
20	1–6	Continue 19	Ending just within exit line
	7–8	Turn to face opposite	
21	1–8	Use a dramatic exchange here	Make sure your music has smashing tag at the end at this point
22 (tag of music)	1–8		

On "Exit" command from team captain, make sure all cross the exit line. Remember, crossover must be within your time limit.

TWELVE

Corps

For us—and for nearly every twirler we know—corps work is the single most rewarding aspect of twirling. Like team twirling, corps twirling gives you the benefits of working in a group: the sense of belonging, the joy of performing and sharing the experience with others, the pleasures of close friendships, and the wonders of traveling.

But a corps is different from a team in several ways. First, it gives far more people a chance for involvement because it has not only twirlers but non-twirlers as well.

The twirling roles themselves are open to solid intermediate twirlers, as well as to advanced. And beginning twirlers can participate as members of auxiliary units. They can carry flags or rifles or pompons or whatever other props the corps director decides to include in the show.

While team twirling is the fanciest and most intricate you'll see in group twirling, a corps can't be beat for sheer spectacle and razzle-dazzle general effect. A corps production is truly an extravaganza. Watching it can send shivers up and down your spine. Performing in a corps is probably the most thrilling and memorable twirling experience a baton student can have.

What is a corps? Very simply, a corps is twelve or more twirlers, called a working twirling line, plus an auxiliary unit, called a national color guard. The minimal color guard unit consists of one flag representing your organization, plus the American flag, plus two people with rifles to guard the flags. That makes a total of sixteen, the minimum number of people needed to make up a corps. But there are several types of corps, as you'll see, and most of these are much larger than this minimum.

What does a corps do? Corps participate in three main activities: The first, and most common, is parades. Most corps begin as *parade corps* and continue to perform in parades throughout their careers, although they may branch out into other areas as well.

Parade routines consist primarily of *forward*-motion marching steps, and they're not difficult to learn. You'll find an example of a parade-corps routine later on in the chapter.

A parade corps can march to a drum cadence, or to the music played by one of the bands in the parade, or to recorded music that the teacher can play from a loudspeaker on the car. Or it can have its own live music of some sort.

Sometimes, parade directors award prizes to the best corps in a parade. Throughout the United States, there are associations of parade corps made up of individual corps that specialize in marching in parades and competing for prizes there. These corps may take part in as many as twenty-five parades a year. There is also a parade corps category in USTA competitions.

If you're in a corps, though, you're not necessarily limited to parade performances. There are other things a corps can do. Corps that specialize in giving concert performances are called *show corps*. You'll often see show corps doing parade routines in nationally televised parades, such as Macy's Thanksgiving Day Parade or the Tournament of Roses. Sometimes you'll see show corps performing out of doors at athletic events. A show corps does a far more complex routine than the basic military forward march a parade corps specializes in. It takes lots of practice for a show corps to look good, about as much rehearsing as a ballet company might do.

A show-corps routine is a very finely choreographed major production, quite spectacular and flashy, with at least one show-stopping number—often more.

The third activity for corps is competition, and corps that specialize in competition are called *floor corps* because they perform on a gym floor most of the time. Actually, competition is the life-blood of baton corps, and it's

308. **MILLER'S BLACKHAWKS,** of Kettering, Ohio. Directed by Mr. and Mrs. Fred Miller. USTA Grand National Music Corps Champions for eighteen out of the last twenty years. Ohio State Champions for seventeen consecutive years. Performances include Macy's Thanksgiving Day Parade, Tangerine Bowl half-time show, Disney World. Founded in 1952, the Blackhawks is the oldest corps of its kind in the United States today.

vital that more competitive floor corps become organized, financially sound and active. Otherwise, even the corps that are currently very active and successful won't be able to survive for long.

A corps can be both a floor corps and a show corps. The Blackhawks and the Thunderers, for example, perform frequently, in addition to competing. They travel throughout the United States and abroad, appearing in parades

309. **HUNTINGTON THUNDERERS,** of Huntington, New York. Directed by Mrs. Gloria Smith. USTA Grand National Music Corps Championship—1969 and 1970; USTA New York State Championship—1966–76; NBTA World Show Corps Championship—1972. Performances include Tournament of Roses Parade, Macy's Thanksgiving Day Parade, half-time shows at Shea and Yankee stadiums. Founded in 1965.

and giving concert performances. Even corps that are basically show corps should compete from time to time, to sharpen their precision.

Types of Floor Corps

Corps are classified, for competitive purposes, according to whether or not they have live music, and if they do, what type of instruments they use. In competition, corps of like types compete against each other. Age divisions are junior (14 and under) and senior (15–21). Beginner, intermediate, and advanced categories are determined by the number of first-place prizes a corps has won, just as in solo competition. (Beginner corps are allowed to compete without a color guard.)

1. *Twirling corps.* This is a corps without any musical instruments at all. It performs to its own choice of recorded music. It consists of a basic twirling line (twelve or more) and a national color guard unit (minimum four people), as described earlier.

However, a twirling corps doesn't have to limit itself to the minimum requirements. It can have a larger twirling line or a larger color guard unit. Although it usually doesn't have other auxiliary units, such as a pompon line, it can. It can also have featured twirlers to lead the working twirling line. No matter how big the corps is, though, it's still considered a twirling corps as long as there is no live music.

2. *Drum-and-baton corps.* This type of corps consists not only of the minimum number of twirlers (or more) and the color guard, but musicians as well. If you add just one drummer to a twirling corps, then you become a drum-and-baton corps.

But there's no need to stop with just a single drummer. In addition to drums, this type of corps can have cymbals, claves, tambourines, triangles, maracas, cow bells, sleigh bells, castanets, gongs—any percussion instrument that doesn't play a melody.

3. *Percussion corps.* Add melodic percussion instruments such as marimbas, glockenspiels, or xylophone to a drum-and-baton corps and you've got a percussion corps. No electrical or amplified instruments are allowed. Everything must be carried and hit with a mallet while marching.

Competitive routines for all three of the above types of corps must last for 6–8 minutes (junior) or 8–10 minutes (senior).

4. *Musical corps.* This is the ultimate in corps. It has a full band, with percussion and brass instruments. Few newly established corps begin as musical corps, but after a year or so it's possible for many corps to expand. Those corps that work hard to establish a strong fund-raising arm have the best chance of succeeding as musical corps—which cost more than other

310. **DALEY DEBUTANTES,** of Milwaukee, Wisconsin. Directed by Nancy Daley. NBTA Drum and Baton Corps Grand Championship, 1976; Parade Corps Championship, 1976. Performances include Chicago's St. Patrick's Day Parade and half-time shows for Marquette University's nationally ranked basketball team. Founded in 1955, the corps began competing in 1962 and has won more than 250 awards.

types of corps to outfit and equip. (You'll find pointers on organizing and raising funds for a corps in the next chapter.)

Musical corps are generally the largest corps, not only because of the full band, but because their auxiliary units are most often enlarged.

One of the most beautiful things about a musical corps is its size. Imagine the impressive effect of a hundred or more people executing precision maneuvers on a gym floor, stage, or athletic field.

The average musical corps has about twenty-six people in a twirling line and four featured twirlers, or captains, who lead the twirlers and give maneuvering commands.

Then there are the auxiliary units. The Thunderers, for example, has a ten-girl pompon line, plus a ten-girl specialty unit (which carries shields and does other novelty things), plus a ten-girl flash-flag unit.

The Blackhawks, on the other hand, has a different type of unusually large color guard. It includes a fourteen-member flash-flag section, which moves its flags in unison for a bright effect of splashing color. In addition, there's a six-person twirling rifle unit.

Musical corps competitive routines must be between 8 and 10 minutes long (junior) and between 10 and 12 minutes (senior).

Should You Join a Corps?

By all means, yes, if at all possible. Since a corps is a family activity, with a parents' club that sponsors fund-raising and social events, you'll have to get your parents' approval and their willingness to become involved. Encourage them to investigate along with you. They should find out what will be required of them. Hopefully, they'll have time to spend working for the corps. Most parents appreciate having an interest to share with their children, and they'll support the corps.

If you (or your parents) have never seen a corps perform, try to attend a contest in your state where corps will be competing. Seeing a corps is usually all it takes to want to be part of one yourself.

If you're either learning to twirl or have been working at it for several years, you've probably developed the kind of discipline you'll need to be in a corps. You've got to be dedicated, practicing the corps routine not only by yourself at home but with the rest of the group as well, in weekend or after-school sessions that may last two hours or longer.

You'll also have to abide by the rules your corps director establishes. You'll have to be on time for rehearsals and not skip practices. You'll have to have your part of the routine learned by the director's deadline. If you don't cooperate, the director will probably ask you to resign from the corps.

Putting a corps together is a big project. It can involve as many as a hundred people—or more—and everyone must abide by the rules. Corps members who do not conduct themselves like ladies and gentlemen at competitive events can cause their entire corps to be disqualified. There's no better way to insure good behavior away from home than to insist upon it at home during practice sessions. It's all part of the discipline needed to make a corps professional-looking.

What Can You Do in the Corps?

1. Non-twirling roles. Non-twirlers and beginners can join the corps as members of an auxiliary unit. The auxiliary unit that's essential to all corps is the national color guard section. People in this unit carry flags or rifles. Although the minimum number of people for a color guard is four, it's better to have more because minimal color guard units can only score a minimal number of points. Many corps have very large color guards, and these include both boys and girls.

Other auxiliary units (such as pompon lines) are considered part of the color guard in the judging. These kinds of units can be added at the director's discretion. They add to the general effect of a corps and give more students a chance to participate. If your teacher has lots of beginners, then a specialty unit is a very good thing for the corps. It helps develop the marching and maneuvering skills and bodywork that all twirlers must have, and prepares beginners to twirl in the corps once they develop better twirling skills.

Other auxiliary units are those that make music. Not all corps have musical auxiliary units, but those that do can have anything from a single drum to a full brass band. Musical auxiliary units are also made up of girls and boys who are music students rather than twirling students.

In the early years of corps competition, the non-twirling units were a less-integral part of the routine than they are now. The musicians and color guard units used to be just a background for the twirling line.

Now these units are choreographed to be an important part of the whole performance. There are sections of the routine devoted to highlighting the talents of the auxiliary units, to show off the precision work of the color guard or the musical skill of the band.

Just as the various instruments in a jazz band play solos during a number, the music section and the color guard unit have their "solos" during a corps performance.

2. Twirling roles. The essential twirling unit for a corps, the working twirling line, must have at least twelve twirlers. All must be solid intermediates, at the least, although advanced twirlers are often included.

Although it's not essential for a corps to have featured twirlers in addition to the working twirling line, many corps do. These girls function as leaders, standing or marching in front of the line. They're often called captains as well because they give commands to the entire corps.

The featured twirler isn't necessarily the most skilled with the baton. In fact, the best twirlers usually aren't the leaders. The most important quality for a leader is not advanced twirling ability, but liveliness, strong projection, superb bodywork, and showmanship.

The best featured twirler upgrades the appearance of the whole corps. She's naturally vivacious and spirited. Her exuberance energizes the entire corps.

Competitive Floor Corps Requirements and Judging Procedures

Corps competitions may be judged by as many as twenty people who are experts in different areas, such as twirling, marching and maneuvering, music, etc. Every effort is made to be fair to the performers. Even so, there are inevitably disappointments, and very often losers judge the judges harshly.

While it's true that the judges sometimes do make mistakes, and very obvious ones at that, they are usually very sharp. However, if you develop a truly critical, objective eye, then you can be the best judge of your own performance, and you will know whether your score was truly deserved, or whether the judges were too kind or too rough on you. It's up to the corps director to develop his or her own critical eye and help the group judge itself properly. He should never let his corps get ecstatic over a win that's due to a judge's mistake. The corps won't be able to depend on a mistake the next time.

There are several things that will help a corps achieve a good score. One we've already mentioned—frequent competition. Another is plenty of practice. A decent routine is paramount. (We'll discuss choreography and routine construction later in the chapter and give some sample routines.) It's also necessary to be familiar with the competitive regulations and scoring systems.

Some of the rules and judging techniques are very technical. We won't go into everything here, but we will give you some sample score sheets and help you to interpret them. If you're going to compete in a USTA competition, you should send for the USTA Corps Manual, which costs $5.00. Study it. It's a course in itself and will give you much of the technical information that can turn your corps into a winner.

All types of competitive floor corps are judged in the same way. That is, both the execution of the routine and the general effect of the performance are judged separately. Also, each different unit of the corps is also judged separately.

For example, the color guard section alone can accumulate a maximum of 20 points; 10 for execution and 10 for general effect. The twirling score itself can be as high as 60. Marching and maneuvering gets a possible 50. The music score maximums differ, according to the type of corps. A twirling corps can score as high as 10 points for music. This makes the maximum number of points a twirling corps can score 140.

Drum-and-baton and percussion corps can score a possible 35 for music. So they can have a maximum of 165 points. Musical corps get a maximum of 40 points for music, so the best possible score for that type of corps is 170.

Of course, there's a separate penalty judge, and penalties are deducted from the final scores. All scores for all corps are public. And not just the final scores, either. For example, if your corps is competing, you'll know what every other corps in your class scored—for each separate section of its performance.

Let's go over the score sheets, briefly, but remember, if you're going to compete, you really should study the complete Corps Manual.

<table>
<tr><td>

UNITED STATES TWIRLING ASSOCIATION, INC.
Color Guard General Effect

Name of Corps _____

CREDIT CAPTION — Possible Points 10.0
(A Minimum Color Guard consisting of 4 people will receive no more than 2.0 points on this Credit Caption).

COMMENTS

C G General Effect Score

Judge's Signature

USTA 332A — THIS SCORE SHEET MAY NOT BE REPRODUCED IN ANY FORM WITHOUT EXPRESS PERMISSION OF THE UNITED STATES TWIRLING ASSOCIATION.

</td><td>

UNITED STATES TWIRLING ASSOCIATION, INC.
Color Guard Executive Sheet

Name of Corps _____

DEDUCT .1 FOR EACH ERROR FROM 10.0

CARRIAGE OF EQUIPMENT
- PIKES
- RIFLES
- SABRES & OTHERS
- UNIFORMITY

EQUIPMENT POSITION
- PIKES ANGLES
- RIFLES ANGLES
- SABRES & OTHERS
- UNIFORMITY

BEARING
- INDIVIDUAL
- ENTIRE UNIT

FLAG CODE: Any violations of Flag Code shall be noted below in complete detail.

EXECUTION SCORE ___ 10.0
LESS PENALTIES ___
TOTAL EXECUTION SCORE ___

Judge

USTA 330A — THIS SCORE SHEET MAY NOT BE REPRODUCED IN ANY FORM WITHOUT EXPRESS PERMISSION OF THE UNITED STATES TWIRLING ASSOCIATION.

</td></tr>
</table>

Color Guard

The color guard unit is judged for its general effect and according to how well it performs. A maximum of 10 points for general effect is possible. As you can see from the score sheet, a minimal four-person color guard cannot earn more than 2 points. So it's advantageous to have a large color guard unit.

The more people the unit has, the more likely it is to make mistakes. So there's more exposure to risk with a large section. A large color guard is bound to give a better show. The more equipment you've got in this section, the more spectacular your effects can be.

A color guard unit can carry a variety of equipment. The minimal re-

197

quirements are one American flag, one organizational flag, and two weapons. Authorized weapons are rifles, simulated rifles (full-scale plastic models made for this purpose), side arms, sabers, or swords. There's no need to limit your color guard to two weapons, or even to one type of weapon.

A crackerjack rifle-twirling unit, such as the one the Blackhawks has, is very impressive. The rifles, because they're twirled, are balanced like batons. But rifle twirling is a very different art than baton twirling, and it's usually impossible for one person to be able to do both.

A baton twirler is so conditioned to the baton that it's difficult to unlearn it all, which is what she'd have to do if she were to learn to twirl a rifle. So the rifle unit the Blackhawks has is comprised of specialists—people who don't twirl batons at all. When the rifle section is highlighted during a routine, all you hear is the click, click, click of the rifles. You can imagine how well-practiced the unit must be. One mistake, and the audience and judges not only see it, they hear it as well. A click an instant too early or too late can damage the effect.

Another terrific effect a corps can have is to use swordsmen, with their steel blades gleaming and sparkling and making a swooshing sound as they cut through the air.

There's no reason to limit your corps to just one organizational flag. Lots of people can carry flash flags—big banners (3'×5') suspended from 7' poles. They make a swishing sound in time with the music and the color flashes in front of your eyes, accenting the music and twirlers and providing a great deal of razzle-dazzle.

On the execution score sheet, carriage of equipment refers to the movements made with the various things a unit carries. Pikes refer to the poles on which a flag is held aloft. Different effects with the flag can be accomplished with various types of movement of the pike—a dip, a spin, a thrust.

It's important to include a variety of movement of the equipment, and make sure that movement is uniform among all the members of the section. All like equipment must be moved to the same degree, at the same angle, and in a uniform relationship to each other.

Position of equipment refers to how the rifles or sabers or flags or whatever are held during the various military commands and ceremonial duties that are carried out by the corps. These rules are given in the Corps Manual.

So is the American flag code, which must be followed to the letter or penalties will be incurred.

You'll also notice that the color guard is judged on its bearing, for both individuals and the unit as a whole. Each person in the guard should stand up straight, carry himself proudly with confidence and authority, show proper respect for the flag, be snappy and alert in response to commands.

Just because the color guard can only accumulate a total of 20 points, don't leave its performance to chance. Make sure the unit is polished, and it will be a big asset.

TWIRLING SCORE SHEET (ROUTINE ANALYSIS)

NAME OF CORPS

	POSSIBLE SCORE	COMMENTS	SCORE
TEAM WORK	5.0		

THE FOLLOWING CATEGORIES ARE JUDGED ON AN INDIVIDUAL BASIS

	POSSIBLE SCORE	COMMENTS	SCORE
DIFFICULTY	5.0		
VARIETY	5.0		
SPEED	5.0		
SMOOTHNESS	5.0		
SHOWMANSHIP	5.0		

POSSIBLE SCORE	30.0	
TOTAL SCORE		

_____
JUDGE'S SIGNATURE

GENERAL EFFECT—TWIRLING SCORE SHEET

NAME OF CORPS

By G.E. is meant all of those elements in the corps performance which collectively present with impressive effectiveness, its Superior Ability, Originality, Appeal and Difficulty.

SCORE

COMMENT BELOW ON ALL OF THE PRODUCTIONS AS THEY OCCUR THAT CONTAINED TWIRLING MOVEMENTS IN THEM . . . (If possible name them by selection name)	
	DANCE TWIRL ROUTINE
	Timing 4.0
	Variety
	Difficulty
	Showmanship
	Appearance
	Expression of Music
	TWIRLING ROUTINE
	Difficulty 4.0
	Variety
	Teamwork
	Fluidity of Routine
	STRUTTING
	Arm & Head 2.0 Movements
	Carriage & Body Lines
	Knee Level
	SHOWMANSHIP
	Audience 4.0 Appeal
	Change of Pace
	Overall Performance
	General Appearance
	Effectiveness
	Professionalism
	ROUTINE CONSTRUCTION
	Correlation 4.0 to Music
	Continuity of Routine
	Originality
	Difficulty
	Variety
	SIZE 2.00
	.1 per every 2 people
	POSSIBLE SCORE 20.0
	SCORE

_____
Judge

BATON TWIRLING

PENALTY SHEET

NAME OF CORPS

DROPS—2/10 Point off for each   UNISON—1/10 Point off for each

DROPS														
	.2	.4	.6	.8	1.0	1.2	1.4	1.6	1.8	2.0	2.2	2.4	2.6	
	2.8	3.0	3.2	3.4	3.6	3.8	4.0	4.2	4.4	4.6	4.8	5.0	5.2	
	5.4	5.6	5.8	6.0	6.2	6.4	6.6	6.8	7.0	7.2	7.4	7.6	7.8	
	8.0	8.2	8.4	8.6	8.8	9.0	9.2	9.4	9.6	9.8	10.0	10.2	10.4	

UNISON														
	.1	.2	.3	.4	.5	.6	.7	.8	.9	1.0	1.1	1.2	
	1.3	1.4	1.5	1.6	1.7	1.8	1.9	2.0	2.1	2.2	2.3	2.4	
	2.5	2.6	2.7	2.8	2.9	3.0	3.1	3.2	3.3	3.4	3.5	3.6	
	3.7	3.8	3.9	4.0	4.1	4.2	4.3	4.4	4.5	4.6	4.7	4.8	
	4.9	5.0	5.1	5.2	5.3	5.4	5.5	5.6	5.7	5.8	5.9	6.0	

PENALTY TOTAL FOR DROPS_____

PENALTY TOTAL FOR UNISON _____

TOTAL PENALTIES _____

_____
Judge's Signature

Twirling

The backbone of any corps is its twirling line. Here's an opportunity to score up to 60 points—the most given in any single category. (Marching and maneuvering is next, with a possible 50.)

Twirling is judged in three different ways. First, there's a thorough *analysis of the twirling routine*. Maximum points to be earned here—30. Some of these categories will look familiar to you because you also saw them on the team score sheets. Go back to refresh your memory if you need to.

Because a corps usually has a larger twirling line than even most large teams, and because there are so many other effects in a corps besides twirling, corps twirling is not as intricate or as difficult as team twirling. But it can't be sloppy and it can't be too simple. Solid intermediate tricks will generally bring a good score in the *difficulty* factor. And don't forget exchanges. They won't be as tricky as those done by a team, but they shouldn't be the simplest you can think of, and they should be around in fair numbers.

Sometimes a corps director might be tempted to devise a special routine for the more advanced twirlers of the line. Or the director might think it would be cute to give the captains or featured twirlers something special in the way of twirling.

Whatever you do, don't make this mistake. A corps twirling line should always be operating in unison. If every girl in the line can't perform a certain baton maneuver, then change the routine. If girls are having trouble, *smoothness* will suffer. The idea is not to look like twenty-four twirlers, but like one body, moving in unison. If your corps twirling line can do this, then you'll rate high in *teamwork*.

Showmanship is one of the most important aspects of a corps twirling line's performance. After all, this is the most showbusinesslike aspect of twirling. While the twirling itself might not be superadvanced and intricate, the footwork and bodywork must be very special and must be used to create an unusual effect. And don't forget to let your spirit, energy, enthusiasm, and self-confidence show through, not just during brief flashy sections, but throughout the entire routine.

Your corps can score up to 20 more points in twirling, for the *twirling general effect*. This general effect score, like all GE scores, is a comparative evaluation. That means the judges will be rating you in comparison with all the other corps that are competing against you.

If you look at the twirling GE score sheet, you'll again see some familiar terms. Most are fairly self-explanatory or have been discussed in the corresponding sections earlier in the book. And the precise technical corps defini-tions of each are included in the Corps Manual—which, again, we urge you to send for. Partly, the Corps Manual is a guide for judges, and it will be helpful for you to know what questions the judges will be asking themselves during your performance.

Note the category of audience appeal, under showmanship. The judge should consider himself or herself a member of the audience and must take into account the audience response. (He must also distinguish between ap-plause of the "let's clap for the home team" kind and genuine appreciation for a superb performance.)

In addition to general effect and routine analysis, there are also points given for a routine executed with no faults. A flawless performance gets 10 points, but each penalty is a deduction. (A routine with no penalties never happens, but occasionally some corps come close to getting the full 10 points.)

As you can see on the penalty sheet, points are deducted for drops and being out of unison. Getting away with no drops is impossible. Imagine twenty-four or twenty-six twirlers doing a high-risk routine with no drops. It just doesn't happen. Each drop costs the corps $\frac{2}{10}$ point. A full point off for drops (5 drops) is considered very good.

Penalties for lack of unison are $\frac{1}{10}$ point. Unison, you remember, means that each trick begins and ends simultaneously, each aerial is released and caught at the same moment. If you throw your baton a second later than ev-eryone else, then you're out of unison.

In corps twirling, unison is far more important than difficulty. If you try things that are too wild, you'll never achieve precision, and your impact on the audiences and judges will be far less. The trick is to make the routine just hard enough to stay in unison—with practice, of course. (If the routine is too easy, the difficulty score will suffer.)

Unison is achieved by giving every movement a definite count, linked to the cadence of the march. A short series of counts, with stops or skipped beats in between each count, gives time to execute the maneuver. So while you're twirling, you might be counting in your head (never move your lips): "one and two and three and four and one and two and three and four and . . ." The "and" is actually a beat you're skipping while the maneuver is being completed.

The only way to become advanced in your precision is to practice, prac-tice, practice. Completely breaking down the maneuvers into tiny parts, counting, etc. makes it possible to achieve unison, but without continual practice, these steps are useless. Your corps director might have you spending an entire evening on an 8-count exchange that takes less than half a minute in your total routine.

Marching and Maneuvering

While the twirling that a corps does isn't as fancy as that done by a team, the marching and maneuvering for a corps is far more spectacular than team M and M. A corps is on the floor for a longer time than a team, so its routine must include more marching and maneuvering. A corps also has a lot more people than a team, so it's a lot more difficult for a corps to maneuver. And it's a lot more impressive, too, because corps M and M formations are generally far more complex than team floor patterns.

A corps has many different units—color guard, twirlers, musicians perhaps —and, while each unit may be doing its own thing, the performance must be an integrated whole. This integration is not easy to achieve.

There have been times when Gloria wished she could just throw out a unit. She choreographs for each unit and rehearses them all separately, and she thinks they all look great. Then she puts them all together and it's terrible—like two different colored socks.

This happens to nearly every corps director. Maybe the twirlers and musicians will look fine together. Or the twirlers and color guard really complement each other, but the musicians look like excess baggage. Or people keep bumping into each other. The thought of getting rid of one unit or a couple of people can't help but occur.

But, of course, we couldn't (and wouldn't even if we could) eliminate a unit. And neither will you. You'll just keep changing things until everything blends the way it should—which is what we do.

Marching and maneuvering is judged in two separate ways, as is twirling and color guard. *Execution* is scored by two technical judges, who are watching from different places on the floor for errors in marching precision and uniformity. Each time they spot an error, they make a mark on the score sheet. One-tenth point is deducted for each, from a possible high of 25.

If you look at the M and M execution score sheet, you may see some unfamiliar terms, as well as some you already know. I'll briefly go down the list. But again, remember to send for the USTA Corps Manual, which will give you far more technical information on requirements and judging technique. There simply isn't space in this book to include all the details.

Interval—the space between the centers of people who are standing next to each other. The intervals must all be even, at all times. Judges will be looking for interval errors in the corps' *lateral* lines, in its *curved* semicircles, in its *obliques* (formations at an angle to the original line of march), and in its *echelons* (staggered lateral lines as in the illustration below).

```
X X X
    X X X
        X X X
```

Distance—the space between the centers of people who are standing one behind the other, in a *column*. Several columns standing side by side are a *file*. Whatever the formation, the distance between you and the person ahead of you and the person behind you must be equal.

Cover—the straightness of a line from front to back. Below is a cover error.

```
X   X X
X X   X
X X X
X X X
```

Dress—refers to the straightness of a lateral line. A dress error is illustrated below.

203

THE COMPLETE BOOK OF BATON TWIRLING

There are four types of lateral lines that can commit dress errors. They are (1) a *company front*, which consists of 90 per cent or more of the corps proper, with or without the color guard; (2) a *platoon*, which consists of six or more people, but not as many as in a company front; (3) a *squad*, smaller than a platoon—any group of five or less in a lateral line; and (4) a *section*, either all the drums, or all the color guard, or all the twirlers, or all the musicians, in a lateral line.

Breaks—timing errors, motions that come too early or too late. They don't apply to turning maneuvers, however. A *false start* is one that comes either before or after the cue to begin moving. A *false stop* is any stop or pause that comes before the actual cue to stop.

Turn—any change of direction by any member of the corps. *Pivot* is the type of footwork needed to make a turn. All members of the corps who are executing a turn should pivot on the same foot. *Anticipation* is turning ahead of cue. *Hesitation* is turning too late. *Sagging* is not making your turn wide enough, and thereby falling behind. *Fanning* is making the turn too wide.

In addition to the group errors, there are also *individual errors*. *Heels at halt* refers to the proper foot position for standing still. *Moving at halt* refers to any unplanned movement when the corps is standing still, such as in the presentation of the American flag. *Out of step and phasing* refers to being out of total unison when marching.

IGA means individual general appearance. It refers to the person's posture, military bearing, etc. If all heads are pointed toward the audience, and you turn yours in some other direction, it's an error. Talking in the ranks, chewing gum, smiling when you're supposed to be serious are also errors that fall into this category.

The *general effect* score for marching and maneuvering is less technical and more interpretive than the execution score. Again, this is a comparative ranking, with a high possible score of 25. The judge wants to see how you stack up against the competition.

At the top of the score sheet you'll notice some general areas the judge will keep in mind during each part of the performance. *Superior ability* means better than good. It's a near-perfect performance, with no errors, smoothly executed. It's doing something very difficult and making it look easy.

Originality means a unique approach. You can do something completely new and score high in originality. Or you can do something distinctive— something that's not totally new but has a new twist. That's considered originality also.

NAME OF CORPS

By G.E. is meant all of those elements in the corps performance which collectively present with impressive effectiveness, its Superior Ability, Originality, Appeal and Difficulty.

COMMENT BELOW ON ALL THE PRODUCTIONS AS THEY OCCUR		SCORE
	ENTRANCE 2.0	
	COLOR PRESENTATION 2.0	
	TWIRLING & DANCE 2.0 TWIRLING Entrance Formation Exit	
	EXIT 2.0	
	COLOR GUARD 2.0	
	SHOWMANSHIP 7.5 Precision Coordination Skill of Execution Flash Training Esprit de Corps Dignity & Military Bearing Appeal Professionalism	
	REPERTOIRE 7.5 Originality Utilization of Time Worthwhile Patterns Maximum Effects Without Repetition Theme Continuity Intricacy Difficulty Adaptability Floor Coverage	
JUDGE'S SIGNATURE	TOTAL MAXIMUM 25.0	

Appeal has to do with the effectiveness of the marching presentation. Is it something the judge enjoys watching? Is he or she reluctant to see it end? If so, the production is very appealing.

Difficulty refers to how much the corps exposes itself to error. There are certain M and M moves that are difficult to accomplish. Some of them are exaggerated arm swing and exaggerated footwork; rapid changes in direction; open single-man symmetrical maneuvers and extended interval fronts. The more difficult maneuvers included in your routine, the more credit you'll be given.

Variety must also be considered. Lots of change in formation and no repetitions of floor patterns are important for variety. A lot of very impressive, applause-getting floor patterns lose impact if they're repeated within a performance. Once is great, but if you do it again, the audience is likely to say, "Oh, I liked it the first time," or, "I've seen that one. Can't they think of something else?"

The judge will be criticizing and commenting upon each part (or *production*) of your performance, as it occurs. *Entrances* should be exciting and arouse the audience's interest. The best, most effective entrances will make good use of all the components of the corps, and serve as a real introduction. It should say, "Here we are, all of us. Look at us. Now you're really going to see something exciting."

During the *presentation of the colors,* dignity and observation of proper flag etiquette must be highlighted. This is a very dramatic production and should move the audience to feeling patriotic emotions and respect for the flag.

Twirling productions are judged on the entrance of the twirlers, their floor patterns, and the exit. (A twirling line's entrance is coming into position to do the twirling number. The twirlers are already on the floor, of course. Exit means relinquishing floor position to the next production—not actually leaving the floor.) Visual effects are important. Is the routine too short or tiresome because it is overly long? Does it move too slowly or just fast enough? Don't shortchange the audience, but it's better to leave them wanting more instead of feeling they've had too much.

The *exit* is an opportunity for the corps to say "good-bye" to the audience. Does the exit make this statement? Does it say, "We've really enjoyed performing for you, but we've got to go now," in an original and appealing way? Is it a fitting conclusion to the rest of the performance?

The *color guard* is an integral part of the corps. Does it add to the overall visual effectiveness? Is the guard effectively used? Does it try to do anything unusual or unique? Does it catch the audience's eye and provide something to look at? The type of equipment and how it is handled will be considered in judging the color guard. The squad handling the American flag must always be very dignified.

Showmanship is judged throughout the entire performance. A large corps using its size to good advantage will be credited for showmanship. Does the corps have a particular style? (The Blackhawks, for instance, specialize in a military style, while the Thunderers have a jazz style.) Does the routine show off the corps' style? Is there a theme? Does the performance enhance the theme? Do the drum majors and corps captains add to the show? What is the mood of the performers? Is it appropriate to the routine and the theme?

Repertoire refers to how well the corps uses its time on the floor. Are the patterns valuable in contributing to a maximum effect? A performance should show theme and continuity while displaying intricate and difficult formations. In a musical corps, does the music and/or drum line enhance the show and help achieve a visual balance?

Inspection and Other Penalties

During the first minute of a corps' performance, the corps will be judged on its overall appearance and uniformity. The inspection judge is to be fair in determining whether each individual has done the best he or she could to maintain his uniform and equipment.

Penalties are assessed for such items as obviously different colored shoes (all boys' styles must be the same, all girls' styles must be the same), spots on costumes (even water spots, so be careful when taking a drink at competitions), bent or twisted chin straps, or anything that is obviously the result of negligence.

But these things should not be penalized: labels on the backs of tennis shoes, a dent in a horn, a pair of trousers or skirt that's too short (if it has been let out as much as possible), or replacement articles that differ slightly from the original.

Other penalties include not starting on time, being overtime or undertime, not observing proper boundaries, etc.

All the specific information you need about these rules is in the USTA Corps Manual.

INSPECTION SCORE SHEET

NAME OF CORPS_____

Moving Inspection will take place in the first one minute (1 minute) of the performance.

Corps are not required to wear a military type uniform. Units with non-military uniforms should not receive any advantage, but should be thoroughly inspected for uniformity, neatness, cleanliness, etc. No deduction if unit wears different styles and colors of uniforms than its color guards.

Do not deduct for imperfections obviously due to age or use of equipment which cannot be corrected short of new equipment. No deduction if corps has instruments of different styles and finishes.

Do not keep unit standing at attention; only those individuals being inspected need be at attention.

Mark 1/10 for each error.

Note as many errors as possible, writing in errors not listed. It is not implied that those printed are the only matters to be considered. Call attention to Drum Major or Corps Captain to all errors.

DESCRIPTION OF ERRORS AND COMMENTS

GENERAL CLEANLINESS AND UNIFORMITY

Uniforms: _____
Hats: _____
Shoes: _____
Personal Appearance: _____
General Appearance: _____
Position of Attention: _____
Instruments: _____
Drums: _____
Batons: _____
Color Guard Equipment: _____
Note for Chief Judge and Timing Sheet: TOTAL NUMBER OF ERRORS:_____
Late reporting to Inspection 2.0 penalty _____

JUDGE

PERSONNEL AND EQUIPMENT COUNT

Total Color Guard (including American Flag squad, silks, rifles, etc.)
_____Instrumentalists _____Drummers

Total number of Twirlers (including_____non-twirling drum majors and/or captains and _____twirling captains)

Others (pompon girls, banner carriers, etc.)_____ Total number of Corps_____

AFFIDAVIT—"I hereby certify that every participant of this corps is qualified to compete under the rules of this contest."

Corps Director or Manager

Music

We've already discussed music pretty thoroughly in the team chapter. Most of the information there is valid for a twirling corps as well. Of course, for a corps you'll need a longer selection, with more songs, since its performance is longer and has more components. You'll probably want to use one number for the entrance and different numbers to highlight the different units of the corps and the different productions. The color guard can have its own theme, and the twirling production can have several different songs —one or two for the twirling and perhaps something different for the dance twirling. Then you can use a new song for the exit.

The score sheet for music selection for a twirling corps is reproduced below. It's fairly self-explanatory. (Of course, there's no execution score in music for a twirling corps since the music is recorded.)

EFFECTIVENESS OF MUSIC SELECTION—TWIRLING CORPS

NAME OF CORPS   SCORE

CHANGE OF PACE 2.0	
APPROPRIATENESS 5.0 OF MUSIC IN CORRELATION WITH ROUTINE	
AUDIENCE APPEAL 3.0	
TOTAL MAXIMUM 10.0	

JUDGE

In corps with live music, the drums are always judged separately from the rest of the instruments. (In a drum-and-baton corps, of course, there are no other instruments.) Both drums and other instruments are judged on execution and general effect. And the GE score is, again, a comparative one.

The score sheets and judging techniques for music are included in the Corps Manual. If you're forming a musical or drum-and-baton corps or percussion corps, your music director should see the Manual.

But we'll discuss the GE music score sheet here. It's reproduced opposite. The judges will evaluate each musical selection separately.

Repertoire deals with the musical effect of the written arrangement of the music. The execution is not being judged here, unless the playing is so bad that the arrangement doesn't come through clearly. A repertoire is original if the approach to the musical material is fresh, or if its way of being performed is new. It is effective if it is a first-rate arrangement and conveys strong emotion to the audience.

208

Coordination encompasses the harmonious blending of all the musical effects. Is the entire production pleasing? Does the music fit the performance? Does any part seem out of place? Or too harsh?

How is the musical presentation? Are the musicians highlighted at some time during the performance? Does the music complement the performance as a whole?

With a corps, as with a team, a poor choice in music can ruin a performance. You'll find some recommendations for musical selections and arrangements in the Appendix.

GENERAL EFFECT MUSIC

NAME OF CORPS _____

_____ SCORE _____

		Comment below on all of the production as they occur
REPERTOIRE originality effectiveness	2.0	
COORDINATION	2.0	
SHOWMANSHIP	2.0	
DIFFICULTY	2.0	
QUALITY	2.0	
TOTAL MAXIMUM	10.0	

_____
JUDGE

Choreographing a Corps Routine

Planning a corps routine requires some specialized knowledge, especially with regard to marching fundamentals and drills for various units within the corps. (See Appendix for where to get additional "how to" material.)

We recommend organizing a corps routine according to the following general pattern. It's not the only way to plan the routine, but it is effective and not terribly difficult for beginning directors to adhere to.

Start from a company-front formation on the starting line and proceed onto the floor in a fast field drill, presenting the color guard.

First impressions are important, so your first drill should be very flashy, saying "Hello" and catching the attention of audience and judges.

If the corps has some type of theme (Spanish, Scottish, Western, or whatever) it should be apparent from the very beginning and continued throughout the whole performance. Arm positions, body positions, music, and uniforms are great aids in getting your theme across and in increasing the general effect.

Once the corps reaches a position on the floor, it's time for a dance routine, fast-twirling routine, and possibly a strutting routine. You decide which comes first. This portion of the performance should be original and reflect the corps' style.

Creating different moods is important. Make sure there's good contrast between the twirling and dance-twirl sections. Use different musical selections to create change of pace and mood.

Remember to keep twirling simple. Two-hand spins, back passes, whips, flat wrist twirls are all fine—especially if you're creative about bodywork and positions of hands and feet. These should be planned and precise—never left to chance.

Twirling and dance sections should be followed by additional marching and maneuvering to highlight the corps' drill abilities. A good variety of short drills is preferable to one or two long drills. The basic rule is to keep the routine moving fast without dwelling too long on any one section. Never let the audience or judges get bored. Keep changing what you do rather than repeat anything, unless repetition has a definite purpose or a specific desired effect.

Save your flashiest drill for last. It should be the climax of the routine and leave the audience applauding wildly. The final drill should say a definite, "Good-bye. We've really enjoyed entertaining you." It should also carry the corps to the finish line, where members give a final salute, bow, or pose before leaving the floor.

Below are a few simple drills and a corps twirling routine to help you get started. Don't forget to choreograph each unit separately. And expect to make some changes when you put all units together. Unless you've had a lot of experience, making the entire corps look like a unified whole will take some trial and error. Try not to get discouraged.

Before you can interpret our drills or effectively write down your own, you'll need to know some basic corps drill and twirling terminology and abbreviations, which follow.

1. CF—company front
2. ST—squad turn

3. MT—mark time (march in place without going anywhere)
4. WT—wheel turn (a type of squad turn to the left, right, or to the rear march)
5. TTR—to the rear (turn around, go the opposite direction)
6. R—right
7. L—left
8. RT—right turn
9. LT—left turn
10. RH—right hand
11. LH—left hand
12. RL—right leg
13. LL—left leg
14. RS—right side of a company front
15. LS—left side of a company front
16. X—pivot (mark time as your squad moves around in a turn, being sure to keep your line straight)

BASIC CORPS DRILL
ENTRANCE OR EXIT DRILL

A simple but effective drill, it can be done in squads of 3, 4, etc., and begins and ends in a CF.

STEP 1. CF

x x x x x x x x x x x x x x x x x x x x x x x x x x x x x x x x x x x

STEP 2. As the CF moves down the floor each squad starts dropping off from each end. Then they go into a WT immediately in 4 counts.

STEP 3. Continue with each squad dropping off every 4 counts. All squads on right side turn to the left, while all squads on the left side turn to the right. They keep turning a quarter of a turn and mark time for 4 counts.

211

STEP 4. After each squad turns completely around they march forward and pick up each squad as they go until they are back in the original CF.

Make sure all members understand that all quarter turns are executed in 4 counts and that they'll then mark time for 4 counts. (Time on this can be increased by leaving out the mark times if you want.)

After the corps is back in the CF, you can have them move to the center line of the gym floor with the following:

STRAIGHT-WALK DRUM-CORPS DRILL TO CENTER OF FLOOR

This is also a very simple, effective drill. Have the group walk to the center of the floor in a walking fashion. All members should turn heads to the right to make sure they keep in line. Then they swing their batons and arms up to shoulder height.

CF CHANGE DRILL FROM DOWN THE FLOOR TO FACING AUDIENCE

STEP 1. Entire corps is in the middle of the floor in a CF.

STEP 2. The last 4 on the RS will do a TTR march in a squad and turn so that they're in line with the 4 that turned the opposite way. (This takes place on both ends of the CF.)

STEP 3. From this formation, squads that did turn will then march straight forward for 4 counts, then do a TTR march turn with the outside person being the pivot. The rest of the corps left in the center will do center pivots, turning into two CFs facing the audience.

STEP 4. The corps then does the following: Squads of 4 will turn toward the audience in a WT as the CFs move up the middle, thus creating 2 CFs covering each other and facing audience.

```
S   X       X
T   X       X
A   X       X
N   X       X
D   X       X
S   X       X
    X       X
    X       X
    X       X
    X       X
    X       X
    X       X
    X       X
    X       X
    X       X
    X       X
```

STEP 5. Have the first CF do WT in squads of 8. One squad turns to the L and the other to the R. The back CF moves up to the first row, thus creating a single CF.

BREAK AWAY FROM CF IN TURNAROUNDS

STEP 1. From the CF, have the corps count off in 4s starting backward 4-3-2-1 from the left side of the CF. Be sure to stress that *a TTR march must be done to the left.*

STEP 2. Number 1 does a one-turnaround aerial to the left in place, while numbers 2, 3, and 4 march away from the stands. They did a TTR march on count 1. When number 1 catches the aerial, they all lunge to the left and follow through with a reverse figure 8 and then bring the baton behind their backs with a figure 8.

STEP 3. Numbers 2, 3, and 4 march back 4 steps as this is going on. Then number 2 does a TTR march after 4 steps and then does the one-turnaround aerial, as number 1 did. This continues every 4 steps with number 3 doing the aerial next, followed by number 4's 4 steps later. Every 4 steps someone is doing a one-turnaround aerial. After they've finished, they should end up in the following position to go into the twirling routine.

SIMPLE CORPS-TWIRLING ROUTINE

Keep in mind that the most important things in corps twirling are simplicity, unison, perfection.

SET	COUNTS	TRICK	FOOTWORK
1	1–2	Blind catch (1 revolution) from RH to LH	Step L to LS and bring RF in
	3–4	Slide to tip and pass baton over R shoulder	Up on toes, LF crossed over R
	5–6	Bring baton down in pass behind back (tip first)	Step L to LS and bring RF into L
	7–8	Time toss in back, catch in RH	Scoot back to RS and up on toes
2	1–4	Time tosses on each side	Step point, start LF first
	5–8	Time tosses on each side catching under legs	Step and pick leg up, toe down
3	1–4	1 turnaround to L	Step out with RL, push off and turn L
	5–8	Rev. fig. 8 to LS and then fig. 8 back pass	Lunge L and then bring feet together. Swing L arm over to RS, lifting high
4	1–2	Fig. 8 to RS	Step across RF with LF
	3–4	2-finger twirl	Lunge to R, make sure toe points
	5–6	Whip	Step with LL
	7–8	2-finger in front	Cross RL over LL
5	1–2	2-finger on LS	Lunge L, point R toe
	3–4	2-finger in front	Step with RL
	5–6	2-finger in back	Kick LL to side and end in lunge with back to stands
	7–8	2-finger on side	Feet together, up on toes
6	1–2	2-finger on side	Lunge L
	3–4	2-finger in front	Feet together, up on toes
	5–6	2-finger, come around to front	Step turn to R
	7–8	4-finger pose	LF out straight ahead in pose
7	1–2	Time-toss throw up under L arm	Step with LF and swing L arm over baton
	3–4	Catch in LH (2 revolutions). Catch under R arm	R arm swings to L, and pose with sit-down pose with RF
	5–6	Short toss in back	Up on toes
	7–8	Whip	Come on around to front
8	1–2	Pass under LL	High LL kick straight
	3–4	Rev. fig.-8 flip	Step with LL
	5–6	Catch in RH	Cross RL over and catch in lunge
	7–8	Pass behind back with rev. fig. 8	Bring feet together

SET	COUNTS	TRICK	FOOTWORK
9	1–4	Fig. 8 in RH, then slide baton to tip and circle under LL	Circle with arm. Pick LL up facing to R
	5–8	Pass baton around LL on floor and then up into flat throw	When leg comes down, put it out into a lunge to R. Feet together on throw
10	1–4	Flat turnaround to L	Step turn to L
	5–8	Pass to LH and then behind neck	Step point LL, then bring feet together
11	1–4	Flat 2-finger down and then up overhead	Lunge L (head down). Up on toes for overhead
	5–8	Flat 2-finger down then up overhead	Lunge R and then up on toes
12	1–4	Taffy pull to the back	Step turn to L
	5–8	Flat toss from LH, turnaround	Step turn
13 (End)	1–2	Cradle	Feet together
	3–4	Roll baton down both arms	L step point
	5–6	Flip-turn baton	Feet together
	7–8	Salute	Feet together

Parade Corps

In addition to the four types of competitive floor corps, there is, in the USTA, a separate category for "parade corps." Floor corps may enter parade-corps competition if they desire.

Parade corps are divided into three age groupings: juvenile (11 and under); junior (12–14); and senior (15–21). There are only two musical categories: corps with live music and corps using recorded music.

The most significant difference between a parade corps and other groups involve the personnel required and the time of the routine. A parade corps need not have a color guard. Its only requirement is a dozen twirlers. And it performs for a very brief time, 2–3 minutes. Floor patterns are forward motion.

Other, more technical differences between parade- and floor-corps regulations are included in the Corps Manual.

If you're a new corps director who hasn't had much, if any, competitive experience, a parade-corps competition is an excellent starting point, especially if many of your students are very young with a short attention span. (It's pretty hard for a little tot to do a six-minute routine, but three minutes is fine.)

No matter how much you rehearse your corps, and no matter how often your group performs in local parades and whatnot, there's no substitute for the real thing, the actual experience of competing.

Corps Name _____

Marching and Maneuvering 30 Points

VARIETY 15 Points	Comments
a) Change of formation on the march b) Diverse maneuvering of corners c) Utilization of time in floor area without repetition	

DIFFICULTY 15 Points	Comments
a) Degree of intricacy of drill b) Degree of intricacy of body movements and handling of equipment c) Difficulty created through combination of (a) and (b)	

	GROSS TOTAL
EXECUTION	
	TOTALS
Interval	
Distance	
Alignment	
Turns — Pivot Execution	
Anticipation	
Hesitation	
Sagging	
Fanning	
Out of Step	
I.G.A.	
Incorrect Timing (2.0)	
Incorrect Entrance or Exit (2.0)	
Using Instruments Taking Starting Line (2.0)	
	TOTAL PENALTY

Judge _____   TOTAL SCORE

Corps Name _____

GENERAL EFFECT 40 Points

I. SHOWMANSHIP WHILE STRUTTING OR TWIRLING		Comments
15 POINTS	a) Carriage b) Body lines c) Appearance d) Facial expression e) Poise f) Enthusiasm g) Audience appeal h) Effectiveness of repertoire i) Uniqueness of content presentation j) Overall presentation	

II. SHOWMANSHIP DURING MARCHING AND MANEUVERING		Comments
15 POINTS	a) Precision b) Skill of execution c) Espirit de Corps d) Effectiveness of repertoire e) Uniqueness of content presentation	

III. FOWARD MOTION		Comments
10 POINTS	a) Routine designed for maintaining a general forward motion of members	

Judge _____   TOTAL SCORE

There's no faster way to sharpen up your group than by frequent competition. The improvement can be quite dramatic. You'll notice that you can accomplish nearly as much in one hour of practice as you used to accomplish in two. Through competition, you'll become more knowledgeable and your students will gain the confidence they need to look professional. You'll quickly notice a change in your corps' performance. If you don't believe us, just try it. And be sure to write and let us know about the "before" and "after."

Here are some sample score sheets for parade corps. Terms are defined in the same way as for other corps.

A parade-corps routine is included. Analyze it in terms of the score sheets, and then adapt it for your own parade corps to use.

PARADE ROUTINE

SET	COUNTS	TRICK	BODYWORK
1	1–4	March fwd., baton on arm	Knees up, toes pointed, arms shoulder level
	5–6	Fig. 8, flourish down	Step L, hop, RK up
	7–8	Rev. flourish up	Step R, hop, RK up (toes next to opposite knee)

216

Corps Name_____

Strutting and Twirling   30 Points   SCORE

DIFFICULTY		Comments	
10 POINTS	a) Challenging combinations of baton and body work creating a degree of risk for perfect execution b) Exchange work		

VARIETY		Comments	
10 POINTS	a) Diversity of arm movements b) Diversity of leg movements c) Diversity of baton movements		

TEAM WORK		Comments	
10 POINTS	a) Precision b) Timing c) Execution as one harmonious performance		

DROPS	.2	.4	.6	.8	1.0	1.2	1.4	1.6	1.8	2.0	2.2	2.4	2.6	2.8	3.0	3.2	3.4	3.6	3.8	4.0	4.2	4.4	4.6	4.8	5.0	SUB TOTAL
	5.2	5.4	5.6	5.8	6.0	6.2	6.4	6.6	6.8	7.0	7.2	7.4	7.6	7.8	8.0	8.2	8.4	8.6	8.8	9.0	9.2	9.4	9.6	9.8	10.0	
UNISON	.1	.2	.3	.4	.5	.6	.7	.8	.9	1.0	1.1	1.2	1.3	1.4	1.5	1.6	1.7	1.8	1.9	2.0	2.1	2.2	2.3	2.4	2.5	
	2.6	2.7	2.8	2.9	3.0	3.1	3.2	3.3	3.4	3.5	3.6	3.7	3.8	3.9	4.0	4.1	4.2	4.3	4.4	4.5	4.6	4.7	4.8	4.9	5.0	
	5.1	5.2	5.3	5.4	5.5	5.6	5.7	5.8	5.9	6.0	6.1	6.2	6.3	6.4	6.5	6.6	6.7	6.8	6.9	7.0	7.1	7.2	7.3	7.4	7.5	
	7.6	7.7	7.8	7.9	8.0	8.1	8.2	8.3	8.4	8.5	8.6	8.7	8.8	8.9	9.0	9.1	9.2	9.3	9.4	9.5	9.6	9.7	9.8	9.9	10.0	

TOTAL PENALTY

Judge_____   NET TOTAL

SET	COUNTS	TRICK	BODYWORK
2	1–2	L shoulder roll	Knees up
	3–4	R shoulder pass	Knees up
	5–6	2 R vert. wrist twirls	R, low position, L arm up
	7–8	2 L vert. wrist twirls	R, high overhead, L arm down at sides
3	1–2	Tip toward floor	Arms down at sides
	3–4	Neck twist	L arm extended to LS
	5–6	Baton LS to RS of neck	2 hands on baton, palms in
	7–8	Horiz. neck roll	
4	1–2	2 L horiz. wrist twirls	R arm extended to RS
	3–4	Release on 3, toss L to R	
	5–6	Catch on 5	L arm out to LS
	7–8	2 R horiz. wrist twirls	
5	1–2	R flat 2-finger down	L arm up
	3–4	R flat 2-finger up	L arm down
	5–6	Repeat 1–2	Left lunge
	7–8	Repeat 3–4	Pull up on toes
6	1	Baton flat out to LS	Both hands at ball, palms down, arms straight
	2	R pulls baton through LH, so LH is at tip	LH extended straight out to LS

SET	COUNTS	TRICK	BODYWORK
	3–4	RH slides to tip as baton moves vert. down, out to RS	Both arms extended out to sides, ball to R
	5–6	Pull baton back onto R shoulder in flat plane (hand leaves baton to switch to thumb under shaft in half toss, half slide—no revolutions)	
	7–8		L arm circles on 7 and back out to side. Hold on 8
7	1–4	RH circle (rev. at LS, fig. 8 at RS)	LH on hip 1–8
	5–8	Repeat	
8	1–2	Hitch-kick pass to LH	Point toes
	3–4	L rev. at RS, pass behind back to RH	Legs straight
	5–6	R fig. 8, pass behind back to LH	
	7–8	Hold	Still marching
9	1–4	LH circle (rev. at LS, fig. 8 at RS)	RH on hip
	5–8	Repeat	
10	1–2	L rev. at LS	R arm out to RS
	3–4	L to R vert. flip	
	5–6	Catch on 5, carry to RS with fig. 8	
	7–8	R fig. 8 down to RS on 7	Both arms down at sides, hold on 8
11	1–4	Snake (back line of twirlers run diag. R for 4 counts to line up with front line at R of girls in front line)	Goose step—run with legs straight, kicking forward. Baton off arm, with both arms swinging.
	1–4	Front-line twirlers do toss turnaround. Recover on 3 in L lunge, tip touching ground. Hold for counts 5 and 6.	Deep lunge, with L arm out to side. Freeze pose on 5 and 6
	5–8	Back line. Run 4 counts diag. L to get in front of the line	Pose in Y position
		Front line (becomes back line) pull up on toes at count 7 and hold for 8	
12	1–8	Repeat above. Since front line is now in back, each line does opposite of what it did in Set 11	

THIRTEEN

Organizing a Corps

If you've ever seen a corps perform, you've probably felt the excitement a corps generates. As a result, you might like to get in on the thrill of it all by having a corps of your own. What do you do to get started?

First, decide what kind of corps you can have. Remember, you'll need at least sixteen students (twelve twirlers and a color guard of four) to make up a corps. If you plan to enter competitions as well as march in parades, then all your corps members will have to be in the same age division (14 and under for junior, 15–21 for senior).

The easiest kind of corps to start with is a parade corps. Put in all your students, give them a routine everyone can do, and rehearse them. Sample parade routines can be found in the previous chapter.

This kind of corps is a terrific thing for a new twirling teacher who has a batch of young students. And it's a good first step toward competitive corps work—for teacher and student alike.

You'll want all your students to be dressed alike for a parade. You can do this quite inexpensively. Let each student supply her own costume—unless you're trying to establish an ongoing competitive floor corps, in which case costumes should be corps property. But more about that later.

For a parade corps, keep the costume simple and appropriate for marching out of doors. A tank-type leotard, white socks, and gym shoes are fine for hot weather. If it's cool, the girls can wear a long-sleeved orlon turtle neck with tights. Design a corps emblem and have it imprinted on the shirts. If you put pompons on the sneakers, you'll get a nice, colorful effect. Hats are appropriate for corps twirlers, and you may include headgear in the uniform if you like.

Costs on uniforms can be cut in several ways. Leotard and/or uniform companies often give discounts or sell wholesale to corps. Have corps stationery printed and use it to request prices from various suppliers. Be sure to shop around for the best price. If you buy in bulk, you'll probably avoid having to pay full retail price.

If your members are making their own uniforms, you can still buy all materials and trim in bulk. Have one person do all the cutting. The material will go farther this way—so you'll need less total yardage. Be sure to tell the seamstresses (probably mothers) to make extra-large hems and seams so the uniforms can be let out as the children grow.

Getting a competitive floor corps started is more complicated than organizing a parade corps. It requires some formal structure and more money.

Since outfitting and maintaining a floor corps is very expensive (around $50,000 a year minimum to keep a large musical corps on the road competing and entertaining), your best bet is to start small. Begin with a basic twirling corps or a drum-and-baton corps. If you want to use juniors, it's a good idea—because a junior corps becomes a feeder group for a senior corps later on.

You're going to be very busy, even with a small corps. Not only will you be responsible for developing your group artistically, you'll be in charge of the group's management as well. If, in the first couple of years, you can build a strong, active fund-raising organization, you'll eventually be able to support a large musical corps.

It's unfortunate that there are so few musical corps in the United States today. (Only around a hundred, by our estimate.) One of the major reasons, of course, is lack of funds. We feel that if more young twirling teachers could organize a strong fund-raising arm for a corps, the money would be forthcoming. And there's nothing we'd rather see at competitions than more competitors in the corps categories. The smaller the number of competing corps, the more they are in jeopardy. Without strong competition, corps cannot survive.

With the hope that more and more of you newer teachers will be successful in forming corps, we'd like to share some of our organizational-structure
and fund-raising ideas with you—methods that have kept our corps in existence for a combined total of more than thirty-six years. If you already have
a corps and need additional money to expand into a musical corps, then perhaps our tips will make it easier for you.

If you decide to organize a corps for your students, the first thing to do is
get the whole family involved. This means fathers, mothers, and siblings, if
possible. Send a letter to the families stating your intentions and call a
meeting. Your students will be enthusiastic, so they'll urge their parents to
attend. Hopefully, you'll get a good turnout.

A strong parents' organization is the backbone of a corps. It not only
boosts morale and team spirit, it is responsible for the financial security of
the group and will be raising the funds. For a successful corps, the members
and parents alike should be willing to work for it. If a student is in financial
distress or has only one parent, you might relax the rules on parental participation, but otherwise, everyone must do his share. If you don't make the
corps a family activity from the beginning, you probably won't get very far.

Being active in the parents' organization doesn't only benefit the corps.
It's very much a two-way street, with the parents getting as much out of it
as the kids who are in the corps itself. Naturally, the parents who are the
most involved get the most. If you can communicate this to them through
your own enthusiasm, you'll probably get a lively and responsive group of
parents.

Just what do the parents get out of working for the corps? Well, first
there's the knowledge that the corps couldn't exist without them—that it's
because of them, there is a corps. Second, corps work gives parents a golden
opportunity to meet new people. We find that in our corps many parents
develop solid friendships with other couples, and these friendships last far
beyond their children's years in the corps.

And perhaps, most important, becoming involved in corps gives parents
and teen-agers a shared interest. While many teen-agers are drifting away
from their families, the corps helps to reverse this pattern for its members.
Being in the corps increases contact between parents and teen-agers, and
not only within families. Parents also become better acquainted with the
children's friends, and children make contact with other adults. Furthermore, corps members rarely have the time or inclination to get involved
with drugs or alcohol, and they don't tend to run with kids who do.

Remember, the more of your students you can involve, the more parents
you'll have working. And the more people you can manage, the more im-

pressive your group will be when competing. So give your beginners pom-pons or flash flags and include them if possible.

At your first meeting, be prepared to present to the students and parents your plans for the corps' first year. Present a regular practice schedule, a listing of parades and competitions you plan to enter, and a budget. Your budget should include such items as costumes and equipment, travel costs to and from parades and contests, competition entry fees, rehearsal-room rental (you may need a school gym if your studio isn't large enough to rehearse a whole corps), and a salary for yourself.

Taking a salary for yourself is very important. You're probably so eager to start a corps that right now you're willing to volunteer your time. You'll regret this later. Of course, your main reason for starting a corps is not to make money. But when the initial excitement dies down, when the going gets rough, when the kids aren't cooperating, you're going to realize that being a corps director is a *job*.

You should also have in mind some type of dues program or annual membership fee for the parents, to help cover your initial costs and to commit the parents financially and emotionally.

Other than dues, try to keep costs for parents down. Accept donations gratefully, but don't take them in lieu of fund-raising efforts. If a parent wants to donate a uniform or some other tangible item for his child to use, be sure he understands that such a donation becomes corps property.

Your uniforms, most instruments, flags, rifles, pompons, etc. are all corps assets, and probably the only ones you'll have. A few words about musical instruments. Avoid borrowing them if at all possible—even if it means waiting a year before adding that instrument to the corps. Many brass players will have their own instruments, and it's fine for them to use them—but players of specialty instruments and expensive drums probably rent or use the school's instruments. Most school band directors will be unable or unwilling to loan you instruments. And believe it or not, it's better for you that way.

If you lose or break a borrowed instrument, you'll have to pay for it. So if you can afford to borrow one, you can afford to buy it.

Obviously, to equip yourself, you'll need funds. Make it clear from the start that the purpose of the parents' organization is to form a yearly budget (upon your recommendation) and to raise the funds needed by the corps.

This means—and there should be no confusion about it—that the parents have no authority over the artistic and performing aspects of the corps proper. You make the decisions with regard to music, routine, uniforms, practice requirements, rules for corps members, how the corps performs, when and where, and who will perform in what capacity.

Establishing your authority in this area will help you avoid problems later. And you will have problems. For example, a father decides his daughter is too good a twirler to be in the pompon line and insists you put her in the twirling line. Or a mother thinks her child should be featured twirler. Or a set of parents badgers you to keep their child in the corps despite repeated absences or discipline problems.

Most parents won't hassle you. After all, they trust you enough to employ you as a teacher, and they'll respect your judgment about what the child can and should do in the corps. But some parents find it impossible to believe that their child isn't the best. And some parents, when they see that their children aren't getting the roles they want, will try to intervene. They get up in arms immediately, thinking they've got to fight for the rights of the child.

Now and then someone will try to put the squeeze on. If a parent tries to pressure you, be polite, but firm. Try to empathize with their position and to understand their emotions. Be as honest as you can, without hurting anyone's feelings. Say, "I know Martha is a better twirler than Judy, but Judy's personality is far better suited to the role of featured twirler," or, "I wish Johnny had a more positive attitude because I'd like to keep him in the corps. But if he keeps cutting practice, I'll have to let him go."

Occasionally, we're sorry to say, you may get a parent who threatens to withdraw a child from the corps if you don't give in to demands. Don't surrender your authority and good judgment in this situation. You've always got to be willing to let any member drop out rather than meet the threat—even if you consider him or her the most valuable member of the corps. This holds true no matter who the parent is. Even if the parent is your most energetic fund-raiser or president of the booster club, you can't give in to pressure. If you do, you'll only set a dangerous precedent and, furthermore, sacrifice the artistic integrity of the group.

Most parents don't carry out this kind of a threat because they know it would make the child miserable. But sometimes, in spite of your best efforts to persuade them otherwise, it does happen. In this case, tell the parents you're very sorry, and you hope they'll reconsider. Leave the door open so that the child can rejoin without losing face.

Our corps are legal corporations, non-profit organizations formed in accordance with state laws. Whether or not you incorporate (and it's a good idea to do it), you should have a set of rules and regulations stating the purpose of the organization, the roles of the director and other officers, the internal structure, requirements for membership in the performing corps and in the parents' organization, responsibilities and obligations of the members, etc.

One of the main things you should do at your first meeting is to have the parents elect a committee to help you with the writing of the constitution.

You and the committee should also establish the type of structure you want the organization to have—number of officers, their duties and tenure of office; necessary standing committees; method of insuring equal distribution of the workload among the total membership; etc.

Your constitution's main function is to establish the organization as a legal corporation and to delineate its powers—what it can and cannot do and how it will or won't do it. Design your constitution with room for interpretation, as our United States Constitution was designed. You can put very specific rules and regulations into a set of bylaws that don't conflict with the constitution. This gives your group more flexibility and allows for changes without constitutional amendment.

Constitutions vary from corps to corps, of course. Most of them are very formal documents. If you'd like a copy of an actual corps constitution to use as a model, write to Blackhawk headquarters (2150 E. Rahn Road, Dayton, Ohio 45440) or Thunderers headquarters (22 Youngshill Road, Huntington, New York 11743).

SUGGESTED PARENTS ORGANIZATION STRUCTURE

As a general rule it's a good idea to elect an executive board. You'll want a president, vice-president, secretary, and treasurer at the minimum. Some corps find two vice-presidents and two secretaries useful. As director, you should be a permanent officer and member of the board. Other officers will serve for a designated term. A year or two is standard.

In addition to your officers, you may want to have standing committees to make sure everything is managed smoothly. Some corps prefer to have each officer be a chairman of a standing committee. The corps director should be an ex officio member of all committees.

Suggested standing committees are:

1. Membership and Hospitality
2. Publicity/Promotion/Information
3. Ways and Means
4. Travel and Accommodations
5. Property
6. Contests
7. Programming and Scheduling

Make sure all chairmen and committee members understand the functions of the committee and their responsibilities to it. These are details to include in your bylaws.

Special committees will probably be needed from time to time to handle various specific events or programs the corps decides to sponsor. These committees will be temporary and are dissolved once the event is over. Chairman should write a written report regarding the event and give it to the executive board.

In addition to officers and committee chairmen, here are a few miscellaneous positions you might find useful to fill.

1. *Corps coordinator*. Checks on all committees regularly for progress and problems.

2. *Band coordinator*. Responsible for instruments and keeping band members informed of corps activities.

3. *Point recorder*. Keeps accurate records of each member's accumulated working hours and advises of their standing at any given time.

4. *Message chairman*. Prepares calling lists and hands out calling assignments.

POINT SYSTEM

In nearly every organization, you'll find a couple of really dedicated people who do most of the work, plus a flock of members who do very little and who rely on the energy of others.

This is what you want to avoid, and the point system can help assure an even distribution of the work load.

Basically, the point system assigns a point value to every hour the member works. The organization should have the right to require a certain number of points per season from each voting member. Officers, committee chairmen, and committee members may get a fixed number of points for taking on a specific job.

Sample Point System

1. Required number of points: 200 points per family with one child in the corps. Each additional child requires 50 additional points.

2. Point values: 5 points for each hour of work.

3. Means of accumulation: officer (100); standing committee member (40); special committee chairman (30); special committee member (20); working at various events and doing assigned tasks (5 points per hour). Such tasks might include driving, cooking, typing, telephoning, etc.

4. Rate of point accumulation: All members must accumulate half their work points by March 1; 85 per cent by May 30; 100 per cent by July 1. Those who are not on schedule will be charged $.50 per point.

BUDGET AND FUND RAISING

How much you'll need to raise each year will depend upon the number of people in your corps, the equipment you have, the number of performances you plan, how many competitions you're going to enter, etc.

Below is a sample budget that will give you some idea of the kinds of expenses you can expect if you have a drum-and-baton corps of substantial size. Following the budget, you'll find some suggested ways to raise funds.

SAMPLE BUDGET FOR A NEWLY FORMED DRUM-AND-BATON CORPS

MEMBERSHIP:

Girls in twirling line	24	Flash flag section	8
Captains or featured twirlers	3	Rifle twirlers	4
Drummers	10	National color section	3

Drum major 1

Total number of members 53

INCOME:

Dues—$10 per month per member	$6,360
Contests—4 per year	3,400
Raffle—$2,000 in prize money	3,300
Monte Carlo	2,000
TOTAL	$15,060

EXPENSES:

Practice rentals	$1,540	
Uniforms	3,975	($75 per uniform)
Drums	2,000	(new drums)
Director's salary	4,400	(44 rehearsals @ $100 each)
State entries	200	
National entries	250	
Color guard equipment	650	(flags and poles)
Rifles	125	
Insurance for drums	100	
Insurance liability	125	
Drum instructor	1,100	(44 rehearsals @ $25 each)
Mailing permit	150	
Contest sanctions	80	
TOTAL	$14,695	

Basic Fund-raising Events

What type of events should you sponsor, and what can you expect to earn from them? The kind of fund-raising affairs you decide to plan should be well-suited to the number of people you've got working in your organization and should take advantage of their combined talents, experience, and capabilities.

The following three events have proven successful for nearly every type of corps in all areas of the country. They're not difficult to pull off, but they do require plenty of pre-planning and work from the parents.

1. *Contests.* Approximate net will be $850 per contest. Sponsor four a year. Write to the USTA for the Contest Director's Manual, and follow that format to sponsor a USTA-sanctioned competition. Profit comes from door admission and food sales. Entrance fees will cover judge's costs, school facilities, trophy, and food costs. (Try to get trophies and food donated to increase net profit.)

2. *Raffles.* Hold four a year and raffle off $500 each time. Each member should sell $25 worth of raffle tickets at $1.00 a ticket.

3. *Monte Carlo.* How you handle this depends on the laws in your state.

METHOD A. For $3.50 the ticket buyer gets unlimited free beer and $10,000 in play money. Each additional $5,000 of play money costs $1.00. You can hold an auction at the end of the evening. Bidding is done by each person with the play money he has left over.

METHOD B. Charge $3.50 for admission and have people gamble with their own money.

Other types of events you may want to consider as fund raisers: yearbook; sales of candy, light bulbs, etc.; dinner-dance; flea market; annual fair; clam bakes.

SETTING RULES

The members of your corps should have no doubts as to what's expected of them. It's reasonable to demand that the youngsters be on time for practices and performances, be properly attired, take care of their uniforms, and behave in a way that reflects positively upon the corps.

You can get as specific as you wish with regard to rules and regulations, and it's a good idea to make sure each member has a copy of the rules.

Members should also know under what circumstances they can be suspended or expelled from the corps.

Many corps use a demerit system for discipline, and they set a maximum number of demerits allowed before dismissal proceedings begin. Members undergoing dismissal proceedings should be entitled to a fair hearing before the executive board.

Decide what infractions you're going to penalize, and set a minimum and maximum number of demerits that's appropriate to the seriousness of the infraction.

Some areas you'll probably want to cover:

1. Insubordination, defiance of authority, insolence, etc.
2. Tardiness.
3. Absenses.
4. Damage or destruction of corps property.
5. Actual or attempted theft.
6. Rude or boisterous play that disrupts practice or performance; fighting or threatening or actually inflicting bodily harm.
7. Sale and use of alcohol, marijuana, and other drugs.
8. Failure to meet valid obligations included in constitution or bylaws.
9. Attempting to destroy or damage the reputation of anyone else connected with the corps or parents' organization.
10. When uniforms may and may not be worn.
11. Misconduct that keeps a member from fulfilling his obligations or that adversely affects the whole organization.

YOUR FIRST YEAR

The first year will be the most difficult—both in getting your performing act together and in getting the parents organized. You should expect to make mistakes and to learn from them.

Don't be discouraged if you don't place high in competition your first year. Starting a new corps is like beginning a new athletic team in some ways. It takes time to get used to working together, to develop teammanship, to build a style for yourself.

We hope these tips will help get your corps onto the floor. We look forward to seeing many more corps entering competitions in the coming years, and we wish every new corps a long and successful career.

FOURTEEN

Careers in Twirling

Teaching

Unless you're an advanced twirler or champion, you may not believe you're qualified to teach twirling. You'll probably take one look at the title of this chapter and say to yourself, "Well, no sense reading that. I'm not good enough."

Hold on. There are plenty of twirling teachers who never twirled better than a fair intermediate. And *good* teachers, too. Lots of people can teach better than they can twirl. Even *we* can't do everything our students can do.

One of the secrets of being a good teacher is knowing your own abilities and your limitations. You may be the perfect teacher for a beginner. Once you realize you've done your job well, that you've taught all you know, you send the student on to another teacher who handles more advanced twirling.

Or maybe you've got an intermediate student who is going into advanced work. Maybe you haven't got the dexterity to demonstrate or do the tricks yourself, but you know what that student should be able to do and you can teach her to do it. Maybe you've got a terrific imagination, and you're fantastic at visualizing tricks or routines and know how to communicate and get your point across. Your student will continue to learn from you, even though you can't do all the things you can think up.

So whether you're super-advanced or just intermediate in twirling, you can put your skill and knowledge to work for you. Teaching is a terrific way to earn money. We both know people who've put themselves through four years of college on what they earned as high school students teaching little kids.

We also know ex-twirlers, women now in their 30s and 40s, who've taken up a twirling teaching career. And they love it. They enjoy the contact with their own children who are learning and with other youngsters and their parents. And they especially love earning money in a way that doesn't involve having a boss, sitting at a desk all day, or investing more years of school before making decent pay.

Besides twirling experience, what else do you need to become a teacher? Here again, there aren't any rules. Twirling teachers come in all shapes and with all kinds of personalities. If you've got energy, enthusiasm, patience, a real love of twirling, and a desire to work with children, then you've got a good chance at success.

If you organize your students into a marching group and get them into parades from the start, then they'll be enthusiastic themselves. Make your classes fun—after all, twirling *is* fun—but let your students know that learning is also serious business. It takes effort and practice, and you expect them to work hard.

How to Get Started

Before you can teach twirling, you've got to have someone who wants to learn. Fortunately, this is no problem. Nearly everyone who has the opportunity wants to learn how to twirl.

If you're a twirler and in high school, you've probably got people begging you to teach them baton tricks. This is what happened to both of us when we were teen-age twirlers. Not only younger kids, but kids our own age and older were dying to learn. Before we knew it, we were each teaching over twenty-five students.

As a teen-ager, you can charge a dollar or two for group lessons of thirty to forty-five minutes. For private lessons, charge more—around $4.00—a little less if your skills aren't terribly advanced.

Word of mouth will probably bring you more students than you can handle. If you feel you can't maintain your authority with your friends and peers, then only teach younger children. You can have business cards printed with your name and telephone number and hand them out to people in the neighborhood. Maybe you've got clients you baby-sit for who'd be interested.

Or take out a small ad in the Classified Section of your local newspaper. You'll probably get a big response. Early fall, by the way, is a good time to do this. That's when most parents are setting up schedules for after-school activities for their children. Or if you find yourself without a job one summer, get a summer group of little tots started. If you only work in the mornings, you'll probably find you can earn as much as your friends who have full-time jobs.

If you're an adult, there may not be people who are aware of your history as a twirler. So you'll have to spread it around yourself. As soon as word gets out, you'll have students at your doorstep.

An ad in the paper will work just as well for you as for a teen-ager. You can also check around to see if there are any twirling schools in your area. Maybe they'll need an extra instructor, part time. Or maybe they're overcrowded, with a waiting list they can refer to you. You never know.

Call up the dancing schools in your area. Lots of dancing teachers are including twirling lessons in their offerings. Most dance teachers know less about twirling than you do—no matter how long ago you twirled or how out of practice you've become. The dance teacher herself might want to take lessons from you, so she can pass the knowledge on to her students. Or maybe she would hire you to teach baton in her school. Better yet, she'll give your name to students who want to learn twirling. Since dancing skills are always useful to twirlers, you can also recommend dancing schools to your students.

Public and private schools also want twirling teachers. We get calls from schools and band directors over fifty miles away, asking us to send instructors. Get in touch with the band director of your local high school or with the physical education department. If there's no room in the budget for your services once or twice a week, the physical education teacher herself might want to learn twirling, so she can include it in the phys. ed. curriculum.

Go to a couple of high school athletic events and pay attention to the twirling level of the majorettes. Sometimes you'll see that they don't really twirl much at all. They just carry the baton. If this is the case, then you've probably got willing students right there. Those majorettes are more than likely starving for lessons.

As soon as you get students, put them on display. They're the best advertising. Other children will see your students in parades and will ask for the name of their teacher. Have a recital in the spring and invite the public. It doesn't have to be a big, lavish show, but it should be well-rehearsed and include all your students. They'll bring their families and invite friends—potential new students.

Your rates will depend upon your twirling experience and skills. If you were once a state or national champion, then even $8.00 for a private lesson isn't too much.

Where to Teach

Of course, you're fortunate if your home can be used. Perhaps you've got a spare room, or an expanse of space in a recreation room or family room. Finished basements can be converted into twirling studios. Keep in mind that if you've got a low ceiling, though, you won't be able to teach high aerial throws. If you're teaching mostly beginners, this doesn't matter much. You can always go outside when the weather permits and work on high aerials.

If your home isn't suitable, then you'll have to find some other space. Probably this will cost you some rental fee, and you'll want to be sure you can cover it and still make a profit.

Dancing schools sometimes have rooms available for several hours a week. Try them. Also, the "Y" will often rent its facilities. The gym of your local high school may be unavailable and/or too expensive, but the elementary school is a possibility. Don't forget to check with parochial and private schools in your area. If rooms are sitting empty after school hours, they may be happy to rent them inexpensively, especially if a custodian is on duty anyway.

When you're looking for a studio, keep in mind how large your classes will be. If you're only teaching one or two students at a time, they'll feel lost in a school gym. But if you've got six or seven people in a class, then they'll need room to spread out.

How to Teach

If you don't have your own method in mind—or even if you do—why not teach tricks in the order we've given them in this book? Of course you'll have to adapt our methods to your own style—and to your individual students as well. But we've written this book to help teachers teach, as well as to help students learn. So please, now that you've got it, make use of it.

232

Maybe you'll want to recommend it to your students. If you disagree with anything, or want them to do something your way instead of ours, just tell them. Exposing students to views different than your own can't hurt you or them. It can help your students learn to think for themselves.

Knowing Your Students

Not all students will learn at the same rate. Nor will they all take the same approach to learning. Just as teachers have different styles of teaching, so students have different learning styles. Here are a few of the most common ones.

1. *The innovator.* Likes to make up twirls or variations. Unfortunately, she also sometimes does it on the floor during a contest. Requires careful guidance, but be responsive to her ideas.

2. *The quick kid.* Can often catch on to a trick the first or second try. Good ability, of course, but this type often thinks she's licked the trick right away. With discipline, this type can often become a real champion.

3. *The concentrator.* Doesn't learn instantly. Has to concentrate and work it out for herself. Requires patience from the teacher. This kind of student often has lots of self-direction. They are usually well-disciplined from the start, and turn out to be excellent twirlers.

4. *The slow learner.* Resembles the concentrator, but needs (and perhaps requests) your help in working through the twirl.

5. *The casual learner.* Takes the whole process nonchalantly. Try to inspire them enough so they become a bit more dedicated and serious.

6. *The attention craver.* Demands your attention constantly. She may pretend she can't do a trick so you'll give extra help. Or she may constantly announce, "I did it." As a teacher, you should give her only a fair share of attention, regardless of behavior. Let her know that her attempts at more attention will not succeed.

7. *The bent-baton kid.* Insists the stick is at fault for all mistakes. This kind needs to learn that the baton only does what she makes it do.

8. *The impossible dreamer.* Works hardest on tricks you say are hard. Tell her lots of tricks are very difficult, and she'll continue practicing with tremendous improvement.

9. *The "I can't do it" kid.* Probably the most frustrating kind of student to have. Usually they say it before they even try a trick. Convince them that the words "I can't" aren't in your vocabulary—and shouldn't be in theirs.

10. *The angel.* Does everything well without showing off or complaining. We're not sure angels really exist.

233

Dealing with Parents

Your relationship with parents is important. You probably see your students only once a week. Parents are responsible for the follow-through of your instructions, especially with the younger students.

We've found that students whose parents are involved learn better and faster. So do everything you can to have parents take an active interest.

Let the parents talk to you about their children. They can tell you how well the child practices, how enthusiastic she really is, what problems they see. Give their comments careful consideration, but form your own objective evaluation of the child.

Observe the relationship between the parent and the child. Sometimes it is better for the child if the parent isn't present during the lesson. You have to speak up in this case. Sometimes, you'll notice that the parents are really of little help or inspiration to the child. You can take over in this role then.

If you think a parent can help the child, speak privately to the parent. Explain your teaching method and explain what particular aspect of twirling the child needs help with the most.

Inform the parents about the various aspects of twirling, twirling associations, and publications.

Try to be aware of the family's financial status. Don't suggest or insist upon things you know are out of financial reach. If you're not sure, keep suggestions mild and don't make the parents feel pressured.

Teaching Sportsmanship

Not every child can become a champion, and it's not your job to make all your students into winners. That would be impossible. But you can help to build character and help your students develop maturity.

We hope that more and more teachers will become more "improvement" oriented, and less "win" oriented. Parents are often all too concerned about winning, and as a teacher, you can help change parental attitudes. Sometimes this is necessary before you can influence the student to change her own attitude.

Students must learn to handle disappointments—even if they deserve a win and don't get it. They must also learn to accept responsibility for their losses. They should not blame the judge, the teacher, the parents, or anyone else.

Teaching your students to control their emotions is also important. When a child drops her baton, she must pick it up with a smile and proceed as though it never happened. Displays of temper on the competition floor can be grounds for disqualification. Losers should maintain their poise and be gracious to the winners. If they've really got the right attitude, then the congratulations they offer will be truly sincere.

Becoming a Certified Teacher

The twirling associations can help you embark on your new career as a teacher. Be sure to write to one or more of them for training information.

In the USTA we have workshops and seminars where twirlers can actually learn to become teachers. You can become a USTA associate teacher at the age of sixteen. An associate teacher has her own students. The title "associate" means you've passed a written examination that tests your knowledge of the rudiments of twirling, your philosophy of teaching, your knowledge of strutting, teams, corps, etc.

Once you're eighteen, you can get a full USTA certificate as an adult teacher. In order to become a certified teacher, you must stop competing. Since a lot of girls continue to compete until they're twenty-one, they remain associate teachers until then.

Completing an association training program and passing the examinations will probably make you a better teacher. Also, becoming a certified teacher will help you get more students since you'll be on a list of association-approved teachers.

Judging

You can further your adult career in twirling by becoming a judge. To judge USTA competitions, you must be a member of the association, must be a certified USTA teacher, and must be recommended by an already certified judge.

Teachers who apply to become judges must attend a special workshop and must pass a difficult four-part test with a score of 90 or more for each section. Part of the exam actually involves judging contestants during competitions. After you obtain your certificate, you must attend a seminar and pass another test every three years.

If these requirements sound tough to you, you're right. But it's all to insure that the young people in twirling get a fair shake and are being judged by people who really know their stuff.

Today, about 10 per cent of USTA teachers become judges. What does judging offer, and how do you know if you can qualify?

The first thing judging can do for you is up your earnings. Judges are paid a minimum of $50 a day for their work, in addition to all expenses being paid.

Second, judging offers travel opportunities you might never have otherwise. We know people who've been from coast to coast, staying in the finest hotels, seeing the United States first class.

Third, judging gives you the chance to form new friendships with other people in the twirling field, or to renew friendships from your days as a twirler.

Fourth, being a judge helps you be a better teacher. It's an opportunity to sharpen your knowledge of twirling and thus give your students some really professional advice. (Judges do not judge contests in which their own students participate.)

And last—and possibly most important—it's a lot of fun.

How do you know whether or not to become a judge? Many teachers aren't really suited to judging. They're reluctant to go out on a limb and say that one child is better than the next. Or they have trouble making decisions. When you're judging a contest, you can't do the job if you're worried about how others will react to your decision. Everyone may disagree with you. It happens from time to time. Can you stick by your decision and tolerate standing alone? You may have to, if you're a judge. How fast can you make decisions? When you're judging, you may only have a few seconds. If making quick decisions frightens you, then you should think twice about becoming a judge.

And although judging is fun, it's also a lot of hard work. So to be a judge, you've got to thrive on busy schedules with lots of pressure. After all, you're on the floor for eight or more straight hours during a contest. And if it's a weekend contest, you'll be working yourself to the bone two days in a row. You've got to enjoy it to do that.

Then there's the travel. A tremendous advantage for some, but how about for you? Do you really enjoy being away from home? Are you able to get away fairly easily, leaving someone behind to manage the household, or is it difficult for you to take trips? Remember, if you're going to make a career of judging, you also have to be available. It's not always practical or possible to judge contests close to home since that's where your own students are most likely to be competing.

Are you willing to study from time to time—keeping up on new rules and regulations? Are you observant, analytical, open-minded? All these qualities will help make you a good judge.

If you're a teacher who'd like to look into judging, write to one or more of the twirling associations for more complete information. Remember, teacher certification must come first.

APPENDIX

Equipment and Uniforms for Twirlers

BATON MANUFACTURERS

1. ABC Baton Company, 300 S. Wright Rd., Janesville, Wis. 53545.
2. Imperial Baton Company, 2150 E. Rahn Rd., Dayton, Ohio 43440.
3. Kraskin Baton Company, 219 Master Ave., Savage, Minn. 55378.
4. Selmer Clark, P. O. Box 310, Elkhart, Ind. 46514.
5. Star Line Baton Company, Box 5490, Pompano Beach, Fla. 33064.

COSTUMERS

1. Algy, P. O. Box 090490, 430 N.E. First Ave., Hallandale, Fla. 33009.
2. Costume Gallery, Amber and Willard Sts., Philadelphia, Pa. 19134.
3. Cranbarry, P. O. Box 488, 2 Lincoln Ave., Marblehead, Mass. 09145.
4. Leo's Advance Theatrical Co., 2451 N. Sacramento Ave., Chicago, Ill. 60647.
5. Show-Off, 429 Norman Ct., DesPlaines, Ill. 60016.
6. Taffy's, 701 Beta Drive, Cleveland, Ohio 44143.
7. Wolff, Fording, 119 Braintee St., Allson, Mass. 02134.

MAJORETTE SUPPLY (Materials, trims, etc.)

1. Art's Majorette and Theatrical Supply, 3053 34th St., Lubbock, Tex. 79410.
2. C of C Champion Supply Co., P. O. Box 26767, El Paso, Tex. 79926.
3. Cote Majorette Supply, 203 W. Bridge, Morrisville, Pa. 19067.
4. Fred J. Miller Studios, 61 Westpark Rd., Centerville, Ohio 45459.
5. Galaxy Enterprises, Inc., 6808 Laurel Bowie Rd., Bowie, Md. 20715.
6. P & D Supply Co., 10890 Kendig Rd., New Carlisle, Ohio 45344.
7. Western Majorette Supply, 7930 S.E. Stark, Portland, Ore. 97211.

Uniform Suppliers for Corps

1. De Moulin Bros. and Co., 1061 S. Fourth St., Greenville, Ill. 62246.
2. Graceful Costumes, 1933 Dubonet Ct., Allison Park, Pa. 15101.
3. Fechheimer Bros. Co., 4545 Malsbary Rd., Cincinnati, Ohio 45242.
4. Fruhauf Uniforms, Inc., 2938 S. Minneapolis, Wichita, Kans. 67216.
5. Ostwald, Ostwald Building, Staten Island, N.Y. 10301.
6. Sol Frank Uniforms, Inc., P. O. Box 2139, San Antonio, Tex. 78206.
7. Stanbury Uniforms, P. O. Box 100, Brookfield, Mo. 64628.

Color Guard Equipment

1. Colorguard Sales, 3601 W. Devon, Chicago, Ill. 60659.
2. Corps Line, P. O. Box 638, Danville, Ky. 40422.
3. Flags Up, 404 College Park Dr., Lynchburg, Va. 24502.
4. Intermedia, Inc., Box 676, Westwood, N.J. 07675.
5. McCormick's, P. O. Box 97, Elk Grove, Ill. 60007.
6. School Specialties, 211 Kingston Rd., Parsippany, N.J. 07054.

Drums

1. Ludwig, 1728 N. Damen Ave., Chicago, Ill. 60647.
2. McCormick's, P. O. Box 97, Elk Grove, Ill. 60007.
3. Slingerland Drum Co., 6633 N. Milwaukee Ave., Niles, Ill. 60648.

Baton-twirling Associations

1. United States Twirling Association, Inc. (USTA), P. O. Box 177, Syracuse, Ind. 46567. Executive Director: Jack Crum.
2. National Baton Twirling Association (NBTA), Box 266, Janesville, Wis. 53545. Director: Don Sartell.
3. Drum Majorettes of America (DMA), Box 1168, Charlotte, N.C. 28231. Director: David Faber.
4. World Twirling Association (WTA), Box 32, Napoleon, Ohio 43545. Director: Victor Faber.
5. Federation Europeene Et Internationale (FEIM), Des Majorettes, Hotel De-Ville, 88-Saint-Die, France. Secretary: Evelyne Durand.
6. International Twirling Teachers Institute (ITTI), Box 5490, Lighthouse Point, Fla. 33064.
7. Italian Majorette Association (IMA), c/o Pepino Giamminola, Laboratorio Guidotti, Via Sempione Cond. Monterosa, 28047 Oleggio (Novara), Italy.
8. Japan Marching Band Director Association (JMBDA), c/o Tes Cultural Center, 7-2 Shinsen Shibuya-Ku, Tokyo 150, Japan. Secretary General: Genkichi Harada.

Twirling Magazines

1. *Twirl.* Published by USTA, P. O. Box 177, Syracuse, Ind. 46567. Included with full USTA membership. Price $6.00 without membership. 9 issues per year.
2. *Drum Major.* Published by NBTA, Box 266, Janesville, Wis. 53545. Price: $5.50. 11 issues per year.

Twirling Camps

1. Brooks Going Twirling Camp, 3146 N. Sheridan Rd., Chicago, Ill. 60657.
2. Camp of the Dells, Box 266, Janesville, Wis. 53545.
3. Casavant Cavalcade, P. O. Box 1124, Chattanooga, Tenn. 37401.
4. Fred J. Miller's Clinics, 2150 E. Rahn Rd., Dayton, Ohio 45440.
5. Majorettes of America, P. O. Box 5004, Ft. Worth, Tex. 75231.
6. National Majorette Clinics, Box 185, South Hill, Va. 23970.
7. National Spirit Camps, Box 31030, Dallas, Tex. 75231.
8. Robert Olmstead Clinics, 3825 Middlefield Rd., Palo Alto, Calif. 94300.
9. Smith Walbridge Camp, Syracuse, Ind. 46567.

Records, Arrangements, Marching-drill Instruction

RECORD CATALOGUES
1. All Star Records, c/o Star Line Baton Co., Box 5490, Pompano Beach, Fla. 33064.
2. Drum and Bugle Corps Recordings, DCI Records, P. O. Box 1972, Villa Park, Ill. 60181.

RECORD ALBUMS (Suggested for twirling teams, dance-twirl teams, twirling corps.)
Enoch Light on Project 3 Recordings
    PR 2-6017/6018SD—*The Beauty of Brass*
    PR 5063SD—*Movies*
    PR 5048SD—*Permissive Polyphonics*
    PR 5077QD—*Future Sound Shock*
Command Recordings
    RS 875SD—*Keyboard Kaleidoscope* ("How Dry I Am" by Dick Hyman is especially good.)
    RS 826SD—*Sound 35 MM* (Enoch Light)
    Command 14SD—*Command Sampler* ("Begin the Beguine" good for dance twirl.)

MISCELLANEOUS RECORDINGS

    Concert in the Park in March Tempo—André Kostelanetz. Columbia CL 2688.
    Mancini Concert—Henry Mancini. RCA LSP 4542.
    Jalousie—Arthur Fiedler. RCA ANLI 1439. ("Carioca" good for dance twirl.)
    Blue Tango—LeRoy Anderson. Decca DL 8121. ("Seranata" is especially good.)
    Give My Regards to Broadway—Montivani. London PS 328.

NOTE: Records listed here are just to start you off. Remember, the secret of finding good music is constant listening for continual new discoveries.

MUSICAL ARRANGEMENTS FOR CORPS

1. McCormick's, P. O. Box 97, Elk Grove Village, Ill. 60007.
2. Hal Leonard Publishing Co., 64 E. Second St., Winona, Minn. 55987.

You can order catalogues from the above companies. Both offer a variety of arrangements for bands of all sizes and capabilities. Prices are moderate, with many arrangements available for $10 or less.

INSTRUCTIONAL FILMS FOR CORPS AUXILIARY UNITS

1. McCormick's "How To" Film Series, McCormick's, P. O. Box 97, Elk Grove Village, Ill. 60007. Films can be rented or purchased. Write for brochure with descriptions and prices of films available.

Twirling Scholarships

The following colleges and universities have twirling scholarships available.

ARIZONA
    Arizona State University, Tempe, Ariz. Contact: Director of Bands
    University of Arizona, Tucson, Ariz. Contact: Jack Lee

GEORGIA
    University of Georgia, Athens, Ga. Contact: Roger Dancz

HAWAII
    University of Hawaii, Honolulu, Hawaii. Contact: Richard Lum

ILLINOIS
    Northwestern University, Evanston, Ill. Contact: John Payntor

INDIANA
    Ball State University, Muncie, Ind. Contact: Roger McConell
    Indiana State University, Terre Haute, Ind. Contact: Director of Bands

IOWA
Iowa State University, Ames, Ia. Contact: Director of Bands

KANSAS
Wichita State University, Wichita, Kan. Contact: Dave Catron

KENTUCKY
Eastern Kentucky University, Richmond, Ky. Contact: Robert W. Hartwell

MARYLAND
University of Maryland, College Park, Md. Contact: John E. Wakefield

MICHIGAN
Michigan State University, E. Lansing, Mich. Contact: George Cavender

MISSISSIPPI
University of Mississippi, University, Miss. Contact: Luther Snavely

NEBRASKA
University of Nebraska, Lincoln, Neb. Contact: Robert Fought

OHIO
Bowling Green University, Bowling Green, Ohio. Contact: Mark Kelley
Miami University, Oxford, Ohio. Contact: Nickolas Poccia
University of Cincinnati, Cincinnati, Ohio. Contact: Woodrow J. Hodges

OKLAHOMA
University of Tulsa, Tulsa, Okla. Contact: Jonathan Ebersole

PENNSYLVANIA
Temple University, Philadelphia, Pa. Contact: Arthur Chodoroff

TENNESSEE
Tennessee Tech. University, Cookeville, Tenn. Contact: Wayne Pegram

TEXAS
Baylor University, Waco, Tex. Contact: Dick Floyd
University of Houston, Houston, Tex. Contact: Bill Moffit

UTAH
University of Utah, Salt Lake City, Utah. Contact: Gregg Hanson

INDEX

5.06